MATTHEW BOULTON

MATTHEW BOULTON

INDUSTRY'S GREAT INNOVATOR

JENNIFER TANN AND ANTHONY BURTON

Cover illustrations. Front: An engraving of Matthew Boulton of 1787 from a wax medallion. (Authors). *Back, top:* Soho House, on the hill overlooking the lake. (Authors); *back, below:* A steel button, most likely made in England around 1750–70. It has Matthew Boulton cut steels around a Josiah Wedgwood centre showing a Merfamily. (Northeast Regional Button Association)

First published 2013

The History Press
The Mill, Brimscombe Port
Stroud, Gloucestershire, GL5 2QG
www.thehistorypress.co.uk

© Jennifer Tann & Anthony Burton, 2013

British Library Cataloguing in Publication Data.
A catalogue record for this book is available from the British Library.

ISBN 978 0 7524 6292 9

Typesetting and origination by The History Press
Printed in Great Britain

Contents

Preface

Readers may wonder why this book has two authors and how the work was divided between them. The answer to the first question is that we are friends with a common interest in the history of technology and we have both been fascinated for some time by Matthew Boulton, his life and his contribution to the Industrial Revolution that swept through eighteenth-century Britain. Jennifer Tann has done extensive research on the Boulton & Watt and Matthew Boulton archives, and Anthony Burton became interested in Boulton while writing biographies of Josiah Wedgwood and Richard Trevithick.

We divided the writing between us on a roughly 50:50 basis, and when each of us had completed a chapter, sent it to the other for criticism and comment. When we were both happy with the results, we made a final check to make sure that nothing important had been omitted simply because we each thought the other would be doing it. Once this criterion was met, the chapters were put together. We hope the seams do not show.

Jennifer Tann and Anthony Burton

1

Eighteenth-Century Birmingham: Birthplace of Matthew Boulton

Early eighteenth-century Birmingham had grown up at the intersection of three shire counties – Staffordshire, Warwickshire and Worcestershire. It was not an ancient city or borough and its emergence as a significant settlement was due to the metalworking trades in the town and its environs, with the coal and iron industries of east Shropshire as well as the coalfield area between Nuneaton and Coventry.

Birmingham's emergence might be explained by the resource endowments of iron, limestone, fireclay and coal, and certainly later eighteenth-century visitors to the region attributed the miracle of Birmingham to the abundance of coal. Yet, in the mid-eighteenth century Birmingham was not really on the beaten track at all. Visitors had to leave the main highway to reach it; there was no river communication such as the Severn, which was navigable as far as Shrewsbury. It was not well supplied with water power, the small streams rising on the edge of the Midlands plateau being shallow and generating little power. It was developments in transport – the turnpiking of roads and the construction of canal and river navigations – that promoted the integration of Birmingham into the West Midlands. In this way the relative isolation of Birmingham was resolved.

Turnpikes came early to the region. The first public stage coach service to London was established in 1731, notice being given that the journey would take two and a half days at a cost of 1 guinea per passenger. And canal building was incentivised by manufacturers such as Josiah Wedgwood, Matthew Boulton and Samuel Garbett, who all had good reason to promote canals either for bringing in raw materials or for enabling more effective access to markets for their products.

While Wedgwood promoted the Grand Trunk Canal, which was begun in 1766, it was not until 1777 that travel along its entire 140 miles was possible. The Birmingham Canal Bill passed both Houses of Parliament in 1768, enabling a waterway to be constructed through the Black Country with the aim of joining up with the Staffordshire & Worcestershire Canal. This made it easier to bring coal and iron by boat and provided a route for Birmingham wares to go to the Severn and down to Bristol. In 1772, with the completion of the Staffordshire & Worcestershire Canal, the West Midlands had its first access to the sea. The Birmingham Canal gave a huge boost to the economy of Birmingham and the Black Country, as did the Birmingham & Fazeley Canal of 1783, which made a shorter route possible to the port of Hull and northern European markets and also provided a link to the southern canal system and, via the Thames, to London. William Hutton noted how, before the opening of the Birmingham Canal, 'it was common to see a train of carriages for miles, to the great destruction of the road, and annoyance of travellers'.[1] Whereas pit coal from Wednesbury had sold in Birmingham for around 13s per ton before the opening of the 22-mile cut, the price fell to 7s per ton in 1772.

Matthew Boulton was not only a promoter but benefited from the new canal system in two ways. First, it greatly reduced the cost of raw materials and, second, investment in judiciously purchased canal shares proved profitable. And, of course, the canal provided a ready market for Boulton & Watt pumping engines, besides promoting canalside locations for new factories. In 1795, Matthew Robinson Boulton and James Watt junior selected a canalside site in Smethwick for their new Soho foundry.

Moreover, improvements to roadways reduced the passenger journey times between London and Birmingham to fourteen hours by 1782. The turnpikes enabled Boulton and Watt to travel to Paris in six days. And when French visitors came to see Joseph Priestley in 1785 they noted that the road between Birmingham and Wolverhampton – 14 miles – was almost 'one continuous town'.[2]

Birmingham's emergence as a centre of metal trades can be traced to at least the sixteenth century, for by this time it was more than a village – indeed a small market town. After the Civil War, minting and gun-making trades came to Birmingham, as did brass working and in 1689 a French visitor wrote that, while he had seen fine swords, cane heads, snuff boxes and works of steel in Milan, they 'can be had cheaper and better in Birmingham'.[3] The town had supported Cromwell in the Civil War and there were many nonconformists there, particularly after the 1660s when they were banned from worshipping in the chartered towns. Nonconformists were excluded from public office, from teaching and from the universities in the Test Acts of 1673 but, after the Toleration Act of 1689, some chapels and meeting houses were built. The Baptists, Presbyterians and Quakers brought energy to Birmingham; its citizens were independently minded and made the most of the lack of corporate regulations.

Birmingham became a town noted for the manufacture of toys: ornamental fashion and decorative goods such as buttons, buckles, snuffboxes and much else besides, which had been made there from the late seventeenth century. Buckles were worn by men, women and children, and were made mainly of white metal to resemble silver. (It was fashionable for them to be worn not only on shoes but also on men's knee breeches.) The variations in design seemed endless and sometimes, depending on fashion, they could be up to 6in in width. But the market for buckles collapsed at the end of the eighteenth century; buttons seemed to be a safer bet, less liable to market fluctuation. Between 1770 and 1788, the number of button manufacturers more than doubled. Meanwhile, the more utilitarian ironwork and edge tools migrated to the Black Country, to be replaced by workshops for goods which produced greater value-added to the raw materials than mere metal bashing.

As early as the 1670s, Birmingham had grown in size to equal some of the county towns of the region. Whereas in 1700 there were over 2,500 houses in twenty-eight streets, by 1781 there were just over 9,500 houses in 133 streets. A visitor in 1776 reported, 'half the town is new, and they continue to build with greater rapidity than ever'. In 1791, William Hutton estimated that there were just over 12,500 houses and 203 streets, by which time Birmingham had become the third largest town in England in terms of population.[4]

Arthur Young, the agricultural writer, visited Birmingham in the 1760s and 1770s, and in 1791 called it 'the first manufacturing town in the world'.[5] By the end of the eighteenth century it was the most significant centre for hardware (pots and pans) manufacture and toys, a position that it maintained into the mid-nineteenth century when the British Association for the Advancement of Science met in Birmingham, the Handbook noting that 'within a radius of 30 miles of Birmingham nearly the whole of the hardware wants of the world are practically supplied'.[6]

Entrepreneurship and innovation characterised Birmingham industries in the later eighteenth century – both product and process innovation; the former to increase market share in businesses subject to rapid changes in fashion, and the latter to secure cost reduction and produce consistency. Birmingham was a noisy place, a German visitor to Soho noting the incessant 'hammering, pounding, rubbing and chiselling' that assailed him on entering the town. Peter Jones draws attention to the rapid response to opportunities in the marketplace which characterised Birmingham's 'formula for commercial success', buckles and buttons being frequently changed in shape, materials and design.[7] And, while Prosser justifiably celebrated the inventiveness of Birmingham manufacturers, as evidenced in the number of patents granted between 1760 and 1850, it is clear that much of Birmingham's inventiveness never reached the patent books.[8] Edward Thomason, for example, successively invented a self-steering fire-ship, a one-sail windmill for pumping water from ponds, folding steps for carriages, an improved corkscrew, a sliding toasting fork, a metal walking cane incorporating a cigar lighter, and a dice-throwing machine.[9] Speed of response to perceived demand was vital, for, as Hutton commented, 'the fashion of today is thrown into the casting pot tomorrow'.[10]

In the early eighteenth century, Birmingham manufacturers largely supplied a domestic market with its more basic hardware. However, by mid-century much of the ornamental work was being exported. In the mid-1760s, Matthew Boulton remarked that 'more than half the letters we receive are wrote in the German language'.[11] It is likely that overseas trade was dominated by the larger manufacturers such as Boulton, John Taylor and others, while the smaller manufacturers focused on the home market. John Fothergill, Boulton's partner in the toy trade, had been travelling in northern Europe from the late 1760s, and in 1776 went to St Petersburg. By 1790, around a quarter of Birmingham's hardware output was directed overseas, but this was severely disrupted when European markets were blocked during the French Revolution and its aftermath. France declared war on Britain in 1793 and much of the Continent rapidly became closed to Birmingham manufacturers, with catastrophic consequences for many. Boulton managed better than some, not least because his London bankers were supportive but also because he had by that stage diversified into a number of different businesses.

In 1757, Josiah Tucker drew attention to the fact that 'almost every Master Manufacturer hath a new Invention of his own, and is daily improving on those of others'. This was, he asserted, a 'Specimen of practical mechanics scarce to be paralleled in any part of the World'.[12] As an example, Dickinson draws attention to the invention of the fly press which was used for stamping buttons in the latter part of the seventeenth century.[13] A simple mechanism, the press was operated by pulling a lever by which the upper die was brought down on to the lower with great impact which could force a thin piece of metal placed between them into almost any shape. The fly press had a great many uses in button, buckle and trinket manufacture, besides minting.

There was considerable differentiation and specialisation within Birmingham and the Black Country. Nail making, which had been important in Birmingham in the sixteenth century, had largely migrated to Dudley and Stourbridge in the seventeenth. Edge tools, knives and sword manufacture, which had been located in Birmingham in the seventeenth century, had left the town altogether. The trades that developed in Birmingham were ever more highly skilled. Buckle manufacture began in Walsall, but as the designs became more and more elaborate it migrated to Birmingham where it grew rapidly.

Birmingham, not being a borough or city, did not have trade guilds or compulsory apprenticeship. This gave entrepreneurs the freedom to employ people based on their demonstrable skills rather than the fact that they had served an apprenticeship, as was compulsory in the corporate towns up to at least the seventeenth century. Trades in incorporated towns were highly regulated, but in Birmingham no one was asked whether they had served an apprenticeship or not. The absence of restriction attracted dissenters of all kinds, particularly Quakers in the eighteenth century, and the new industries attracted skilled craftsmen from some distance. Boulton recruited from France, later in the eighteenth century, for example. Thus new blood coming in facilitated the spread of new techniques and ideas. Birmingham must have been an energetic town in which to live and work. William Hutton identified it as the place for a man to make his fortune; many arrived on foot and left in chariots.

Matthew Boulton's grandfather, John, married an heiress, which may have enabled the family to set up a reasonably capitalised business early in the eighteenth century. His son, Matthew senior, was a toymaker specialising in the steel toy trade. The business was located in Snow Hill, then almost on the outskirts of the town on the road to Wolverhampton. Matthew Boulton, the subject of this biography, was born on 3 September 1728 (14 September in the new calendar) in the house behind the workshop in Snow Hill which abutted on to Slaney Street. The name Matthew had been given to the firstborn son of his father who had died, aged 2, in 1726. Matthew was a double namesake and, while he had a brother John and two sisters, it was clearly he who embodied his father's aspirations.

Boulton went to school at the academy of the Rev. John Hausted, who was also chaplain at a chapel in Deritend. He did not have the classical education of a gentleman, but he certainly had some knowledge of both the classics and English literature and throughout his life actively pursued learning. As he walked to school he would have passed the houses in Temple Row occupied by well-to-do businessmen and professionals and would then have gone down High Street, the nearby lanes and courts being filled with workshops and all sorts of markets. Corn and garden produce were sold in the Bull Ring and there were a number of bookshops along the route. Distraction was everywhere for a boy with curiosity. The town and its workshops taught Boulton as much as the classroom.

While his many notebooks kept in adulthood demonstrate his inquisitiveness, they also show a knowledge of mathematics, science, engineering and much else besides. Boulton probably left school aged 14, as was usual at the time, and entered into his father's business. It would seem that he had both energy and enthusiasm for this.

In 1755, Boulton made a note of the books he had bought to set up in his study. The list contained many items that would have been found in a gentleman's library. There were four collected volumes of *The Tatler* and eight of *The Spectator*. There were English, Italian and French dictionaries and the complete works of Pope, Swift, Shakespeare and Locke. Then there were the more practical works such as Clare's *Introduction to Book Keeping*, besides a number of books on electricity.

His father specialised in buckle manufacture and it is said that at the age of 17, young Boulton produced an inlaid buckle which broadened the product portfolio and helped to enlarge his father's business. He became a partner at the age of 21 and, from that time on, was entrusted with the management of the business.

Matthew was a sociable individual, a trait remarked upon throughout his life. Amongst his friends were Samuel Garbett, button and hardware maker; Garbett's partner John Roebuck, the industrial chemist; and the great printer John Baskerville. All were independently minded, 'risktakers pursuing their ends with dogged perseverance'.[14] Garbett taught Boulton how to finance large projects, and Roebuck showed him that science was important and could be made to pay, while Baskerville demonstrated that art and experiment were good bedfellows.

Later on, Boulton was an engaging host to the many Soho visitors, as well as to members of the Lunar Society. He was dark, with curly brown hair and a wide smile, well dressed, perhaps slightly flamboyantly, and had a sense of humour and an eye to the main chance in looking for a wife. He sought both love and money, and found this not once but twice through family connections in Lichfield. In 1749, at the age of 21, Boulton married Mary Robinson, daughter of a prosperous Lichfield mercer. The marriage settlement brought both land and money which were to benefit him as his businesses grew. Mary died ten years later, in 1759, being buried not in Birmingham but near Lichfield. Boulton was heartbroken and wrote a poem which he placed in her coffin (having carefully made a copy first). But only months later, he was sending love letters to Mary's sister, Ann, his 'lovely, dearest, sweetest charmer', whom he married in 1760, despite family and public disapproval. Ann brought additional land and capital and, on the death of her brother Luke, this was greatly increased.[15]

In 1759, his father died leaving his property to Matthew junior. He got on well with other manufacturers in Birmingham and the surrounding area and was probably regarded as an eligible bachelor. This brought Boulton more into the public domain, and his demeanour and a degree of diplomacy must have singled him out to be prominent in petitioning the House of Commons in 1760, at the age of 32, when he appeared before a Parliamentary Committee as a representative of the buckle makers of Birmingham, Warwick and Wolverhampton. It is not known how he was selected, but this was only the beginning of a remarkable career as a parliamentary lobbyist.[16]

It was reported that more than 8,000 people were employed in buckle making in the counties of Warwick and Stafford, and this excluded those employed in making tools and preparing materials. Buckles were made of copper, brass, iron, tin and spelter and many were set with glass in imitation of jewellery. The purpose of the inquiry was the buckle makers' petition to the House of Commons for leave to bring in a Bill to prohibit the export of buckle chapes – the part of the buckle by which it was fastened to a strap or ribbon. Chape making and buckle making were distinct and independent, only one example of the huge subdivision and specialisation within the toy trade. The division of labour and its separation into distinct businesses was a characteristic of a number of Birmingham industries, notably the gun trade in the nineteenth century.

Boulton's evidence showed that the great part of the consumption of buckles was overseas. He thought that there were around 2,500 iron chape makers in the counties of Warwick and Stafford and, owing to the great demand for export, the price of chapes had risen. The petitioners argued, that if their export was prohibited, it would prevent foreigners acquiring them and would keep the buckle trade at home while not diminishing the number of chape makers. Another witness said that 'the Buckle is by far the most considerable article in the Toy Trade'. On further examination, Boulton claimed that chapes could not be made in Spain or Portugal as well or as cheaply as in England, for there were no rolling or slitting mills there and if they were to import iron the price would be too high. The chape makers petitioned against the Bill and finally it was dropped.

While this dispute between buckle makers and chape makers may present Boulton in an illiberal light, at other times he could be magnanimous and generous. However, another example of his focus on self-interest was the petition for the extension of Watt's engine patent for a term of twenty-five years which, combined with the pursuit of pirates in the courts in the 1790s, suggests that where business was concerned, self-interest came first. Another example of this was his determination not to allow the war with France to prevent Boulton & Watt from exporting a steam engine to France, and on this occasion Boulton applied 'a little gold dust' to the eyes of the customs official, also ensuring that the engine parts were exported from different ports so as not to raise suspicion.[17]

The Birmingham in which Boulton grew up and flourished was an exciting and vibrant town, full of noise and bustle, where invention and innovation ranged from the frankly weird to the highly marketable, from the flamboyant to the practical; where raw materials and labour could be readily sourced. This was an excellent background for a young and ambitious man.

Notes

1   W. Hutton, *An History of Birmingham*, 1795, p. 402.

2   Quoted in Peter M. Jones, *Industrial Enlightenment: Science, technology and culture in Birmingham and the West Midlands*, 2008, p. 27.

3   Jenny Uglow, *The Lunar Men*, 2002, p. 19.

4   Hutton, op. cit., p. 69; Jones, op. cit., pp. 34–36.

5   *Annals of Agriculture*, Vol. 16, 1791, p. 532.

6   S. Timmins (ed.), *Birmingham and the Midland Hardware District*, 1866, repr. 1967, quoted in Jones, op. cit., p. 39.

7   Jones, op. cit., p. 24.

8   R.B. Prosser, *Birmingham Inventors and Inventions – Being A Contribution to the Industrial History of Birmingham*, 1881.

9   'Sir Edward Thomason's Memoirs during Half a Century', Vol. I, pp. 3–4, quoted in Jones, op. cit., p. 40.

10 Hutton, op. cit., p. 107.

11 Peter M. Jones, 'Birmingham and the West Midlands in the eighteenth and early nineteenth centuries', in Malcolm Dick (ed.), *Matthew Boulton: A Revolutionary Player*, 2009.

12 Josiah Tucker, *Instructions for Travellers*, 1757, p. 20.

13 H.W. Dickinson, *Matthew Boulton*, 1937, p. 13.

14 Uglow, op. cit., p. 2.

15 Shena Mason, 'A New Species of Gentleman', in Malcolm Dick (ed.), op. cit., pp. 32–33.

16 E.g., in achieving an extension to Watt's engine patent.

17 Jennifer Tann, 'Marketing Methods in the International Steam Engine Market: The Case of Boulton and Watt', *Journal of Economic History*, XXXVIII, 2, 1978.

2

The Soho

Soho Manufactory

The Birmingham toy trade was characterised by a highly sophisticated division of labour between 'small masters' in specialised trades. Each small master might have from two to ten workmen, the work being done in a multitude of 'shops' built along the backs of houses and garden boundaries. Boulton recognised that the centre of Birmingham, while it had some convenience, was nevertheless too crowded, so he looked for a site beyond the town in 1761. What he found was some land, a watermill and a house on Handsworth Heath, about 1¾ miles from his previous works. With a ½-mile mill leat providing power, Boulton began to plan the construction of an elegant factory within which his manufacturing businesses would be housed and, in the wings, some of his workers too. He depended upon water power (supplied by Hockley Pool and the leat) for a while and, in a period of water shortage in 1771, (for which, in part, he blamed the Birmingham Canal Navigation, suspecting leaks) he had to stop half the machinery in the mill and resort, in part, to using horses to work it.[1]

Boulton was one of the few manufacturers of the mid to late eighteenth century to employ an architect for his factory. The building, designed by William Wyatt and built by his father's firm, Benjamin Wyatt & Sons (the original architect, T. Lightoler, being found unsatisfactory), was three storeys high with gables at each end and a porticoed centrepiece of four storeys enclosed within a dome. Vertically sliding sash windows were a feature of the main and side elevations; the last three bays of windows at either end of the building projected slightly forward, emphasised by pediments. Building work probably began early in 1762, the main building being completed between 1765 and 1767; in 1765, Boulton's partner, John Fothergill, told Boulton, 'Mr Wyatt has been wrote to for to send you the requested elevation immediately.'[2]

Soho Manufactory is a prime example of 'the factory as country house', an early engraving showing a carriage in the driveway, emphasising the appearance of a landed estate, representing Boulton's social aspirations. Later assessment of the building was less complimentary: 'It was a plain brick building with a clock cupola, looking like a stable block.'[3] Parallel ranges of workshops enclosed a courtyard. A range of the chimneys indicates furnaces. Boulton continued to improve the Manufactory – John Rennie, who spent some time at Soho before setting up on his own in London, noted 'the old mill pulled down and the new one founded', a probable reference to the lap mill for polishing steel.[4] And two successive mints were constructed near to but not adjoining the Manufactory. Through Boulton, the Wyatts gained the commission for the new General Infirmary in Stafford, Boulton being appointed one of the trustees. He remained a faithful patron, helping Samuel Wyatt, another of Benjamin's sons, to be commissioned to design the new façade of the Theatre Royal in Birmingham in 1777, and Heathfield House for James Watt in 1787. In turn, the brothers recommended Boulton's manufactures to their clients.[5]

The Manufactory at Soho was soon included in the itinerary of tourists to the latest manufacturing and mining sites. Boulton revelled in entertaining visitors, much to James Watt's chagrin. The first foreign visitor recorded as coming to Soho was an Italian chemistry professor. In 1766, Lord and Lady Shelburne arrived. 'The front of this house is like the stately palace of some Duke,' reported one visitor.[6] Boulton recognised the marketing benefits of Soho and, along with other manufacturers in Birmingham, sought to promote the town to visitors. The Manufactory was the jewel in Birmingham's crown and sightseers, tourists, technologists and scientists had almost unlimited access until the mid-1780s.

In 1771, Boulton added a showroom to demonstrate his move into silversmithing and ormolu. Wedgwood considered it to be a 'superb gallery'. However, it was not only a marketing showcase, for Boulton craved fame and praise for his good taste, which seems 'to have outweighed all other considerations'.[7] But Boulton's steam engine partner, James Watt, disapproved of the stream of visitors, particularly those from overseas, fearing that some, rather than coming to admire the Manufactory, might be intent on stealing inventions and business ideas. And, by the late 1780s, a number of manufacturers in the region were beginning to deny access to their premises for fear of industrial espionage.

Soho Manufactory became the centre for the complete portfolio of Boulton's business interests. Here the Boulton & Fothergill partnership manufactured toys, ormolu, and plated wares; Matthew Boulton & Plate Co. made plated and silverware; Boulton & Watt manufactured some of the smaller precision parts of steam engines (the heavy castings and forgings being made by specialists); Boulton & Eginton had their mechanical painting business (copying pictures for those who could not afford the originals); Matthew Boulton & Button Co. and Boulton & Scale made buttons and buckles; and there was the M. Boulton Mint Co.

Soho House

As Boulton prepared to marry his second wife, Ann Robinson, he turned his attention to preparing his Snow Hill home to bring it to the kind of standard she would have expected, having been brought up in a smart home in Lichfield. Much shopping and redecoration began. Soho House, built *circa* 1757, was valued at a little under a third of the total price paid for the leasehold estate. Boulton moved his mother and one of his sisters there, but in 1762 they had to leave in order to accommodate Boulton's business partner, John Fothergill. Boulton commuted between Snow Hill and the Manufactory, but this was tiring and inefficient and by 1766 he urgently felt the need to live nearer to his work. He thought up a whole range of reasons why it was essential that Fothergill should move out: it was far too much of a strain to be constantly making the journey between Birmingham and the Soho works; being nearer the works would make for greater efficiency and thus larger profits of which Fothergill would have a share; and, finally, that Fothergill had not cared for the grounds and gardens. Fothergill, disgruntled and protesting, was evicted and Boulton and Ann moved in.

His plans for an elegant manufacturer's house began to take shape and he turned to his architect friends, the brothers Samuel and James Wyatt. Samuel was the first to be employed, writing in 1787, 'I sent you a few days ago the sketches for your house, which may afford you some amusement at a leisure hour and when I know your determination, I shall proceed as you desire.'[8] In the 1790s, Samuel's brother James became Soho House architect and proposed a new front elevation dominated by a pediment carried on Ionic columns. Boulton's response was that the design, being more than 2,000 years old, had 'stood the test of Cricks and Time'. He approved the plan but wavered over the new study and library: 'The plan of the offices I have repeatedly try'd to mend, but I have allways returned to the point I set out from & have decided to conform exactly to your plan.' He considered one alteration, 'but I will not adopt it without your approbation & advice'.[9] Sometime later, Boulton introduced a warm-air central heating system.

Boulton's genteel lifestyle demanded servants to support it, including a butler, footman, valet, cook and housekeeper, besides maids and outdoor servants, including a liveried coachman and gardeners. He paid great attention to the interior of the house, commissioning carpets to be woven, cabinets and bookcases to be made. He had a wide range of books on chemistry, 'handmaid to ye arts', agriculture, optics, medical essays, matrimonial precepts and Ovid's *Metamorphoses*.[10] There was gilded furniture in the drawing room, gilt-framed mirrors, silverware produced in Boulton's workshops and Wedgwood china on the dinner table. In Boulton's small library and study, besides books there was scientific equipment. In 1771, he wrote in one of his notebooks of his ideal 'hobby horsery' which would be a round building with storage for all his equipment and books and a 'skylight in ye middle of the domical roof'.[11] His pipedream did not end there, for he imagined a private door from this room opening into a passageway leading to cold and warm baths, laboratory, dressing room, powdering room and an observatory. He was still thinking about this the following year; indeed his dreams had grown to include a museum – 'abt 800 feet area wd be big enough for me'.[12] He was an avid learner throughout his life as his notebooks demonstrate: they include notes from the classics, novels, fine art, geology, medicine, physics, chemistry, biology and even accountancy.

The Gardens

The fine, well-known drawing of the Soho estate by Francis Eginton junior, engraved by Stebbing Shaw, shows Soho House perched on a hilltop overlooking the lake on which is moored a monogrammed boat – the complete gentleman's estate – until we remind ourselves that the lake also provided water power for the Manufactory. A number of sketches and watercolours of the estate were done by John Phillp in the 1790s. Phillp's sketches of the garden buildings show Boulton's aspirations to have a landscape garden in imitation of the landed gentry and aristocracy. A sketch of Soho Pool shows a boathouse enclosed in shrubbery, while a small classical pedimented Temple of Flora adjoined the lake. The lake served a dual purpose – as a decorative landscape feature and as a source of power for the Manufactory.[13] Boulton studied the lifestyle, homes and garden grounds of landed society, even to the extent of carefully noting how long the Earl of Hopetoun had his eggs boiled for breakfast and how many he ate. In July 1772, Boulton visited Charles Hamilton's grounds at Painshill Park in Surrey. It would have interested Boulton greatly because, in creating the gardens, Hamilton had faced much the same sort of problems that he confronted at Handsworth. When Daniel Defoe visited the Park in the 1720s, it had just been laid out over what had been heathland, 'most of it so poor as not to produce anything but *Heath* and *Broom*'.[14] Boulton decided that what had been done on poor ground in Surrey could be repeated on equally impoverished land at Soho. He took extensive notes and made sketches of the various features.

This was just at the beginning of the great period of English landscape gardening, when the strict formality of the past was giving way to a more natural look, with an emphasis on the picturesque. There were garden buildings, carefully sited to provide focal points in the landscape rather than perform any useful function, and the style was as likely to be Gothic as Classical. The firs that had been planted primarily as a windbreak when Boulton first bought the estate were now supplemented by more exotic trees and shrubs. Boulton's landscape was particularly inspired by Painshill, and his estate evoked a number of eulogies, including a poem from an unknown hand in 1796:

Where nature seem'd to have left a spot for waste
And barren heath defied all human taste
Where tree nor Shrub except the furze bush grew,
Became the chosen seat of art and you.[15]

Food

Food played an important role in life at Soho; Boulton kept a well-appointed household and was a generous host. A stream of visitors arrived as the fame of the Manufactory spread. He revelled in high society, and while he had not had an extensive formal education, was urbane and widely read. The Lunar Society regularly met at Soho House on the night of the full moon, a wise precaution in view of the copious quantities of food and wine consumed and the absence of street lighting. Boulton's cellar was renowned.

Food was supplied from Birmingham sources and, for the more unusual items, from London where Boulton shopped when there on business. Wine and spirits were sent by canal boat, but Boulton regularly dispatched food by stagecoach or by Deykin's wagon. Goods included such items as oysters, costly spices, pasta and varieties of tea and coffee, besides mineral water from Jacob Schweppe, the latter packed in hampers of twelve dozen half-pint bottles. In 1802, scientifically minded friends consumed so much fizzy water that Schweppe asked Boulton if a Birmingham agent could be found. (The idea of fizzy water had come from the scientist Joseph Priestley, a friend of Boulton's.) Quantities of fish and other seafood, as well as beef and venison, were regular items of the Soho diet. The household also devoured a great deal of sugar. While this was an indicator of prosperity, an unintended consequence was tooth decay and both of Boulton's children, Anne and Matt, had frequent painful visits to the dentist for extractions, Anne undergoing a tooth transplant at least once.

In one of his early letters to Watt, Boulton called his house 'Hôtel d'amitié sur Handsworth Heath' – his friendship hotel. He revelled in the company of such visitors as Benjamin Franklin, Sir Joseph Banks, Sir William Herschel and others, besides the fashionable Elizabeth Montagu, 'queen of the Bluestockings', and the actress Sarah Siddons. Close friends frequently stayed at Soho House, as well as some business contacts such as the Russian Ambassador, through whom Boulton aspired to export a mint to Russia.

Matthew Boulton was an eminent and active Birmingham citizen, playing a part in committees and taking shares in a variety of enterprises. In 1788, he contributed to the subscription being raised to build a new library in Birmingham[16] and was also an active supporter of the Birmingham Medical & Scientific Library.[17] An enthusiastic promoter of the plan to build a new theatre, Boulton became a shareholder, voicing strong views on redecoration in 1805: the interior was 'very dark, very dirty & disgraceful to the town & to the proprietors in particular'. He requested that the assembly room would not be painted with oils as within a month 'this will smell and be more disagreeable and dangerous to the company than the site or smell of a dirty Bacchanalian apartment'.[18] In 1801, he chaired a meeting to consider a proposal to establish a botanical garden for 'The Purpose of study'g Botany'.[19] Boulton & Watt supplied a pneumatic apparatus to the Birmingham Dispensary, probably out of concern for Watt's son Gregory, who suffered from tuberculosis.[20] He supported the idea of building a Free Church in Birmingham, donating £100, 'since the lower classes of Inhabitants are almost excluded from the Churches and Chapels and consequently deprived of the Means and Advantages of attending Divine Service'.[21] He held 400 shares in the Trent & Mersey Canal and proposed that the Birmingham Canal Navigation Committee consider a cut being made across Handsworth Heath to the Soho Manufactory. In the event, this did not happen, but when Soho Foundry was built, it was located alongside the canal at Smethwick.

Boulton was to the fore in making an alliance with the merchants and manufacturers of Birmingham to establish a 'General Commercial Committee for the purpose of watching over and conducting the public interest of this Town and Neighbourhood'. A number of other towns had similar bodies and, in 1784, Josiah Wedgwood proposed a plan to unite them to prevent the emigration of skilled workmen or the introduction of foreign industrial spies.

This became the General Chamber of Manufacturers of Great Britain, Wedgwood becoming its first chair.[22]

It was probably as much on account of his public works (some underlined by self-interest) as by his fame as a manufacturer that Boulton became High Sheriff of Staffordshire in 1794, an early example of the manufacturer being acknowledged as a member of the landed gentry.[23]

Notes

1   MB to T. Gilbert, 2 February 1771.

2   Fothergill to MB, 12 November 1765.

3   John Martin Robinson, *The Wyatts: An Architectural Dynasty*, 1979, p. 19.

4   J. Rennie to MB, 18 August 1785.

5   Robinson, op. cit., p. 21.

6   Peter M. Jones, *Industrial Enlightenment: Science, technology and culture in Birmingham and the West Midlands, 1760–1820*, 2008, p. 71.

7   Ibid., p. 73.

8   S. Wyatt to MB, 1787.

9   MB to James Wyatt, 7 July 1796.

10 List of books in a bookcase at Soho, n.d.

11 Shena Mason, 'A New Species of Gentleman', in Malcolm Dick (ed.), *Matthew Boulton: A Revolutionary Player*, 2009, p. 36.

12 Ibid.

13 Phillada Ballard, Val Loggie & Shena Mason, *A Lost Landscape: Matthew Boulton's Gardens at Soho*, 2009, pp. 52–53.

14 Daniel Defoe, *A Tour through the Whole Island of Great Britain*, 1724–26.

15 Ballard et al., op. cit., p. 4.

16 M. Boulton Papers, Box Bham, 1, p. 479.

17 M. Boulton Papers, B, 1, p. 64.

18 MB to J. Woolley, 4 September 1805.

19 M. Boulton Papers, Bham Boxes 1–6.

20 Bham Dispensary, 19 November 1795.

21 M. Boulton Papers, Bham Boxes 1–34, 31 January 1804.

22 Robert E. Schofield, *The Lunar Society of Birmingham*, 1970, p. 352.

23 M. Boulton Papers, Shrievalty, 3.

3

The 'Toymaker'

The Boulton family's button and buckle business had been firmly established at Snow Hill, although not on a large scale, by the time Matthew Boulton was born in 1728. At the time, it was one of many small firms producing 'toys' in Birmingham, and Boulton joined the business on leaving school around 1745. During the 1750s, the business flourished, the firm's letterbooks showing many orders. In addition to manufacturing, the family mercantile business, with contacts across the European mainland, continued for the sale of Birmingham wares.

After his father's death in 1757, Boulton continued at Snow Hill, but with his wife Ann's inheritance and his own from his father, he began to make ambitious plans. The constraints on development of the Snow Hill site made expansion there impossible. To be able to combine the activities of merchant and manufacturer, Boulton required larger premises. What he needed was somewhere large enough for a drawing office, raw materials stores, workshops for manufacture and a warehouse for finished products. He did not have power at Snow Hill, so had to purchase metal already rolled. Part of his plan was to have a mill for basic processes such as metal rolling and polishing. In the event, with the acquisition of the Soho estate on a long lease in 1761, he could meet all these requirements, but only with significant capital outlay. Since there was already a watermill at the site, he demolished and rebuilt it while retaining his house and workshops at Snow Hill, but this obliged him to move between the two sites, which, in the wintertime, was not easy. It was clear that he needed help. And, while in London in January 1762, he was approached by John Fothergill, a Birmingham merchant who had only just parted company from his employer. On Midsummer's

Day that year, a partnership agreement was signed and Fothergill went to live in Soho House. Fothergill was born in Russia and brought significant continental European mercantile experience to the partnership. He worried about money and had to borrow his share of the partnership capital. Boulton's Snow Hill clerks took eight days over stocktaking and preparing an inventory in preparation for the partnership. Once the agreement was signed, Fothergill travelled extensively, particularly in France and Germany.

Boulton, whilst at Snow Hill during his father's lifetime, had become accustomed to being in more than one business – the mercantile trade and toys. From the time of his move to Soho his business interests proliferated and he established new business partnerships. In 1766, four years after his partnership with John Fothergill began, he entered into partnership with John Scale for the manufacture of buttons. Buckles, steel chains and sword hilts were added to the portfolio from 1782 until 1796. The Matthew Boulton & Button Co. also commenced in 1782, continuing until Boulton's death in 1809, albeit latterly probably not very actively.

Although Boulton had not initially intended creating a manufacturing unit in which all production processes were brought under one roof, it became clear that it was 'impossible almost to guard against the Losses we were so exposed to by having our Patterns goods & materials scattered about in so many different Streets and places'. And, while he did not distrust his workmen, or the small firms which undertook various processes, Boulton believed it to be prudent to bring production 'more under our Eyes & immediate management'.[1] He decided to move into Soho House, ousting Fothergill, who was not at all pleased. Boulton justified the move, at least to himself: 'As Fothergill is not of the least use in the Manufactory, if he will not live near a warehouse in Town, Query of what use will he be?' What Soho needed, Boulton mused, was 'a master of some resolution some knowledge of human nature & great skill & ingenuity in all mechanick arts both in theory & practice'. He was clearly writing his own job description and added, 'if B hath any claim to that character let it be him'.[2]

Now, with room for expansion, Boulton & Fothergill began to extend their product range. One of the first was steel jewellery, much in fashion until the last quarter of the eighteenth century, made of highly burnished faceted steel which reflected the light brilliantly. A wide variety of wares could be made from faceted steel: buttons, buckles, clasps, frames for purses, and chatelaines (functional ornaments which women wore at the waist and from which chains could be hung for keys, scissors, thimble cases and the like). Later on, enamels made in Bilston and cameos from Wedgwood's Etruria factory were set in faceted steel frames. The steel from which this jewellery was made was produced by the cementation method, using Swedish wrought iron. Wrought iron is a very pure form of the metal, but steel contains a small proportion of carbon, up to 1.7 per cent. In the cementation process the carbon is added by heating the wrought iron with charcoal in a closed fireclay pot.

Buttons were a decorative feature of clothing, and a directory of 1767 highlights the huge variety that was made:

> Gilt, Plated, Silvered, Lacquered and Pinchbeck, the beautiful New Manufacture Platina, Inlaid, Glass, Horn, Ivory and Pearl: metal buttons, such as Bath Hard and Soft White etc ... Link buttons in most of the above Metals, as well as of Paste, etc ... in short the vast Variety of sorts in both Branches is really amazing.[3]

There was a considerable price range, up to 140 guineas a gross, and Boulton & Fothergill had not only an extremely competitive market to contend with, one requiring almost continuous novelty, but the bad reputation of what were known as Brummagem Wares. Of this Boulton was acutely aware, writing to John Fothergill, 'The prejudice that Birmingham hath so justly established against itself, makes every fault conspicuous in all articles that have the least pretensions to taste.'[4]

So, in his new Manufactory, Boulton set about raising Birmingham's reputation as a town in which high-quality fashion goods were made. The button trade grew extensively in the second quarter of the eighteenth century. By 1762, Boulton knew about platina, a silvery alloy of copper and zinc, and experimented with a range of non-precious metals which looked like silver. One, known as tutenague, was an alloy of copper, zinc and nickel which, at the time, could be obtained only from China. Around 1770, he also used another white metal for a range of wares – an alloy of tin, antimony and copper.

The huge range of buttons produced at Soho required a wide variety of materials, including not only these 'new' metals but also steel, brass and pearl. From 1766, Sheffield plate buttons were produced and made in great quantities subsequently. Livery buttons in Sheffield plate were in demand, and a Georgian gentleman might wear as many as four dozen buttons on one set of clothes for coat, waistcoat and breeches. In about 1790, a 'dipping' process was discovered by which a gilt button could be quickly and cheaply produced. This led to pressure by the more reputable manufacturers for a system of marking buttons 'gilt' or 'plated' when they were covered in gold or silver, rather than 'dipped'. Plated wares comprised two layers of rolled silver enclosing one of copper, whereas dipped wares were cheaper, being dipped in molten silver, sometimes very briefly.[5] Between 1790 and 1795, meetings of master manufacturers were held to insist on the necessity of this. At one such meeting Boulton took the chair, denouncing the deception of marking 'gilt' or 'plated' on buttons which were not, and added:

As I am an old button maker, allow me to advise my brethren to make excel-
lence rather than cheapness their principle of rivalry; and pardon me if I
advise the merchant ... to lay aside the arts of reduction, and not expect to
buy his goods cheaper than any other man who has money in his hands.[6]

Boulton's friendship with Josiah Wedgwood, spiced by a degree of rivalry, led
to Boulton & Fothergill's use of cameos, some of which were first used in
the decoration of snuff boxes. Boulton had met Wedgwood in about 1761,
some time before either his Etruria works were built or his London showroom acquired. It was Wedgwood who, after a visit to Soho, suggested other
applications for cameos: intaglios, buttons and jasperware amongst them. This
led to some reciprocal selling – Soho-produced tortoise-shell boxes, inlaid
with cameos, being offered for sale in Wedgwood's London showroom.[7] While
Wedgwood, too, followed taste and ornament, dividing his Etruria factory into
distinct sections for the production of 'Useful Wares' and 'Ornamental Wares',
he had a firmer hold on the implications of luxury goods production for his
overall profitability than Boulton.

These industries required workmen of the highest calibre and Boulton was
keen to extend the skills of willing pupils – for instance, any apprentices who
showed a propensity to draw received lessons. But there were not enough
'home-grown' workmen to meet the need for the highest quality craftsmen
and Boulton sought to recruit from abroad. This was not regarded as espionage,
whereas when foreign firms enticed British craftsmen overseas it was. Self-
interest was reinforced by patriotism when both served the same ends. When
they did not, self-interest won hands down. Boulton's close contacts with John
Ebbinghaus, a German hardware merchant, provided plenty of opportunity for
exchanging trade secrets, such as when Ebbinghaus was asked to discover the
method of manufacturing white metal in Saxe-Gotha, and it was through contacts in both London and France that Boulton was able to acquire details of
French ormolu manufacture (and replicate it). On another occasion, Boulton
sought 'an excellent workman in the silversmith trade' in Paris, and brazier's tools
were purchased via an intermediary in Amsterdam. In 1771, four Frenchmen
were employed at Soho, each having a very specific skill, including a buckle
maker and an expert mathematical instrument maker and gilder. A workman
from Saxony was so skilled that Boulton & Fothergill wished him to be kept
isolated from all other jewellers in London in case he was enticed away. In 1791,
the merchant R.E. Raspe wrote, 'For engravers I have wrote to Vienna, Hanau
and Sweden – as also to Berlin – without compromising you – simply requesting to let you know whether and how they can and will engage with you.'[8]

Boulton did not leave overseas marketing entirely to Fothergill and, in 1765,
went to Paris sufficiently unexpectedly for his wife not to know in advance.

John Baskerville undertook to inform her that the visit was necessary to establish the reputation of the trade and suggested that Mrs Boulton meet him in London on his return 'and observed it would be as useful as a journey to Bath, and the consequence is no doubt a son and heir, at which she laughed heartily and said she would not go'.[9] Some merchants were well connected and supplied lists of foreign houses which Boulton & Fothergill might deal with. In 1764, Fothergill reported to Boulton, who was then in London, that the orders in hand were increasing at a rapid rate and provided a list of merchants dealing in their articles in Italy, America, Germany, Spain and Holland – eighteen merchant houses in all.[10] No wonder that Edmund Burke had called Birmingham 'the great Toy Shop of Europe'. Later, in 1793, Boulton was sent a list of merchants in toys, hardware and buttons in Philadelphia.[11]

Boulton's business optimism appeared to know no bounds. Writing in 1766 to an acquaintance in Leipzig, who he hoped would invest in the business, he reported on the 'great increase in our business', adding, 'if you will advance £2,000 you shall share in our profits'.[12] However, there was the suggestion that Boulton's goods were more highly priced than those of his competitors and that people in foreign markets prefer 'what is showy, pretty and cheap'.[13] Boulton did not give up easily, writing to tell Ebbinghaus that the plated trade was increasing, that he had been offered the opportunity to buy out Peter Capper's business in platina and plated buttons, but that he was already doing too much for the present capital.[14] Ebbinghaus wrote in the following year, warning that 'money in trade is always better than large buildings and dead stocks, for money gains money and dead stocks decrease'.[15] However, ignoring the warning, Boulton purchased Gimlett's trade of gilt chains, boxes and instrument cases in 1768, and was busy making new patterns for this branch of the toy trade.[16]

The profitability of Boulton & Fothergill was variable and, overall, the business was run at a loss to both partners. In 1780, Zach Walker, one of Boulton's right-hand men, compiled a set of accounts for the years 1765–1780, showing capital advanced each year, together with annual profits and losses for each partner. Profits are recorded for five years and losses for five. There was a run of three years of modest profits between 1765 and 1767, but no further recorded profit until 1774, Boulton's profit being £1,598 8s, Fothergill making £1,365 2s. Losses were recorded in 1765, 1768, 1772, 1773 and 1780, the latter three years' deficits for Boulton altogether being around £8,750.[17] It was at this time that James Keir, a fellow member of the Lunar Society, then manufacturing glass at Amblecote near Stourbridge, suggested to Boulton that, in view of the poor glass trade, he should quit and begin a connection with Boulton. In April 1778, Boulton spent fifty days in London and while he was there Keir visited the Manufactory but did not undertake any management duties, save the refining of plated scraps, and making aqua fortis.

On Boulton's return in June, Keir became both an irritant and a consolation.[18] In no uncertain terms he reported on the various elements of Boulton's non-engine businesses: 'I have been making a strict examination into the plated and tortoise-shell business, both of which may be put, I think, on much better management than they are at present … The plated business is well worth cultivating but much depends on management of it.' The tortoise-shell business was in a bad state. 'Your prices are from 15 to 20 per cent lower than any other manufacturers, and yet your stock is very great. The fact is that the goods are made in bad taste, notwithstanding they are made at Soho.' Keir recommended that the stock of tortoise-shell, steel chains and other similar goods be marked down and sold for what they would fetch and that, in future, more attention be paid to fashion.[19] In the following year, Keir reported on his task, which he saw as 'to call your attention to the general state of your affairs'. The first step, Keir suggested, was to understand his business affairs in greater detail, otherwise 'you wouldn't have believed as you did last summer that raising a few thousand pounds could permanently extricate you out of your difficulties'. Keir estimated Boulton's business commitments to be £8,500 and his probable incomings no more than £4,000, intimating that neither he nor, he suspected, Boulton would wish him to continue in any management role at Boulton & Fothergill. Keir urged, 'If you would but give up one or two mornings in a week solely and without interruption to the business of the manufacturing, to enquire into and regulate the detail of it, I would never fail to meet you there.' He sought to sugar the pill:

It is a misfortune common to all men of Genius, that they find it in themselves an aversion to employ their minds up on any subject but where their genius can be exerted particularly to attend to the regular, uniform & daily detail of business. And this I consider as the principal source of your misfortunes. We have however known instances of men of true genius conquering that aversion and subjecting the natural bent of their genius to the rules of prudence and propriety of conduct in their respective stations.[20]

The partnership with Fothergill quickly became strained. The basis of the difficulties was largely financial, Fothergill having persuaded himself that their partnership funds were, in part, supporting the Boulton & Watt engine business. Boulton's banker, William Matthews, wrote that he had examined Boulton & Fothergill's books and found them to be 'simple, fair and just … And that the engine business … is not at all interwoven with the accounts of Boulton and Fothergill'.[21] A memo to Murdoch, employed on the engine side, suggests that this was not entirely so, for in 1781 the engine business was so starved of cash that the company did not have sufficient money to pay Christmas balances or

workmen's wages, 'but have had money from B&F on account for those purposes'.[22] When Vere, Foreman and Garbett examined Boulton & Fothergill's
books they concluded that Fothergill had never lent any money for the conduct of the steam engine business, there did not appear to have been any legal
agreement between the two businesses and for that reason it became evident
that Fothergill had no legal claim on the profits of Boulton & Watt.[23] Boulton,
in these circumstances, did what he frequently did, which was to write notes,
partly as a record, partly perhaps to persuade himself of the force of his own
argument. His 'History of facts B and F' claims that when Watt, Dr Roebuck
and Dr Small met concerning the future Boulton & Watt partnership, they
made clear that they would have no connection whatsoever with Boulton &
Fothergill.[24] By 1780, Fothergill was sick, Keir reporting, 'I saw Mr Fothergill
yesterday, he looks very much shattered by his illness.'[25] In November 1781,
Boulton decided to part company with Fothergill, the latter believing himself
to have been cheated, and Fothergill died bankrupt the following year.

After Fothergill's death, overseas marketing was undertaken in various ways,
one of which, in the 1790s, was through commissioning A. Collins, who also
represented two other mercantile houses, one in Sheffield and another in Leeds.
Collins, for instance, suggested that his salary and travel costs should be divided
between the three houses in proportion to the orders he obtained for each.[26]

Boulton had made silver buckles in the 1760s but, by 1773, he factored those
made by Thomas Mynd, a craftsman whose products he admired. Demand for
buckles, like buttons, steel jewellery and other toys, was subject to the whims
of fashion. But Boulton knew people in high places and did not hesitate to
plant ideas, at least one of which bore fruit. When, in the 1790s, Boulton was
concerned about the falling demand for buckles, he mentioned to an acquaintance his regret that ladies did not wear them: 'If they could be introduced as
a part of fashionable dress, it would render an essential service to the manufacturers in Birmingham.' The suggestion was communicated to the Prince
of Wales, who replied that he would exert his influence with the Queen, the
princesses and ladies of the first rank, 'to introduce the wearing of buckles
during the ensuing season'. The intermediary asked Boulton for patterns and
suggested that some stock be sent to London in time for the Queen's birthday.
The Prince had given him a pattern of the buckle he would be wearing, and
Mrs Fitzherbert, his mistress, had ordered some of her shoes to be adapted so
that buckles could be attached.[27]

Industrial espionage in Birmingham was certainly a perceived threat. How
real it was is difficult to estimate, and espionage could – and did – work both
ways. Soho Manufactory was a target for harmless visitors as well as those
intent on stealing ideas. On the one hand, Boulton was flattered by the opportunities to entertain members of the nobility and visiting dignitaries. On the

other, he became increasingly aware that not only were product ideas being stolen but so too, on occasion, were skilled craftspeople. An acquaintance passing through Thoun in Switzerland saw several men from Wolverhampton and Birmingham who had been tempted by promises of high wages and cheap lodging to establish a steel and gilt toy manufacturing there. They had been 'much disappointed'.[28] Thomas Mortimer, Vice-Consul in Ostend, contacted Boulton in 1766 to enquire whether three named craftspeople, one of whom was said to be one of the best steel polishers in Europe, came from Birmingham. He offered, upon confirmation, to be able to uncover 'a most villainous scene of seduction of your manufacturers into foreign service'.[29] F. Garbett wrote to Boulton in 1767, advising him of a man who had been discovered in London hiring people to go to Vienna. Boulton was encouraged to seek prosecution, for 'this is the man who has done us the great mischief. He is a Birmingham man, a good workman and has got a petty fortune and now lives in London.' Boulton declined to prosecute, chiefly because of pressure of work, on which account he could ill afford to be absent in London.[30]

In 1766, a toy manufactory, modelled on the best in Birmingham, was established at La Charité-sur-Loire, near Roanne. This factory was the target of elaborate counter-espionage by Thomas Ingram, a detailed report being sent to Boulton in 1774, in which he was told that the manufacture of English buttons was conducted 'as ours at Birmingham and the tools are exactly the same'. The millwork for rolling metals was turned by horses, and the employees were chiefly women and children. In addition to buttons, the factory also produced plated buckles and ornaments for coach harnesses. The reporter suggested that La Charité was not an enterprise to fear so much as that at Roanne, which had been established by the Alcock brothers and was 'conducted with greatest skill & to more advantage ... They strangely outdo us in the price of those wire buttns ... They make the best tin silvered buttns I ever saw ... For these I found they have imence orders.' Ingram did not think there were many advantages in materials or labour prices, but the key advantage was the situation of the factory on the banks of the River Allier, by which they were united with wire supplies and also a navigation through a great part of France.[31]

But the boot could also be on the other foot. While on a sales trip to France in 1765, Boulton had coffee with the Duke of Richmond, the British Ambassador to Paris, and while he was not altogether sanguine about acquiring orders, he thought, 'my journey will pay' for he had 'been seeing the manner of French silvery and have learned also ... the manner of boyling ye French brass foundery'.[32]

By the 1790s, the button trade was in its death throes. Boulton wrote in 1797, 'the present humiliating situation of button makers and of their prospects in time to come has induced Mr John Scale for some time past to turn his thoughts towards forming an establishment in some other business of more stability'.[33] It was in the previous year that Boulton, his fingers having been burned albeit his ego having been stroked, stated:

> [branches of the trade which] depend upon the Fashion of the Day, the whim ... caprice and Fancy of Nobility and persons of fashion are never profitable in the end ... MB is convinced that it is much better to work for the Gross mass of the people of the world, than for the Lords and Princes of it. He is so much convinced of it That he has abandoned all his manufactories which depend on Fashion and taste such as Golden toys, and Or Moulu ornaments, paintings, etc.

Boulton earnestly recommended to his son, 'never to engage in any Manufactory that depends on fashion ... but to confine his pursuits to things usefull rather than ornamental'.[34]

Perhaps the last word on Boulton's approach to toy manufacture and his other non-engine businesses during the 1770s should go to Jabez Fisher, an observant young Quaker from Philadelphia, who wrote in his diary:

> He is a sensible, ingenious, and enterprising Man, who plans and executes with equal Expedition, but like many other great men he has his hobby horse. He is scheming and changeable, ever some new Matter on the Anvil to divert his attention from the steady pursuit of the grand object. He is always inventing, and by the time he has brought his Scheme to perfection, some new affair offers itself. He deserts the old, follows the new, of which he is weary by the time he has arrived at it. This volatility prevents him from becoming very rich.[35]

James Keir could not have put it better.

Notes

1   Notes on dispute with Fothergill.

2   Quoted in Jenny Uglow, *The Lunar Men*, 2002, p. 69.

3   Sketchley, *Birmingham Directory*, 1767.

4   Quoted in H. W. Dickinson, *Matthew Boulton*, 1937, p. 51.

5   Quoted in Malcolm Dick (ed.), *Matthew Boulton: A Revolutionary Player*, 2009.

6   S. Timmins (ed.), *Birmingham and the Midland Hardware District*, 1866, repr. 1967, p. 215.

7   Nicholas Goodison, 'I almost wish to be a Potter: Matthew Boulton's relationship with Josiah Wedgwood', in Malcolm Dick (ed.), op. cit.

8   Quoted in Eric Robinson, 'The International Exchange of Men and Machines', *Business History*, Vol. 1, No 1, 1958.

9   J. Baskerville to MB, 9 December 1765.

10   Report dated 8 February 1764.

11   R. Mather to MB, 4 February 1793.

12   MB to J. Ebbinghaus, 26 June 1766.

13   Ferdinand de Mierre, Bristol, to MB, June 1771.

14   MB to J. Ebbinghaus, 28 October 1767.

15   J. Ebbinghaus to MB, 24 March 1768.

16   MB to J. Ebbinghaus, 6 February 1768.

17   Z. Walker to MB (M. Boulton Papers, Z. Walker snr).

18   M. Boulton Papers, Keir, 70.

19   J. Keir to MB, 14 October 1778.

20   J. Keir to MB, 1 February 1779.

21   W. Matthews to Mainwaring (attorney at law, Birmingham).

22   MB to Murdoch, 19 June 1782 (M. Boulton Papers, 328), quoted in Uglow, op. cit., p. 364.

23   M. Boulton Papers, Foth.

24   M. Boulton Papers, Foth.

25   J. Keir to MB, 17 May 1780.

26   A. Collins to MB, 4 January 1791.

27   R.B. Prosser, *Birmingham Inventors and Inventions*, 1881, repr. 1970, p. 43.

28   H. Vyse to MB, 9 September 1769.

29   T. Mortimer to MB, 27 September 1766.

30   F. Garbett to MB, 14 January 1767.

31   Thomas Ingram (from Lyon) to MB, 11 March 1774. Michael Alcock died in 1785, 'formerly an eminent button manufacturer of this place, some years since went to France where he was encouraged to establish his button Manufactory', *Aris's Birmingham Gazette*, 4 July 1785.

32   MB to Mrs Boulton, Paris, 27 November 1765.

33   James Alston to MB, 5 January 1797.

34   MB to Eckhardt, 1796.

35   Kenneth Morgan (ed.), *An American Quaker in the British Isles*, 1992, p. 255, quoted in Jones, op. cit., p. 56.

4

Family Life

Very little documentation has survived to give an indication of what life was like for Matthew and Mary Boulton. We know that Mary gave birth to three daughters, who all died in infancy, and that her own health was poor. She died in 1759, and Boulton recorded that when he saw Mary in her coffin, he went away and wrote a eulogy, which he placed with the body. He also made a copy, which seems an odd thing to do at such a time of grief, almost as though he felt he needed to make a public declaration of his feelings rather more than he wanted to express his personal sorrow. Alternatively, he may simply have felt that he wanted future generations to know his feelings at this tragic time. Here is the first part of what he wrote:

If Sincerity to all & Flattery to none
If a good natur'd Hand: & Compassionate Heart
If being truly affectionate & dutyfull to her Parents,
If a sincere Regard to her Brothers & Sisters
If Loveing to Excess her weeping Husband
If bearing many Children & endureing many Pains & illnesses, with Patience under his Eye
If preserving fair Virtue around her unpolluted Bed
If passing through Life without one Black Spot upon her Fame
If these things can endear a Wife to a Husband
Thou wert dear to me.
If these things are worth the Remembrance

Thou shalt not be easily forgot.

If these things can recommend thee to the throne of Grace,

Thou shalt find Mercy & Happiness in Heav'n.[1]

He ended this eulogy with a prayer for comfort for himself in his sorrow and for acceptance of Mary into 'thine Heavenly, Glorious & Eternal Kingdom'. Shortly afterwards, his father died and was buried in Lichfield.[2] He would have appeared to be inconsolable, yet only two months after Mary's death he was writing in the most passionate terms to her younger sister, Ann. In a typical but undated letter he wrote: 'With what words can I describe the true state of my Heart, the anxiety of my mind & the extream sincerity of my Love; without carrying the appearance of Servile flattery & Romantic nonsense.' He soon found exactly the words to make it perfectly clear exactly what he thought and where his hopes for the future lay:

> Think not my Dearest Creature that it is in the Power of Enemys or Friends, or Absence, Sickness, or any other Circumstance to abate one Spark of that Fire thou has kindled in my Breast. No I will sooner be torne to pieces by Savage Wolves than I will ever abate one jot of that Resolution I have so often repeated to thee … I again most Solemnly declare to thee, that I will never live to see thee in the Arms of another; for if I do my brain will be overturn'd with madness, & I shall do some desperate deed: but if I was once assured my dear that thou wert mine, & that it was out of the Power of all my Conspiring Enemys to delude thee from me (for they are now busy) then should I be Chearfull & happy … Adieu, God bless & preserve & keep your heart & mind in Sincere & Constant Love towards me who am Dear Creature, Your unchangeable Lover & most affectionate Friend I wish I could say Husband, MB[3]

It is clear from the correspondence that Boulton was a regular visitor to the Robinson family at Lichfield, where he was warmly welcomed by his mother-in-law Dorothy Robinson, who seems not to have had any objections to his transferring his affections from one daughter to another. That leaves the question of who exactly were the 'Conspiring Enemys'. One possible contender was Ann's brother, Luke. Ann's father had died in 1749, so Luke may well have regarded himself as the man of the family, with special responsibilities for preserving their good name and reputation. Boulton wrote to Ann:

> The behaviour I perceived in your brother yesterday, his non acceptance of the trifles I brought him, & the information you & your Mamma gave me of his insinuations & conduct, added to what I have otherwise heard makes

me so very uneasy that at present I am incapable of either eating, drinking,
sleeping or minding any business & indeed I am quite ill with uneasiness.[4]

There could be many reasons for Luke's antagonism. He might well have
thought it inappropriate for Boulton to be wooing one of his sisters so soon
after the death of another. He might even have considered that Boulton was
little more than a fortune seeker. Mary had brought an estimated fortune of
£14,000 to the marriage, which is the equivalent of over £1 million at today's
prices. Ann had inherited an estate that brought in £80 per annum, today
worth over £7,000 a year, and could reasonably expect to inherit more in
time. It was a far from inconsiderable inducement. There was also the prospect of a scandal affecting the family. Marriage to a sister-in-law was not then
accepted as legitimate by the Church of England. This was something Boulton
obviously worried about. In April 1760, he bought not just one but 180 copies
of John Fry's book *The Case of Marriage between Near Kindred particularly with
respect to the Doctrine of Scripture, the Law of Nature, and the Laws of England*, published in 1756. Fry stated quite unequivocally that 'marriage with a deceased
wife's sister is fit and convenient being opposed neither to law nor morals'.
His views may not have been those of the Established Church, but they were
warmly welcomed in other quarters. John Wesley himself wrote: 'It is the best
tract I ever read upon the subject.'[5] It would seem likely that Boulton ordered
so many copies so that he could distribute them among his friends who might
be shocked by his proposed marriage. When one of those friends, Richard
Lovell Edgeworth, was planning a similar marriage, Boulton recommended
him to read Fry, and then 'to say nothing of your intentions but go quickly and
snugly to Scotland or some obscure corner in London, suppose Wapping, and
there take Lodgings to make yourself a parishioner ... I recommend Silence,
Secrecy & Scotland'.[6]

In spite of Luke's opposition, the courtship continued and Ann went to stay
with Boulton at Birmingham, presumably with her mother's agreement and
suitably chaperoned. Dorothy may have approved the relationship between
her daughter and son-in-law, but that did not necessarily mean that she would
accept a complete break with convention and church law by condoning
an actual marriage. Then, in May 1760, Dorothy died and was buried near
Lichfield. Ann no longer needed to seek parental permission for a marriage,
and the couple clearly wasted no time at all in making their plans. They set off
immediately for Rotherhithe, a suitably 'obscure corner in London', where
they needed to establish a month's residence in the district to qualify as parish-
ioners. They were married there in the June of that year.

What can one make of this marriage? The speed with which Boulton began
his courtship and the rush to get married at the very earliest opportunity,

taken together with the passionate tone of the surviving letters, all seem to point to a genuine love match. We shall never know if Boulton wrote in similarly romantic terms to Mary, because no letters have survived. But the eulogy quoted above shows none of the passion that fills the letters to Ann. A cynical interpretation would be that Boulton was attracted to the two sisters from the first, but convention demanded that the elder sister should also be the first to get married, and that proved the decisive factor. What we do know is that Boulton retained a deep affection for Ann throughout his life. They now had to make a home together.

Boulton had spent a considerable amount of money on Soho House. In an undated note in his own hand he gave an account of the expenditure. When he bought the Handsworth estate for £1,000, he estimated that £300 of that was for the house and the rest for the mill. He kept a record 'of ye money lay'd out on either of these Accts & did accordingly expend a large sum same yr in furnishing ye House Within (wch before was almost bare walls) & in making a new Kitchen Garden building planting above 2000 Firs & a great variety of Shrubs wch in ye whole amtd to abt 500 additional expence to ye House'.[7] Yet in spite of the large investment, he let the house to Fothergill and the couple began their married life together in the Birmingham house at Snow Hill. That was fitted out to become a fashionable home, maids were employed for Ann, and Boulton announced in 1763 that all they needed was a manservant to complete the household.

Boulton not only lavished affection on his new wife but was equally generous with more material demonstrations of his love. No visit to London was complete without a shopping expedition to find something new and grand for Ann. On one of these buying sprees he bought a 'suit of lace' for 65 guineas, and it is easy to see how hugely expensive that was by comparing it with the £300 it cost him to buy the house at Soho. It was not just generosity towards Ann. Boulton obviously loved fine clothes and was no less extravagant when it came to dressing himself. When they went into society they appeared as a fine couple, decked out in the very latest style. Boulton's business mind was never idle, and he well knew that his profits came in large part from pandering to the latest taste. They both enjoyed their finery, but it did no harm if his aristocratic customers saw that Mr and Mrs Boulton were always dressed à la mode.[8]

Everything appeared to be going well for the family and there even seemed to be a reconciliation with Luke. Ann made several visits to see him in Lichfield and, in 1764, Luke eventually came to stay in Birmingham. But his health was not good, and in September of that year his condition deteriorated so far that he was urged to make out his will. By this time he seems to have been very far from clear in his mind, and as a result had to be prompted by his solicitor to make appropriate bequests to his servants. Inevitably there were disappointed relatives, none more so than his cousin Charles Blackham. He was angry that nothing had been left to his mother, who had cared for Mrs Robinson throughout her last illness. In the event, the main beneficiaries were the Boultons, and Matthew Boulton was appointed the sole executor. This is all the more surprising, given the acrimony that had existed so recently between the two men. Blackham thought that Luke was not in a fit state of mind to understand what was going on, but the family solicitor insisted that as the will had been drawn up before the signing day it was valid. Soon after the will was signed, Luke Robinson was dead.[9]

Luke's death was not the only tragedy to overtake the family. Ann was pregnant at the time of her brother's death and although no birth is officially recorded, it seems likely that the baby was born shortly afterwards. In a letter to one of his agents, dated 9 March 1765, Boulton added in a postscript that his baby son had died the previous day. Death and illness seemed to be haunting the family, in spite of receiving the best possible medical care. By this time Boulton had a new doctor. William Small had been introduced to him by Benjamin Franklin as 'an ingenious Philosopher, & a most worthy honest Man'. Boulton was delighted with the introduction and replied:

… the addition you have made to my happiness in being ye cause of my acquaintance with the amiable & ingenious Dr. Small deserves more than thanks & therefore I take this opportunity … by introducing you to my good friend Mr. Samuel Garbett who is an admirer of Mr. Franklin in particular, a Friend of Mankind in General, a Lover of his Country, a zealous Advocate for Truth & for ye rights of your oppress'd countrymen.[10]

Small was to become a good friend as well as the family physician and with other friends would meet with Boulton to discuss all kinds of scientific and philosophical topics in what was to become known as the Lunar Society (see Chapter 5). Boulton's letter is also interesting in being one of the few in which he expressed an overtly political, and quite liberal, viewpoint, clearly taking the side of the more progressive thinkers who favoured a less repressive approach to the American colonies. Shortly after the introduction, Small's medical services were needed when Ann suffered what was clearly quite a serious illness, during the course of which her speech became unintelligible. Boulton was away on business at the time, and fired off anxious enquiries about her health. He must, however, have been greatly relieved when he started getting messages from Ann with a shopping list of items she wanted purchased in London. Clearly things were back to normal. Meanwhile, her life in Birmingham during her husband's absences was not lonely. Boulton's sister Mary was a regular visitor, with her husband Zacchaeus Walker, Boulton's chief clerk at Soho.

The job title now suggests quite a lowly position, but Walker was in effect in charge of the company's finances. They often came round in the evening to chat and play whist.

In November 1765, Boulton went to France. He made no mention to Ann that he was going, in order to avoid causing anxiety, but simply added the visit on to one of his regular London trips and only wrote when he had arrived safely across the Channel. Once there, he sent back regular letters about his experiences, few of which he enjoyed, complaining about the food and the general air of frippery:

> … my affection for my dear Nanny encreases with my absence: for all ye Variety I have seen will only teach me to enjoy home & value my good Wife more & more if possible, as all my observations rather induce me to think there is scarcely such a thing in this Country; if paint, patches, powder, Silks, Diamonds & flirting airs render ye Sex agreeable the Garden of ye Tulleries abound, but for that Gem call'd Virtue whose brightness puts ye Diamd out of countenance, I have scarcely seen a glimpse of it in any Face here.[11]

As usual, he compensated for his absence with a present, this time of good silk, which he told her to get made up 'a la mode de Londre'. Even in the realm of fashion he refused to follow the styles of Paris. Ann must have been mollified, for in spite of her recent illness, she set off for London to greet her husband on his return to England – and, no doubt, to indulge in her favourite pastime with some more shopping.

In 1766, the Boultons decided that it was time to leave Snow Hill and move to Soho House. Unfortunately, as we have seen, Fothergill and his family were still in residence and were not at all keen to move out. In the end, the argument came down to one simple fact: it was Boulton's house and he wanted it back. By the end of the year, the Boultons had moved in, but not before making several improvements to the building.

Boulton had not been unreasonable when he claimed that by being permanently settled at Soho he could increase business. The Soho factory was becoming firmly established as a place for the gentry to include in their journeys round the countryside of Britain, and now they could also be entertained at Soho House. It was a house in which Boulton took great pride, and everything in it had to represent the latest in fashionable taste, even including a very modern musical instrument for Ann. Boulton bought one of the first of the square fortepianos by the London-based manufacturer Johannes Zumpe, instruments that had just begun to displace the older harpsichords and spinets. But Ann was not to have much time for practising her music: she was pregnant again and gave birth to a baby girl on 29 January 1768. They named her Anne.[12]

It was an anxious time for both parents, particularly the new father. This was the fifth time that a wife had given birth and none of the first four had survived beyond infancy, but the child appeared to be well. It was only when she reached the toddling stage that it became clear that all was not quite right after all. The child was not walking properly but had a pronounced limp, walking on tiptoe on her left foot. Boulton looked for advice to both Small and Erasmus Darwin, and the little girl had special shoes made, with the left shoe built up to compensate, but neither doctor came up with a real solution to the problem.

In April 1771, the parents took Anne to London to see a specialist surgeon, John Hunter. He made careful measurements and told them that although both legs were the same length, there was a slight lifting of one side of the pelvis, which also caused a twisting of the spine. He advised getting rid of the built-up shoe and recommended having one shoe longer than the other to encourage her to put her bad foot firmly down on the ground. Hunter diagnosed rickets, which he thought might have been caused by the wet nurse having insufficient milk and not caring adequately for the baby. We now know that rickets is caused by Vitamin D deficiency, and that the vitamin is formed by the skin on exposure to sunlight. If rickets was indeed the cause of Anne's problem, then it could have begun simply because the wet nurse herself was suffering from the vitamin deficiency, which could hardly be called her fault. However, given the level of medical diagnosis at this period, the problem could have had quite different origins. Nevertheless, it was perhaps a comfort for the parents to have someone else to blame, although it did nothing to resolve the problem. There are other possible diagnoses. It could, for example, be that Anne suffered from scoliosis, and that her spine was twisted causing the uneven hips, rather than the other way round. Or she may simply have had congenital dislocation of the hip; there is no way of telling. Whatever the cause of the complaint, Hunter's remedy proved no more effective than any other. Anne was to live with this slight deformity all her life.[13]

While the family was searching for medical help for Anne, a new healthy baby was born on 8 August and named Matthew Robinson Boulton.[14] To everyone's relief, he appeared to suffer no problems and grew up to be a healthy, strong child.

During these years Boulton was regularly making visits to London, sometimes accompanied by his wife, but more often on his own. While he was away he wrote home regularly to ask about the children. Anne was often referred to as 'the Maid of the Mill' or together they were the King and Queen, but most often they were simply Nanny and Matt. He wanted to know everything: were they keeping well, what were they eating, and what were they saying and doing? Judging by the number of times he wrote asking for news and complaining about not receiving any, his wife was not a great correspondent.

But one thing the children could be sure of when their father returned was that there would be presents for them in the luggage. Everything suggests that Matthew Boulton was a doting father who loved his 'little dears'.

The time came when the Boultons had to think about the education of their children. In the earlier part of the eighteenth century, education for boys of the upper and wealthier middle classes was still very firmly based on the classics. These were considered all that was required to prepare the student for the life of a gentleman, who, if he was the eldest, would run the family estates, while any younger brother would enter a profession. Most girls were required to do little more than read and write and practise such crafts as embroidery, learn music and paint watercolours. The boys who went on to university would have found the education on offer in England to be in a wretched condition – although things were a good deal better in Scotland. At Oxford and Cambridge many lecturers and professors scarcely bothered to teach at all. The historian Edward Gibbon, who was at Oxford in 1752, described the life of the dons:

> From the toil of reading or thinking or writing they had absolved their conscience. Their conversation stagnated in a round of college business, Tory politics, personal stories, and private scandal; their dull and deep potations excused the brisk intemperance of youth.[15]

It was no wonder that the new generation of industrialists, engineers and scientists had little time for English universities. Sir John Rennie recalled his father, the engineer John Rennie, giving his view on universities: 'After a young man has been three or four years at the University of Oxford or Cambridge, he cannot, without much difficulty, turn himself to the practical part of civil engineering.'[16] Manufacturers such as Boulton, who were looking to their sons to follow them into the family business, had to think very hard about what sort of education to provide. It would need to be quite different from that favoured by the landed aristocracy and squirearchy.

There was no shortage of new ideas, and Boulton would certainly have discussed the question with his friends, and have been offered a wide range of opinions. Some were greatly influenced by Rousseau, whose ideas were set out in the novel *Émile*. Rousseau believed that the young child should be given a great deal of freedom and should learn by experiencing the natural world, not by studying books; that children were naturally good; and their own curiosity would lead them on the road to discovery and education, while society would only ruin them. The idea was much debated. Thomas Day, while still a young man, adopted two girls from orphanages with a view to bringing them up on the best Rousseauesque principles, and to avoid contamination by society he decided to do so in France, where they would not be corrupted for the very good reason that they could not speak a word of the language. James Keir, for one, thought this arrant nonsense: children needed to know how to live in society and control their 'selfish impulses' for the sake of 'general order and happiness'. In the event, Day's experiment proved disastrous. Others were more concerned with providing a conventional education, but making sure that certain subjects, notably the sciences, were added to the usual programme of the 'three Rs' with classics.

The biggest debate, however, was whether to send children away to school or educate them at home. The Wedgwood family, for example, decided in favour of a boarding school, but having packed them off discovered that although they were learning well, their health was suffering. They then decided to set up a school at home, with appropriate tutors and a rigorous timetable, which started with the school bell ringing to rouse them at 7 a.m. in winter and at 6 a.m. in summer. The curriculum was fairly standard, with emphasis on the 'three Rs', and additional language lessons, exercises and, for the boys, accounting. The Edgeworth family had also tried the conventional route of sending children to school, but like the Wedgwoods, were not very impressed with the results. One thing that disturbed them was the lack of what they considered to be appropriate books. They believed that children would learn far more if the books were actually entertaining to read and if information was expressed clearly, and as they could find none that matched their ideals they set out to write their own. There were a lot of models for the Boulton family to choose from, but none of them seemed to offer the ideal solution.

After considering the options, the Boultons chose the very conventional route for Matt of sending him for lessons at a school at nearby Winson Green, run by a clergyman, the Rev. William Pickering.[17] The boy was obviously bright and must already have learned quite a lot at home, as his schoolmaster offered to reduce his fee at the end of the first year, simply because he had had to do so little actual teaching himself. He was to remain there for only two years before being moved to a boarding school in Twickenham. There is no written evidence of why Boulton made the move. Perhaps a provincial vicar could not supply the breadth and sophistication that his father felt was necessary for his future career. His decision may also have been influenced by the fact that he was now having to spend several months a year in Cornwall on steam engine business, and he wanted his wife to join him there, and knowing Matt was safe in boarding school left them with one less thing to worry about.

Boulton was an anxious parent. Like Wedgwood, he worried a lot about his children's health, and when Matt developed a cough he kept him at home and then started worrying about him missing school: 'The health of my Children is the first consideration with me & next to that the improvement of their minds.' Even so, in the summer of 1779, Boulton decided that London was unhealthy and removed Matt from school again and took him and Anne to Southampton for the bathing. However, he was reassured when a new master, Mr Stretch, informed him that he had instituted a new healthier regime, with lots of salads and fresh vegetables on the menu and regular bathing. Poor Matt must have wondered what was happening to him, for in no time at all another illness, described simply as 'the scratching disease' saw him back home again. Now instead of returning to Twickenham he was sent again to Winson Green, while his father, so decisive in business, dithered about what to do. 'I am really at a loss where to place Matt. I only know that home is the most improper of all places. If I send him again to Twickenham I shall be apprehensive of bad health.'[18] Pickering offered to take Matt as a boarder, but Boulton declined, so it was to be Twickenham once again. There he received a conventional education, where Latin featured very prominently. He would, after all, expect in his adult life to be able to mix with gentlemen who had a similar classical background and feel comfortably at home. He had ample opportunity to dabble in science and learn of the business world during his time at Soho. His later education would be much more closely geared to the needs of a man with interests around the world.

The other question that the parents had to answer was how to educate their daughter. Again, there were many alternatives. The conventional view would be that girls with a secure financial future need only to be educated to become ladies of leisure. Among the books in Boulton's library was *A Father's Legacy to his Daughters* by Dr John Gregory, published in 1774. It was conservative even by the standards of the day. One example of his advice to girls is typical: 'If you happen to have any learning, keep it a profound secret, especially from the men.' Fortunately many of Boulton's friends took a different view. Erasmus Darwin was also to write a book about education for girls, although not until 1794, when he was setting up his two illegitimate daughters with a school of their own to run. He recommended including science in the curriculum, taking the pupils on visits to industrial sites and providing lots of healthy exercise. There were good models of highly intelligent, well-educated women in the mid to late eighteenth century, not least Matthew Boulton's acquaintance, Elizabeth Montagu, the first 'bluestocking'.[19] Girls were not the fragile, delicate blooms that Gregory believed, or perhaps hoped, they were.

As with Matt, Boulton took a long time in deciding what was best, consulting his friends on the three main options: education at home with a governess; being taught at a local school; or being sent off to boarding school. In the end, the Boultons settled for a local school at first, but Anne had hardly spent any time there before she was sent away, in September 1778, to Campden House School in London, leaving her parents free to go off for an extended stay in Cornwall.

Boulton was already paying for his niece Nancy Mynd to be taught there, so he must have been impressed by the school and its principal Mrs Elizabeth Terry. There were three teachers and eight 'young ladies' who 'read French & English constantly'.[20]

Matt and Anne were both now settled in the London area, so Boulton was able to visit them on his regular business trips to the capital and report on their progress in letters to his wife. In one of his letters home he described a visit to see a dancing display by the girls, but Anne was unable to join in: her deformed hip made it impossible – 'my poor Nanny sat modestly behind'. Matt, however, was described as having 'acquired the Character of a Bold Fellow on Horse back'. It was a stark and sad contrast.

Anne's schooling was no more consistent than her brother's. In 1779, Boulton had been to see one of his wealthy clients, Elizabeth Montagu, a famous hostess, who was buying ormolu from him. Her evening parties were attended by some of the great literary figures of the age, including Dr Johnson, and they were not frivolous affairs. There was no dancing, music or games, and strong liquor was strictly forbidden. What there was in plenty was discussion on literary and philosophical topics. Guests were chosen for their wit rather than their social rank. Johnson later fell out with her, but he clearly enjoyed his time spent at her evening assemblies, as Boswell recorded in his biography of Johnson:

> One evening at Mrs. Montagu's, where a splendid company was assembled, consisting of the most eminent literary characters, I thought he seemed highly pleased with the respect and attention that were shewn to him, and asked him on our return home if he was not highly *gratified* by his visit: 'No Sir, (said he,) not highly *gratified*; yet I do not recollect to have passed many evenings *with fewer objections*.[21]

That would count as high praise from that gentleman. It is obvious that Elizabeth Montagu was widely recognised as a well-educated woman, so when she offered advice on schooling, Boulton listened. As a result, Anne left Campden House for a new school that she personally recommended in Richmond, run by Mrs Elizabeth Wilkes. It had the further advantage of being reasonably close to her brother's school at Twickenham.

Boulton constantly fretted about the health of his children, and when they both caught measles he was deeply concerned, especially on Anne's behalf. He received comforting news from Mrs Wilkes, who assured him that she was getting the best possible care and the services of a professional nurse. He was still sufficiently worried, however, to have qualms about letting Anne endure the long journey home for the Christmas holidays. Again Mrs Wilkes was reassuring and gave an interesting account of Anne's schooling:

I hope Sir, you will think your dear child already something improved; although I generally appropriate some time at first to the purpose of gaining the affection & confidence of those intrusted to my care & laying the groundwork of improvement; rather than venture the disgusting them of those things I wish to inculcate by too much hastening their acquirement. Miss Boulton's health being so very delicate & her spirits in consequence weak, makes this treatment particularly necessary with regard to her & I make no doubt it will succeed to my wish – I beg you to believe that no attention on my part shall be wanting & from her good sense, great memory & sweet disposition I dare hope that sometime hence, her progress in her learning will be very apparent.[22]

The two children seemed to be well settled in their different schools and everything in the family was going well. Then, on 11 July 1783, Ann Boulton was discovered drowned in the ornamental pond at Soho House.[23] Estate workers cutting hay saw her walking towards the pond, but no one saw what happened next. There was the inevitable speculation about suicide, but as she had seemed in both good health and high spirits the only possible verdict at the inquest was 'accidental death'. Boulton was devastated and took his friends' advice to forget business in order to take time to recover. He could only do that by getting well away from Soho. He decided to go on a tour of Scotland and Ireland, setting off on his travels on 22 August.

Dublin was his first stop, and from there he took the boat to Portpatrick in Galloway. He may have been advised to forget business altogether, but he was a man for whom industry had as much fascination as any natural wonder. His was not to be the standard tourist itinerary. He visited the Carron Ironworks, famous for the high quality of their castings and for their 'carronades', short large-bore cannon that were used on board Nelson's flagship *Victory* and which Wellington described as the finest artillery available. This was a company which was noted for innovation and one in which his old friend from Birmingham, John Roebuck, had an interest. Boulton also called on notable scientists, such as Dr Joseph Black, and visited Lord Cochrane to see the process he had developed for extracting tar from coal. It was proving to be something of a busman's holiday. However, he did find time to add many new mineral specimens to his collection. He finally got home on 11 December and, according to his meticulously kept notebook, the whole tour had cost him precisely £232 5s 6d. He was ready to get back to work.

Boulton now had sole charge of the children, which he never regarded as a chore. He clearly loved being with them whenever the various demands on his time permitted, and was always anxious to know just how they were getting on whenever they were apart. They seemed equally keen to spend time with their father. The following summer, plans were made for Matt and Anne to join their father in Cornwall and they were both looking forward to the experience when Anne caught whooping cough. Instead they were forced to spend their time at Soho House, which had been loaned out to friends, Dr and Mrs Withering, while Boulton was away. They sent regular reports to Cornwall, and when Anne had recovered she made preparations to make the long journey to the West Country, together with Matt, Nancy Mynd and a maid, following elaborate instructions from their father. Then she caught a cold and was considered too ill to travel and, to her extreme disappointment, had to watch her brother leave without her. Her feelings would hardly have been improved by letters saying what a good time Matt was having, visiting mines and collecting fossils. As soon as she was declared fit, she too was off with Nancy to join the family.

Once the holiday was over, Matt was sent to yet another new school, this time at Stoke-by-Nayland in Suffolk, an establishment for 'young gentlemen'. Here the efforts were concentrated on Latin and European languages, and his teacher, the Rev. Samuel Parlby, explained that he would not be making any attempt to teach him philosophy – which would have included natural philosophy, the name used then for science – as he could not hope to match the instruction available at Soho. It is interesting to compare Matt's education with that of his near contemporary, friend and neighbour James Watt junior. The two boys were being groomed by their fathers to follow them into their respective businesses – Boulton to be the businessman and entrepreneur, Watt the practical engineer. So, while Matt was being packed off to study Latin, young James was being sent to John Wilkinson's ironworks at Bersham in Wales to study the practical world of engineering. James was not to spend a lot of time there, for an opportunity arose to go to Switzerland to study under Pierre Aimé Argand. He was the inventor of a new lamp of a type that is now familiar, an oil lamp with a wick and a glass chimney, that was being manufactured at Soho. It was an exciting opportunity for the boy, and Matt in his letters made it very clear that he would far rather be with his friend in Geneva than parsing Latin in Suffolk.

While Matt was being sent to Suffolk, Anne's schooling came to another temporary impasse. It had been constantly interrupted due to her health problems, and now she stayed mainly at Soho House, where she spent a lot of her time at the keyboard. Music remained one of her great pleasures in life; for some reason, she did not follow her mother in learning the piano but preferred the harpsichord. Perhaps she preferred the Baroque repertoire of Bach and Handel to what was then the modern music of the age, the classical compositions of Haydn and Mozart. Her father would hardly have had time to learn an instrument, but he was an enthusiastic concertgoer and Handel was one of his musical heroes. But the stay at Soho was again short-lived, and she was sent off to Leicester to study embroidery with an accomplished needle-woman, Mary Linwood. She was just 30 years old, famous for her needlework pictures and was also a competent musician and composer, even writing a number of novels in whatever time was left. Her portrait shows a very good-looking woman, and Boulton, who always had something of an eye for the ladies, especially if they combined intelligence with beauty, was quite gushing in his praise of her. Anne seems not to have been quite so enthusiastic, but her father was firm:

> I hinted to you in my last that I wish you not to be in a hurry to leave Leicester unless it be to return to it again speedily, for it is impossable that you can keep company with Miss Linwood without improving your tast & your hand.[24]

Boulton went so far as to invite Mary Linwood and her mother to join them at Soho for Christmas, but was politely turned down. Whatever Boulton may have had in mind, romance was clearly not on her itinerary. She was, however, able to use Boulton's connections to obtain an audience with the Queen to show off her embroidered pictures that were full-sized copies of old masters. Royal patronage helped her to stage major exhibitions, and her work was greatly admired. Back at Soho House, Anne was having fresh instruction on the harpsichord and, in 1786, her father bought her a new instrument by the foremost maker of the day, Jacob Kirkman.

Anne returned to Leicester after the holidays and Matt went back to his Latin studies, with the addition now of Greek, but it was to be a short visit. Boulton decided that Matt needed to broaden his horizons and continue his education in France, with a French tutor in Versailles. Boulton may have been scathing about French frippery, but the 16-year-old boy loved it and promptly set about ridding himself of his provincial background. His father accompanied him to Paris and saw the transformation: 'I actually did not know Matt this morning when I first met after his Hair was dressed a la Francois.' While Matt was revel-ling in France, Anne was moping at home and complained to Matt about being forced to play cards, which she thought was a game invented for the King of France: 'I should much sooner have believed it to have been for an old woman of eighty who was incapable of amusing herself by any other means.'

Matt was discovering a whole new way of life, managing to persuade his indulgent father to move him from Versailles to Paris itself. Boulton sent his son a flannel waistcoat to ward off the cold, but Matt's taste ran to swaggering around in a dress coat with a sword at his side. His father was, not surprisingly, a little concerned.

There is some danger in a young Englishmans head becoming giddy by the pageantry of Courts & the Folly of Fashion ... It seems to be agreed on all hands that Germany is the place to make a Man & Paris the place to make a Man of Fashion (i.e. a Gambler & a Rake). I wish, & beg you will constantly be employd & that you as speedily as possible get possession of the language & that you read such History, such anecdotes & such sentiments as tend to teach & to inspire sentiments of Honour & Benevolence for it is the possession of such like principles that constitute the real Gentleman. Fashion & Foppery has nothing to do with it.[25]

There was a constant stream of letters from father to son, offering advice, begging him to go to lectures in subjects such as chemistry and mineralogy, and to look after his health by taking plenty of exercise and recommending horse riding. But it was getting close to the time when Matt was to be made a man. He was to go to Germany in 1788, to study with the Rev. M. Reinhardt, who had also taught young James Watt. His tutor was very pleased with his progress, writing to Boulton that he had learned more in nine months than young Watt had in a year. There was only one brief alarm, when he met the Baroness of Wangenheim, a young lady with a dubious reputation, and announced they were engaged. It did not last. He was persuaded that he was too young and his disappointment was short-lived. The baroness promptly confirmed her reputation by starting an affair with a footman. Matt finally returned to England, his continental education completed, in 1790.

It is interesting to compare his life at that time with that of young James Watt. Both were being groomed to take over from their fathers, but the attitude of the two families was very different. James was constantly being nagged about spending too much money and being berated for not working hard enough. In July 1787, his father wrote to complain that his expenses 'have run as high as Matt Boulton's in <u>Versailles</u> except in the article of board & yet he is employed from morning to night with his masters. Which of you have made the best use of your time?' While Boulton was always delighted to receive a letter from his children, Watt could only find fault. He complained that his son had written on only one side of the paper, 'which is bad economy & needless piece of ceremony towards me'. Where Boulton sent Matt all the latest news, Watt set his son geometry problems. When he returned to England, his father declared that he was 'dogmatic, contemptuous of others, self-opinionated and impatient' and dispatched him to a textile firm in Manchester to learn the trade. He had an allowance but soon overspent it by £80 and received another dressing down from his father:

Your Shoemakers bill was more than 4 times as much as mine; partly because you would not be contented to wear serviceable shoes, but wanted to have them made so as to do as little good as possible following a nonsensical fashion … These things may suite people of fortune but do not answer tradesmen.[26]

The debts were paid, but James had his allowance reduced. He realised from experience that there was little hope of a change of heart in his own home, but he knew someone who would be more sympathetic. He wrote to Boulton when he found himself in a mess again at the end of the following year, and must have been delighted to receive a draft for £50, and although the accompanying letter indulged in a little sermonising, it was clear where Boulton's sympathies lay:

> I made it payable to myself that I might thereby conceal your Name from all persons & you may tranquillise yourself in respect to your Father as I promise that he shall not know anything of the Transaction. Although I would not willingly give you pain yet I must honestly tell you that I am not very sorry you have experienced some pain & anxiety by my delay that you may not only feel how uncomfortable it is to be in debt but you may experience e'er long how pleasant, how cheerfull independence, which no man can possess that is not out of Debt.[27]

Having delivered the rebuke, he went on: 'It is possible your Fathers Ideas may be too limited in regard to the quantum necessary for your expences.' Boulton explained that he could not himself approach Watt on the matter, but James should set out his own case.

The two young men might appear to have had very different temperaments, but one suspects that James might have been less rebellious had he received a little more encouragement instead of constant criticism. In the event, they were not only to remain good friends but were to become, for a while, successful business partners in the way their parents had always hoped.

Anne's life was altogether less exciting, although she did her best to liven things up for herself. But she was always plagued by ill health and subjected to treatments that must often have seemed as bad as the complaint. In the summer of 1787, she had toothache in one of her front teeth and consulted a French dentist resident in London, Charles Dumergue. No young lady wanted to go around with a gaping hole in the front of her mouth, so Dumergue recommended a transplant. Boulton described this bizarre operation to Matt.

> Your sister had a tooth drawn & at the same time another was drawn out of a young Girls head about 14 & after cleaning it & washing it in Spirits of Wine & Camphor it was planted in your Sisters jaw where it seems to fix firm & I have no doubt but it will prove a good tooth & usefull.[28]

It was an agonising affair in the days before anaesthetics, but one also sympathises with the young girl who had a perfectly sound tooth pulled just to make a little money.

The one constant in Anne's life was the loving relationship with her father. They spent as much time together as possible, and regularly exchanged chatty letters when they had to be apart. But, inevitably, business drew him away and he was absent for her twenty-first birthday – which he actually miscounted and thought was her twentieth. But he wrote a letter expressing his feelings, which were clearly heartfelt and genuine. 'I cannot let slip this happy day without congratulating my dear daughter & congratulating my Self upon the return of that day which gave Birth to the greatest blessing & comfort of my old age.'

Anne and Matt grew up and followed their very different paths: Matt for the great world of business and enterprise; Anne (who never married) for an altogether more constrained life at home. The one thing they had in common throughout their childhood was the security of a loving family.

Notes

1   Shena Mason, *The Hardware Man's Daughter: Matthew Boulton and his 'Dear Girl'*, 2005, pp. 2–3. The book is the story of their daughter Anne's life, but has a very full account of the life of the whole Boulton family.

2   Ibid., p. 212.

3   MB to Ann Robinson, 1759, ibid., p. 2.

4   Ibid., p. 3.

5   Journal of John Wesley, 11 September 1756.

6   MB to Edgeworth, 20 November 1780, quoted in H. W. Dickinson, *Matthew Boulton*, 1937, p. 34.

7   Phillada Ballard et al., *A Lost Landscape: Matthew Boulton's Gardens at Soho*, 2009, pp. xii, 15–22.

8   Mason, op. cit., p. 8.

9   Ibid., p. 9.

10   MB to Benjamin Franklin, 22 February 1766.

11   Mason, op. cit., p. 13.

12   Mason, op. cit., p. 18.

13   Mason, op. cit., pp. 19–21.

14   Mason, op. cit., p. 2.

15   Edward Gibbon, *Memoirs of My Life*, 1796, ch. 3.

16   Sir John Rennie, Autobiography, 1875.

17   A. E. Musson & Eric Robinson, 'Training Captains of Industry: The Education of Matthew Robinson Boulton (1770–1842) and James Watt, Junior (1769–1848)', in *Science and Technology in the Industrial Revolution*, 1969, pp. 200–15.

18 MB to Anne Boulton, 13 January 1780, quoted in Mason, op. cit., p. 44.

19 Norma Clarke, *Dr Johnson's Women*, 2005, pp. 127–54.

20 Mason, op. cit., p. 55.

21 Clarke, op. cit., pp. 127–54.

22 Mason, op. cit., p. 48.

23 Ibid., pp. 61–62.

24 MB to Anne Boulton, 17 August 1785, quoted in Mason, op. cit., p. 72.

25 MB to MRB, 29 June 1787, quoted in Mason, op. cit., p 80; Musson & Robinson, op. cit., pp. 200–21.

26 J. Watt to J. Watt jnr, 31 December 1788.

27 MB to J. Watt jnr, 26 December 1789, quoted in Mason, op. cit., p. 91.

28 Ibid., pp. 87–88, 90.

5

The Lunar Society

R eaders of Georgian fiction will be left with a distinct impression that polite society was based on land ownership and hereditary wealth; those who earned their money by trade were likely to be boorish and ill-educated. Such views were not limited to the world of novels. John Byng, Viscount Torrington visited Cromford in Derbyshire where Sir Richard Arkwright had established his cotton mill and was building a new, grand house for himself. Byng was contemptuous: 'It is the house of an overseer surveying the works, not of a gentleman wishing for retirement and quiet.'[1] Industrialists might be making the nation rich, might even get knighted for their efforts, but they would never be in the same class as those who inherited wealth. Philip Thicknesse, a genuinely eccentric travel writer who was notoriously quarrelsome and positively enjoyed making enemies, undoubtedly intended to insult Boulton when he addressed him as 'Tradesman of Birmingham'. Boulton sent a stinging reply:

If you had known how much the Tradesman you shot at had been out of reach of your venom'd arrow, you would not have shot it, for if I glory in anything it is in being one of those exporting importing tradesmen whose connections are not circumscribed by the bounds of Europe ... Early in life Fortune gave me the option of assuming the character of an idle man commonly called a Gentn, but I rather chose to be of the class wch Le Baron *Montesque* describes as the constant contributors to the purse of the commonwealth rather than of another class which he says are always taking out of it without contributing anything towards it.[2]

Boulton was happy and proud to accept that he was a tradesman. That did not mean, however, that he was prepared to accept any of the implications that some attached to that name. He was intelligent, of inquisitive mind and, unlike many of the gentry, was very aware that the world was changing and changing rapidly. He knew it from his own working life, where he could see the gathering pace of a technological revolution. He was also keenly interested in the other worlds being discovered in the sciences in many different fields, from the investigations of electricity to the often startling findings of the very new science of geology. Even as a young man he started collecting scientific books for his personal library, and electricity fascinated him from the first – Benjamin Franklin's three-volume work on the topic had pride of place. He would, he declared, very much like to add 'my mite to the Science', but felt that he lacked the expertise.

An amateur scientist in the literal meaning of that word, Boulton did it for the love of satisfying his own intellectual curiosity. He made collections of fossils and minerals. He collected scientific instruments: he had a telescope and an orrery (a clockwork model of the solar system) to further his interest in astronomy; he had microscopes through which he could peer at the strange creatures that could be found in a glass of water; and a variety of measuring instruments of all kinds to help with his researches in any subject that took his fancy. He was fascinated to hear of any new advances made in any scientific field. This was an interest he shared with many of his friends who got into the habit of meeting regularly at Boulton's house. The original group consisted of Boulton, Erasmus Darwin, Josiah Wedgwood and Joseph Priestley. They were joined by James Watt on his arrival in Birmingham, James Keir, John Whitehurst, Dr William Small, Thomas Day, William Withering and Richard Lovell Edgeworth, and somewhat later by Samuel Galton junior, Robert Augustus Johnson and Jonathan Stokes; fourteen in all, although it was probably very rare that they could all sit down together for dinner.[3] And, on occasion, distinguished visitors joined them.

Meetings often took place at Soho House. There they would be treated to a sumptuous meal, offered fine wines, all at their host's expense, and then retire to talk over ideas, discuss experiments and share opinions. They would cheerfully discuss each other's theories, however fanciful. Boulton's friend and physician Dr Small, for example, expounded a view that the earth was cooling and that in time the whole planet would be as barren as the moon, which he believed was also covered in ice. But the nature of the moon was more than an interesting topic of conversation. As the conversation often lasted well into the evening, and as this was a time before street lamps, it was most convenient to meet on a night near the full moon that would light them on their journey home, and so they became known as the Lunar Society.[4]

The Society had no fixed rules, published no learned papers (although a number of members, including Boulton and Watt, became Fellows of the Royal Society) and there was no fixed membership. It was an open forum for like-minded men who had shared interests in science and technology. Some of them had business interests in common, others did not. Each of them, however, was distinguished in his own field. These were men who, although very different in many ways, above all enjoyed each other's company. The Lunar Society may have had a serious purpose, but that did not stop it being a great deal of fun. There was always room for a little frivolity, especially when Darwin was involved. One of the best-known examples was their interest in a new technological marvel – the balloon.

Hydrogen was identified as a gas only in 1776, and it was Watt's old mentor Joseph Black who first filled a calf's bladder with the gas and watched it float up to the ceiling. He never followed up the idea that it might be a means of achieving flight, and it was left to three French physicists – Jacques Alexandre César Charles and Aîné and Cadet Robert – to give the first public demonstration of a hydrogen balloon in August 1783. It was no easy matter. They used almost 500lb of sulphuric acid and 1,000lb of iron filings to make the gas. So when we read of the Lunar men playing with hydrogen balloons we are actually looking at people who are experimenting with something very new and exciting. It was just four months after the French demonstration that Darwin made the first hydrogen balloon in Britain, and in the January he tried to send a message by balloon to his friends. It was not quite successful: 'You heard we sent your society an air-balloon which was calculated to have fallen in your garden at Soho, but the wicked wind carried to Sir Edward Litteltons.'[5] Had it arrived as planned, it would have been the world's first airmail letter. The description 'air-balloon' might be misleading – hydrogen was still known as 'inflammable air' at this time.

Boulton was soon enthused with the idea of balloon experiments. At the end of 1784, he was in Cornwall with Watt and decided to take time out from dealing with the problems of mines and engines. He made a paper balloon that he coated with varnish and filled with a hydrogen/air mixture. He attached a firecracker to the balloon, lit the fuse and let it go. The fuse was burning for rather a long time and it was well over a mile away before the cracker went off and the balloon exploded to the accompaniment of loud cheers from the spectators. According to Watt, this was a serious experiment to investigate the noise of thunder, and he bemoaned the fact that the noise made by the onlookers ruined the effort. But one cannot help feeling that Boulton simply enjoyed the spectacle. It was typical of the Lunar Society that the members did not see why research should not be entertaining as well as instructive. The atmosphere of those days comes across very strongly in a letter written by Darwin apologising for not being able to attend a meeting:

I am sorry the infernal divinities who visit mankind with diseases, and are therefore at perpetual war with doctors, should have prevented my seeing all your great men in Soho today. Lord! What inventions, what wit, what rhetoric, metaphysical, mechanical, and pyrotechnical will be on the wing, bandied like a shuttlecock from one to another of your troupe of philosophers! While poor I, I by myself I, imprison'd in a post-chaise, am joggl'd, and jostl'd, and bump'd, and bruised along the King's highroad to make war upon a stomach-ache or a fever.[6]

Who were these men who, in the words of one of the members, Richard Lovell Edgeworth, were 'all devoted to literature and science. The mutual intimacy has never been broken but by death'?

Erasmus Darwin was one of the most remarkable of all the Lunar men, if only because of the breadth of his interests and his originality of thought.[7] Darwin was born at Elston, near Newark-on-Trent in 1731. His father was a barrister, who was also a man of scientific curiosity: he discovered the fossil of a plesiosaur that he presented to the Royal Society, and his interest in fossils was passed on to the son. Erasmus was educated at Chesterfield School and Cambridge University where he studied Classics and began writing poetry. The family, however, was not wealthy and as he had a living to earn he chose to go on to study medicine. His early practice in Nottingham was not a success, but he moved to Lichfield where his career flourished. In 1757, he married Mary Howard and they had five children, two of whom died in infancy. Mary also died young in 1770, and a 17-year-old Mary Parker arrived to look after the children and soon developed a very different relationship with her employer. She had two children, both of whom were acknowledged by Erasmus. He set them up in a school of their own and supplied them with a book of instruction on education for girls. While he was certainly not a believer in the notion that girls and boys should receive identical educations, he did believe in girls going to school rather than being educated at home and proposed a wide range of studies, including the sciences, and, even more surprisingly, suggested that pupils should be taken on outings to see industries at work.

As a doctor, Darwin was keen to keep up with all the latest thinking and techniques. He was among the first to appreciate the role of the lungs in exchanging oxygen with the bloodstream, but many of the techniques he applied were based as much on novelty as on genuine scientific principles. Although he railed against quackery, he was always willing to treat his patients as guinea pigs. Among them was the family of another Lunar member, Josiah Wedgwood, and when one the daughters, Mary Ann, suffered convulsions he diagnosed teething trouble. She lost the use of one arm and one leg, and Darwin gave her electric shock therapy and lanced her gums, keeping the wound open to allow the teeth through. Sometimes he proved less than sympathetic. When Wedgwood complained of constantly seeing spots before his eyes, Darwin replied rather unhelpfully that many people had such spots, 'but everybody did not look at them'.[8]

In spite of his busy practice, he found ample time to study a huge variety of subjects. Mechanical matters fascinated him and he contrived a number of devices that were put to practical use. He built a windmill for driving grinding machinery at the Wedgwood factory and worked on innovations to make his own life more comfortable. One of the disadvantages of having a widespread practice was the amount of time the doctor had to spend bumping along bad roads to visit his patients. He invented a carriage that he claimed could not be turned over and, more ambitiously, devised a totally new way of steering. Up to then, the carriage changed direction by moving the whole axle, but in Darwin's carriage the wheels themselves pivoted – the device used in modern cars. Many of Darwin's notions were far ahead of their time. He proposed a rocket powered by cylinders of hydrogen and oxygen, and would have been delighted to know that two centuries later just such a device would be hurtling into space. He was very willing to join Watt and Boulton in considering steam engines and their development, even proposing a design for a steam carriage. It was never built. This was one of the differences between Darwin and Boulton. The former overflowed with brilliant ideas and schemes, but only a few were ever carried forward to a practical conclusion. Boulton's ideas were less extravagant but were more likely to be fully developed. In the steam engine world, Darwin was free to let his imagination roam where it would; Boulton needed to think about practical applications that were within the bounds of current technology, for which there was a market.

Darwin did make very real contributions to the scientific world. Botany was among his many interests, and he became very interested in the work of the Swedish scientist Carl Linnaeus. The latter was the first to establish a systematic method of naming all plants using two names: the first to identify the genus, the second to give the particular species within that broader category. He was later to extend the system to the animal kingdom. His original book *Species Plantarum* was published in 1753, and Darwin used his classical training to make the first translation into English. He then decided to produce a work of his own. He had always been fascinated by poetry and was even considered for a time as a possible Poet Laureate, but when he decided to combine verse and his botanic studies in an immense epic poem the result was bizarre. *The Botanic Garden* attempted to combine descriptions of the world of plants with accounts of new advances in technology using rhyming couplets and a wealth of classical allusions. What would a modern reader make of this?

Where Derwent guides his dusky floods
Through vaulted mountains and a night of woods
The nymph *Gossypia* treads the velvet sod
And warms with rosy smiles the watr'y god.

It helps to know that *Gossypia* is the botanical name for the cotton plant, but it might not be at all clear that what follows is going to be an account of Richard Arkwright's water-powered cotton mill. The second half of the work is called *The Loves of the Plants* and is based on Linnaeus' discovery that plants had sexual characteristics; Darwin's plants were given characters that were quite flirtatious. Some found it quite shocking – a sort of botanical pornography. His next major work was even more controversial. *The Temple of Nature* of 1803 followed the same verse pattern as *The Botanic Garden*, but put forward far more startling ideas:

ORGANIC LIFE: beneath the shoreless waves
Was born and nurs'd in Ocean's pearly caves;
First, forms minute, unseen by spheric glass,
Move on the mud, or pierce the watery mass;
These, as successive generations bloom,
New powers acquire, and larger limbs assume;
Whence countless groups of vegetation spring,
And breathing realms of fin, and feet, and wing.

The verses continue describing developments until he arrives at 'imperious man' who 'styles himself the image of his God'. This is quite clearly a description of evolution and it is notable that he is not saying that it is God who makes man, but man who declares himself to have been made by God, which is not the same thing at all. Darwin's basic belief seems to have been that there was a divine being who set creation in motion, but after that left it to evolve – a long way from the Bible story in Genesis. What the poem lacked was an explanation of what drove evolution forward. It was to be another two generations before that explanation was to appear. Darwin's son Robert married Josiah Wedgwood's daughter Sukey, and it was their son Charles who would write the famous book *On the Origin of Species*. The story of evolution was not very different from that of his grandfather's, but he provided the essential mechanism – natural selection.

It is said that one can measure the value of a man by the company he keeps. Boulton was in many ways a quite conventional man and it says a great deal about him that he was such a close friend of the very unconventional Darwin, who held views that many considered deeply shocking. It is also an indication of the values of the Lunar Society that all opinions would be given serious consideration, even those which seemed to challenge the most deep-rooted conventions of the age.

Darwin was responsible for introducing another member to the group, William Withering. He was a doctor, with a rather unsuccessful practice, and when Dr Small died, Darwin suggested that he make the move to Birmingham. They had more than an interest in medicine in common and he became interested in Darwin's botanical theories. Withering had been treating a young lady, Helena Cookes, a keen amateur artist, who particularly enjoyed painting plants and flowers. He began collecting specimens for her and became more and more fascinated by both botany and Miss Cookes. He and Helena were married, and he was soon sharing Darwin's interest in the latest Linnaean theories. But where Darwin expressed his ideas in the rather whimsical poem, Withering produced an altogether more sedate work, with the ponderous title *A Botanical Arrangement of All the Vegetables Naturally Growing in Great Britain*. It was the first serious attempt to describe all known British species and give them scientific names.

His chief claim to fame rests, however, on just one plant, the foxglove, *Digitalis purpurea*. He had heard of an old lady in Shropshire who had what was claimed to be a herbal cure for dropsy. He identified the foxglove as the active ingredient and began a series of experiments, using the leaves in various forms to make concoctions. He discovered that digitalis had a far more important use than merely treating dropsy – it was invaluable in treating cardiac difficulties, and is still used today. Darwin and Withering, who had been friends, had now become rivals, and each disparaged the other's work, claiming plagiarism and more. It was a rare case of two Lunar members squabbling rather than co-operating on scientific work. Broad areas of interest brought most of the Society members together, but there were also strong business connections to draw on as well.

Josiah Wedgwood, the famous potter, was a core member of the Lunar Society, a good friend of Boulton's, a business colleague for a time, and briefly a potential rival. They had a great deal in common. Both were determined to take an old craft and convert it into a modern industry, with all that entailed in terms of mass production. Both needed to keep a close eye on changing patterns of taste and adapt their products to meet them. Their work together will be dealt with more fully in the next chapter. They appear to have met as a result of Wedgwood's drive towards mechanisation. He made a number of visits to Birmingham in the 1760s to look at metal-working lathes, with a view to adapting them for use in his pottery. It was inevitable that he would visit Soho, and it seems that there was an instant rapport between the two men. He bought a lathe from Boulton in 1767, and described the meeting in a letter to his business partner Thomas Bentley. 'He is I believe the first – or most complete manufacturer in England, in metal. He is very ingenious, Philosophical, and Agreeable. You must be acquainted with him. He has promised to come to Burslem.'[9] Wedgwood was grateful for Boulton's advice and encouragement, and sent him a selection of fine vases that were much admired: '... my wife returns you a thousand thanks. She admires your vases very much & indeed so do I, even so much that I almost wish to be a potter.'[10] The following year, Wedgwood went to stay with the Boulton family and wrote an effusive letter of thanks. They were to remain good friends and often exchanged visits, but there were occasional strains in the relationship. Boulton was always on the lookout for new ideas and new directions in which to develop his business. He greatly admired what Wedgwood was achieving and began to think that he might indeed try going into the pottery business himself. At first Wedgwood was quite alarmed, but soon took a very different attitude. 'It doubles my courage to have the first Manufacturer in England to encounter with – The Match likes me well, – I like the Man, I like his spirit. He will not be a mere snivelling copyist like the antagonists I have hitherto had.'[11] The moment passed; Boulton soon found other pursuits to absorb his energies.

Wedgwood, like Darwin, took an interest in the new science of geology. As a promoter of the Trent & Mersey Canal he was fascinated by the material being excavated by the navvies tunnelling through Harecastle Hill. They found a fossil of what he described as 'a monstrous sized Fish', that the local 'connoisseurs' thought was actually the whale that had swallowed Jonah. He was even more intrigued by the stratification of coal and sandstone and fossilised plants. He could think of no explanation of how they came to be not on the surface but deep under the earth. This, he decided, was not an area that he could profitably investigate:

I am got beyond my depth. These wonderful works of nature are too vast for my narrow, microscopic comprehension. I must bid adieu to you for the present & attend to what better suits my small capacity, the forming of a Jug or Teapot.[12]

The self-deprecating comment was not meant to be taken too seriously. When it came to the practical world where he made his living he was among the pioneers of applying scientific methods to industry. At a very early age he began a series of experiments on all aspects of pot making, carefully recording all his results. Every time he tried a new clay, glaze or colouring, he kept a sample that was given a coded number. He was as aware as Boulton of the dangers of piracy. One of his main concerns was to produce consistency, and that was only possible if all the conditions could be replicated. His major difficulty was regulating kiln temperatures, as there was no thermometer that could measure such high values. So he set about inventing one, which was so successful that he was elected a Fellow of the Royal Society on the strength of its success. The Lunar men were often quite happy to explore fanciful theories, just for the sheer pleasure of argument and conjecture, but they were also essentially practical men, who could see where science could be useful in their everyday lives. Many of the members were dilettante scientists, but others made genuine and important contributions to knowledge, and men such as Boulton were always seeking ideas that could be converted into commercial propositions.

One of the most remarkable facts about the Society was the great diversity of the interests of its members. Some, such as James Watt, play a prominent part in the story and their lives will be dealt with in later chapters. Some were business associates, others friends of friends. But all had one thing in common: they were successful in their chosen fields.

John Whitehurst was in some ways typical of the Lunar men. He was a clockmaker and manufacturer of scientific instruments, who supplied many of the instruments that Boulton bought for his personal laboratory and was later to supply complex clockwork mechanisms for Boulton to mount. His other passion, which he shared with Boulton, was the study of rocks and minerals, but whereas Boulton was content to collect, Whitehurst meticulously observed, recorded and built theories on his observations. He published his theories in 1778 in his book *An Inquiry into the Original State and Formation of the Earth*, which Boulton ordered in advance of publication. The most important part of the work was the appendix in which he described his field studies into the geology of Derbyshire. He concluded that the various strata must have formed at different times and by different means. For example, he correctly identified the volcanic origins of basalt. If the theory was correct, then it directly challenged the Biblical story that the earth had been created just as it is today. He was not the last member of the Lunar Society to arrive at theories that challenged orthodoxy. The views caused considerable debate within the Society, but one of the distinguishing features of the loose grouping was that different opinions were tolerated. Whitehurst did his best to fit his ideas into religious orthodoxy. Boulton was a conventional member of the Church of England, although not a particularly regular attender, and was not unduly perturbed by Whitehurst's findings. Wedgwood found the book quite shocking. Other members had even more heterodox ideas.

Richard Lovell Edgeworth was introduced to the Lunar Society by Darwin, who wrote to Boulton in an undated letter: 'I have got with me a mechanical Friend Mr Edgeworth from Oxfordshire – the greatest conjurer I ever saw. Can take away polarity or give it to the needle by rubbing it thrice in the palm of his hand. Can see through two solid oak boards.'[13] Edgeworth was an enthusiastic amateur inventor, and one can see why he and Darwin would get on well together. Darwin was always attracted to novel ideas – Edgeworth obviously enjoyed playing with the currently fashionable but little understood science of electricity and magnetism. He invented a carriage that could be sailed along the road, what appears to be a version of a track-laying machine, and he joined Darwin in thinking about steam traction. Boulton's tastes tended towards the less fanciful, but he did find Edgeworth useful in helping to develop Watt's steam engine. In particular he contributed to the development of what became the standard measure of power – horsepower. He remained in the Birmingham area for only a short time before leaving for Ireland where he inherited estates. But he did introduce another friend to the Society, Thomas Day. They shared a common enthusiasm for the works of Rousseau, particularly his theories of education. The two men were equally radical in their political opinions, which might easily have caused a rift in the Lunar ranks when America went to war to claim its independence.

Manufacturers such as Boulton and Wedgwood had seen the follies inherent in Britain's approach to the colonies; they felt that, given better treatment and a more sympathetic approach, Britain and America could have enjoyed a fruitful relationship. In their world view, they saw America as the provider of raw materials, which Britain would turn into manufactured goods. There was also the good relationship enjoyed between Boulton and Benjamin Franklin, who was a very persuasive advocate for the American cause. Day and Edgeworth were natural supporters of the Americans, although Day had qualms about granting independence to a country that supported slavery. The outbreak of war changed Boulton's views. He saw that an independent America would no longer be satisfied with the passive role in feeding British industries but would be more likely to develop as a rival manufacturing power. He was more interested in preserving his business than in political argument. His change of heart led to a permanent breach with Franklin. Wedgwood's sympathies remained with the Americans: 'All the world are with the minister and against the poor Americans.' In 1778, he wrote, 'I ... blessed my stars and Lord North that *America was free*', and in the same letter he was unusually frank in his denunciation of Britain's foreign policy that had brought the calamities of warfare. 'We must have more war, and perhaps continue to be beaten – to what degree is in the womb of time. If our drubbing keeps pace with our deserts, the Lord have mercy on us.'[14] This, however, was a private letter. In public he kept his opinions to himself. Like Boulton, he put business first, and he was not about to offend his wealthy customers.

Interest in America did not die away with the end of the war. Day had always been a passionate opponent of slavery. In 1773, he and John Bicknell had written a poem *The Dying Negro*, presenting the last thoughts of an African

who chose death over slavery. It presented the hero as being very much one of
Rousseau's Noble Savages. It is more than a little long-winded, but there are
places where it becomes direct and powerful:

And better in th' untimely grave to rot,
The world and all its cruelties forgot,
Than, dragg'd once more beyond the Western main,
To groan beneath some dastard planter's chain.

Day was not the only Lunar member to take up the issue. This time Wedgwood
made no attempt to keep his views private. He became an enthusiastic committee member of the Society for the Suppression of the Slave Trade in 1787,
and he designed a cameo that became the emblem of the movement. It
showed a slave in chains with the inscription 'Am I not a man and a brother?'
It appeared in various forms from brooches to snuff boxes and did much to
popularise the cause among the gentry. This time there was no conflict of
interest, but it is worth noting that this was a cause devoted to ending the trade
in slaves – not slavery itself. It was a cause Boulton was happy to support, but it
did not prevent him supplying steam engines to drive sugar cane mills on the
slave plantations.

Day was prepared to forgive Boulton his indirect support of the slave system,
and went even further by helping Boulton out by making loans to the business
– which were not always repaid very promptly. A typically exasperated letter
was sent to Boulton about a loan of £500: 'You cannot I think complain of my
want of patience since I have waited for the letter you promised me, with the
same patient expectation that the Jews do for their promised Messiah.'[15] On
another occasion, he complimented Boulton on his many qualities, including his mastery of a number of scientific subjects, especially mineralogy, but
added wryly that he hoped he might also spend more time practising the art
of making a fortune. Day's patience may have been strained, but the good relationship remained intact.

The other great event of the times that divided opinion even more sharply
and had even more profound effects was the French Revolution. At first welcomed by the libertarian members of the Lunar Society, there were some
doubts as the more violent events developed into the years of the Terror.
Boulton largely kept his own counsel, but the events were to have a profound
effect on one of the most distinguished of all the Lunar men, Joseph Priestley.

Priestley was born near Leeds in comparatively poor circumstances: his father
was a weaver who, as was usual at the time, worked in his own cottage.[16] When
his mother died in childbirth, his father was quite unable to cope with a growing
family, so 8-year-old Joseph was sent to live with an aunt. The family were all

Calvinists and great believers in education. He finished his education at a non-conformist academy and became a minister. He was a nonconformist, even by nonconformist standards, refusing to accept the doctrine of the Holy Trinity on the grounds that the doctrine was totally illogical. It is perhaps not too surprising that the sceptic became interested in science. His interest in matters outside the normal sphere of religion was given a boost when he married Mary Wilkinson, sister of the ironmaster who was to play such a crucial role in the fortunes of both Boulton and Watt. But his main interest became the study of chemistry, the new science that had grown out of the old ideas of the alchemists.

One of his first successful experiments was based on studying the carbon dioxide produced from the fermentation vats of a nearby brewery. He found that a very interestingly fizzy drink could be made by bubbling the gas through water – he had invented soda water, but never made any money from his discovery, even though it soon achieved huge popularity. Eventually manufacture was begun by a London company, J. J. Schweppe, and Boulton was to be among their best customers. Priestley was to discover a number of gases over the years, but by far his most important achievement was the isolation of oxygen, recognising it as a separate gas from ordinary air. He also observed that it had some interesting properties. For example, candles burned brighter in oxygen than in air, and a mouse trapped in a vessel filled only with oxygen survived twice as long as one in the same vessel filled with air. It was clear that this gas was, as he wrote, much better than air at keeping things alive. We now know that this is because it is essential to life, but occupies only a fifth of the air we breathe. His other great discovery was that if he placed a plant in a closed jar – his first experiments were with mint – it did not die. He had discovered photosynthesis, the chemical process by which plants use the energy in sunlight to take in carbon dioxide and expel oxygen. Others were to make the next big breakthrough, by showing that when substances burned they took in oxygen – and not as scientists believed at the time, and Priestley continued to believe, gave out a mysterious substance called phlogiston.

Priestley moved to Birmingham in 1780. He already had strong connections with the Lunar men, first through his relationship to Wilkinson and then through his long friendship with Benjamin Franklin. He was immediately accepted as a valued member of the group, not least by Boulton and Wedgwood. He became a sort of one-man research department for the two industrialists: they supplied him with equipment and he, in return, carried out analyses of all kinds of materials, from clays to metallic ores. He never had much money and was not greatly concerned by the lack of it. He declared that £100 a year was quite sufficient. There was talk among the Lunar men of raising a subscription to help support his scientific work, but it came to nothing, as James Watt noted:

The Doctor says he never did intend or think of making any pecuniary advantage from any of his experiments but gave them to the public with their results just as they happened & so he should continue to do, without ever attempting to make any private emolument from them for himself.[17]

Priestley was not a man to keep his opinions to himself. He attacked the Church of England and welcomed the French Revolution. In 1791, a dinner was given in Birmingham to celebrate the anniversary of the storming of the Bastille. Rumours soon circulated that revolution was being plotted and agitators worked on the crowds, demanding that they oppose these dissenters and revolutionaries. What followed became known as the 'Church and King' riots. The mob never got round to attacking the actual event, as the organisers had moved the dinner to earlier in the day, but set off to find any who might have been there, Priestley among them, although he seems never to have attended the dinner at all. Having been warned of what might happen, he fled with his family. He was just in time: his house was burned down and all his scientific work went up with the flames. To the mob, anyone associated with Priestley was equally suspect. Boulton had steered well clear of political controversy:

I am happy in living alone in the Country & am almost silent upon this dissonant Subject. By minding my own business I live peaceably and securely amidst the Flames, Rapine, Plunder, anarchy & confusion of these Unitarians, Trinitarians, Predestinarians & tarians of all sorts.[18]

Nevertheless he felt that he too would soon be attacked, being found guilty by association. He barricaded himself in at Soho and armed his workforce with muskets to repel the attack. It never came.

The Lunar men were horrified by what had happened, and Wedgwood was among the first to offer practical help:

Can I be of any service to you upon the present occasion? Assure yourself, my good friend, that I most earnestly wish it. Believe this of me – act accordingly, instruct me in the means of doing it & I shall esteem it as one of the strongest instances of your friendship.[19]

But there was nothing to be done as Priestley left Birmingham for good, staying for a time in London before emigrating to America. He looked back on his Birmingham days with nostalgia, writing to Watt of 'the pleasing intercourse I have had with you and all my friends of the Lunar Society. Such another I can never expect to see – indeed London cannot furnish it. I shall always think of you at the usual time of your meetings.'[20]

The Lunar Society had lost one of its most brilliant lights and others too had moved on. Darwin had left Lichfield for Derby, where he tried to form his own version of the Society, but it could never quite match the brilliance he had found in the Soho meetings. Edgeworth had left to look after his Irish estates, and other members were simply getting old. But, while it was in its pomp, the Lunar Society was one of the most extraordinary meetings of brilliant yet diverse talents that Britain had ever seen. It flourished because all the members shared common interests, in particular in the wonders being revealed by the new sciences. And it owed not a little of its success to the generosity and affability of its host, Matthew Boulton. He provided a forum for discussion, and although he lacked any formal scientific education, he was well able to appreciate the work of his distinguished friends and discuss their scientific insights with sense and understanding. His own scientific work divided into two parts: the science that he felt he could usefully apply to his business; and the science that he studied for the pure pleasure of doing so. It would be hard to say that he applied himself to one more than the other. His old friend James Keir summed it up well:

> Mr Boulton is a proof, how much scientific knowledge may be acquired without much regular study, by means of a quick and just apprehension, much practical application, and nice mechanical feeling. He had very correct notions of the several branches of natural philosophy, and was master of every metallic art, and possessed of all the chemistry that had any relation to the objects of his various manufactures. Electricity and astronomy were at one time among his favourite amusements.[21]

Perhaps the last word on the ideal that permeated the Lunar Society should go to its most distinguished scientist, Joseph Priestley:

> The only method of attaining to a truly valuable agreement is to promote the most perfect freedom of thinking and acting ... in order that every point of difference may have an opportunity of being fully canvassed, not doubting but that ... Truth will prevail, and that then a rational, firm, and truly valuable union will take place.

Notes

1   Private diaries quoted in Anthony and Pip Burton, *The Green Bag Travellers*, 1978.
2   Draft letter, 1781.

3   Two excellent accounts of the Lunar Society are Robert E. Schofield, *The Lunar Society of Birmingham, 1970,* and Jenny Uglow, *The Lunar Men,* 2002.

4   E. Darwin to MB, 17 January 1784.

5   ED to MB, 5 April 1778.

6   Quoted in Anthony Burton, *Josiah Wedgwood,* 1976.

7   Desmond King-Hele, *Erasmus Darwin: A Life of Unequalled Achievement,* 1999.

8   Wedgwood to Thomas Bentley, 27 September 1769, quoted in Burton, op. cit.

9   Ibid., 7 October 1767.

10 MB to Wedgwood, 10 July 1767, quoted in Nicholas Goodison, 'I almost wish to be a Potter: Matthew Boulton's relationship with Josiah Wedgwood', in Malcolm Dick (ed.), *Matthew Boulton: A Revolutionary Player,* 2009.

11 Wedgwood to Bentley, April 1778, quoted in Burton, op. cit.

12 Ibid., 7 October 1767.

13 Schofield, op. cit., p. 45.

14 Ibid., April 1788, quoted in Burton, op. cit.

15 Thomas Day to MB, 14 April 1785.

16 F.W. Gibbs, *Joseph Priestley: Adventurer in Science and Champion of Truth,* 1965.

17 JW to MB, 10 March 1781.

18 MB to Charles Dumergue, 18 August 1791.

19 Undated letter quoted in Henry Carrington Bolton, *Scientific Correspondence of Joseph Priestley,* 1892; Schofield, op. cit., p. 361.

20 Schofield, op. cit., pp. 363–66.

21 H.W. Dickinson, *Matthew Boulton,* 1937, pp. 70–72.

6

Ormolu & Plate

Boulton's interest in studying metals was by no means limited to mere intellectual curiosity: he was concerned with practical applications not only for the useful but also the ornamental. Not content to be known only as a manufacturer of useful objects and toys, he hankered after a reputation as a man who produced highly artistic wares, suitable for the use of the aristocracy and even royalty. Luxury items in the metal trades were generally the work of specialist goldsmiths and silversmiths, and he had no inclination to compete directly in that market. He wanted to produce materials that looked as grand as those crafted out of precious metals but which could be made in the factory using machinery and cheaper materials. His friend Wedgwood had already shown the way.[1]

Porcelain was all the fashion by the middle of the eighteenth century, but Wedgwood was working with the far less expensive earthenware. He needed to find a way of imitating some of the fine points of porcelain, which he achieved by whitening the basic clay so that it no longer needed to be disguised under a thick, heavy glaze. The result, known as creamware, became instantly fashionable, and when he received an order from the Queen he promptly rechristened it Queensware – which encouraged its sale to both the aristocracy and the new discerning middle classes. He also looked to the classical world for inspiration in producing items such as vases. Boulton began by producing a small amount of silverware and then turned to a product that looked like gold of the finest quality: ormolu. He too looked to the artefacts of Greece and Rome for inspiration.[2]

The name 'ormolu' derives from the French *or moulou* or ground gold. As the name suggests, the process was first developed and brought to a very high level of sophistication in France. Powdered gold of very high quality is mixed with mercury to form an amalgam. This is added to the surface of an object of brass or occasionally bronze, which is then fired in a furnace, vapourising the mercury and leaving the gold firmly attached. The toxic effects of mercury vapour were understood at the time, and the results on those who worked with it were all too apparent. The best-known example comes from its use in the hat-making industry, hence the expression 'mad as a hatter'. In one of his notebooks, Boulton wrote, 'When the gilders are Slovenly & do not wash their hands clean before they eat their Dinners, or if the chimney doth not properly draw off the Mercurial Vapour the party will very soon grow Paralytick.'[3] When he brought gilding to Soho he attempted to avoid the worst effects by designing an improved hearth to remove the dangerous fumes.

French ormolu became fashionable in England. Boulton would certainly have been aware of it, and would have seen examples on his trips to France. But, as we have seen, he was not necessarily hugely impressed by all things French. On a visit in 1765, he wrote home to his wife:

> I intended to give my love some idea of this grand & paltry country, a country that abounds with pompous poverty & in most particulars quite in the papier machee style … I am under the necessity of dressing every day in full trim's Black clothes a Bag wig & sword with a little Hat under my Arm for to put it on upon my head would be such a sight as Paris affords not.[4]

Boulton may not have been enthusiastic about French taste, but he was certainly aware of the often exquisite work being done in ormolu by French craftsmen. The craftsmanship could not be faulted, but he viewed the elaboration of the designs with considerable distaste. Nevertheless, as a businessman he knew that the work was steadily gaining in popularity in Britain, as Wedgwood explained to his merchant partner Thomas Bentley in 1768:

> Mr. Boulton tells me I should be surprised to know what a trade has lately been made out of Vases in Paris. The artists have even come over to London, picked up the old whimsical ugly things they could meet with, carried them to Paris, where they were mounted and ornamented them with metal, and sold them to the virtuosi of every nation, and particularly to Millords d'Anglaise … This alone (the combination of Clays & Metals) is a field, to the farther end of which we shall never be able to travel.[5]

It made sense for an English manufacturer to carry out the work at home and to make objects in a rather simpler style more in accordance with English taste. Wedgwood was obsessed with vases at this stage, and the idea of combining clay and metal appeared again before the end of the year, when Boulton asked for some vases for mounting in ormolu. Much as Wedgwood admired Boulton, he was wary of him, seeing him as much as a potential rival as a partner in any enterprise. He wrote to Thomas Bentley to put the point, saying that they were doing very well on their own, but then added, 'Very true, but he will be doing, so that the question is whether we shall refuse having anything to do with him, and thereby affront him, & set him of doing them himself, or employing his friend Garbett.'[6]

The 1760s seemed to be just the time to enter this potentially lucrative and prestigious trade. The taste for classicism was growing, encouraged by the fashion for young aristocrats to take the Grand Tour of Europe, where they were expected to admire the antiquities being unearthed by excavators.[7] The whole movement was given a huge impetus by the discovery of the ancient city of Herculaneum in the Bay of Naples. The reluctance of the Neapolitan authorities to allow visitors to see the discoveries only added to their attraction, surrounding them with an air of mystery. Soon illustrated volumes of engravings were being circulated, such as the very influential *Recueil d'antiquités egyptiennes, etrusques, grecques et romaines* by Count de Caylus, published in 1756, which added a taste for Egyptian styles to those he wrongly attributed as Etruscan. William Hamilton, who was the envoy at Naples at the time, began buying up the treasures to form what was to become one of the most important collections of antiquities in Britain. When an illustrated volume of the works was published, Boulton subscribed to the four volumes, which were to prove an inspiration for later designs. British designers travelled abroad to see these wonders for themselves, including the architect Robert Adam who visited Diocletian's palace at Spalatro in 1758. He too published his results in a book illustrated with engravings. More importantly, he began to apply the same ideas to domestic buildings in Britain. The classic Georgian house, with its elegant symmetries, was only the frame in which to display a variety of objects in the same style – everything from candelabras and vases to door handles.

Boulton's first efforts at producing gilded work appear to date from 1766, when he was asked to provide door knobs and escutcheons for Kedleston Hall, a sternly neo-classical mansion, designed by Robert Adam for Sir Nathaniel Curzon. It was intended as a showcase for antiquities as much as a family home, and Adam ensured that every detail contributed to the overall effect. Samuel Wyatt, who was acting as clerk of works for the project, was not impressed with Boulton's efficiency in meeting the order, writing, 'My Lords patience is quite tired out. I am afraid to mention the name Boulton to him.'[8] The work, when it did finally appear, was very elaborate and imposing. Kedleston Hall was part of a growing trend for ornaments to be in keeping with the architectural style of the whole building. There was a limit to the number of genuine classical artefacts available, but a growing market for ornaments in the antique style. By 1768, Boulton had decided that the time was ripe to start a new business, fitting vases in elaborate ormolu mounts, and took on two new chasers to be responsible for the finer engraving work. The vases could be purely ornamental or could be adapted as perfume burners or candelabra. He later claimed to have been the first to introduce the manufacture of ormolu to England.[9]

He began by putting in modest orders for vases to Wedgwood, who overcame his early scruples and decided to supply what Boulton requested. In the event, Boulton soon lost his enthusiasm for ceramic vases, which were fragile and difficult to mount, and turned to other materials, notably fluorspars and marbles from Derbyshire. The most highly prized was Blue John, which was mined in the Castleton area. It was generally found in natural caverns in the limestone, but in places more elaborate workings were needed. The Speedwell mine, for example, was developed using an underground canal system for transport. Boulton's first idea was to lease one of the Blue John mines to supply all his needs, and he wrote to one of his Lunar friends, John Whitehurst, asking him to make discreet enquiries:

> I have found a use for Blew John which will consume some quantity of it. I mean that sort which is proper for turning into vases. I therefore should esteem it a singular favour if you would enquire whether the mine of it has lately been let or when it is to be let again, for I wish to take it for a year and if you find that it is not possible to come at it then please to learn how I can come at any of the best and largest sort of the produce of it. But above all I beg you will be quite secret as to my intentions, and never let M. Boulton and John Blue be named in the same sentence.[10]

Boulton never did acquire exclusive rights to any of the Derbyshire marble or Blue John mines, although that did not prevent him telling a shopkeeper that he had a monopoly when he thought it helped in gaining an order. He listed the different materials he thought might be useful for vases and similar objects, which included glass, ceramic, various marbles and alabaster, but Blue John remained of paramount importance. The other main raw material he required was brass to form the basis for the ormolu mounts. This is an alloy of copper and zinc, although Boulton often referred to his products as being bronze, which is actually an alloy of copper and tin, and is generally considered rather superior. Bronze was associated with art works, while brass was generally thought of in terms of the sort of cheap ornaments for which Birmingham was already famous – and that was precisely the image that he did not want to portray. At that period, however, the two names were often used interchangeably, and once the gilding process had been completed it was virtually impossible to see what metal lay beneath the surface.

Boulton collected a number of volumes of engravings for inspiration, and consulted a number of architects and designers, but the most influential single individual he dealt with was William Chambers. Although regarded as one of the more conventional of English architects, there was little conventional about his start in life. Born in Sweden to English parents, he joined the Swedish East India Company and travelled widely, spending a considerable amount of time in China. There he studied the language and the buildings, developing an interest in architecture. In those days it was possible to make a fortune in the East, which Chambers duly did and used it to pay for a formal architectural training, first in France and then in Italy. During his time in Italy he not only learned a great deal about classical architecture but also met many of the English aristocracy doing the Grand Tour – connections which did him no harm at all when he decided to set up a practice in England in 1752. His talents and good connections were not lost on the other great classical architect Robert Adam, who wrote to his brother James, 'All the English who have travelled for these five years ... imagine him a prodigy for genius, for sense and good taste ... it will require very considerable interest to succeed against Chambers who has tolerable Friends & real merit'.[11] Nicholas Goodison has argued that it could well have been Boulton's connections with Chambers that prevented him from getting very many orders from the rival Adam, although there was an attempt to form some sort of collaborative partnership with the Adam brothers in 1770 (see below).[12] Chambers' good connections gave him the great breakthrough in his career in 1757, when he was appointed as architect for Princess Augusta's gardens at Kew. Here he made use of what he had learned in China about garden design and gave the gardens one of their iconic images, the Pagoda. At the same time he was appointed architectural tutor to George, Prince of Wales. He became very much the establishment's architect of choice – he remodelled Buckingham House, later to become Buckingham Palace, and designed Somerset House on the Thames in London. Not surprisingly, this was a connection that excited Boulton, who welcomed any possible connection with the royal family and saw Chambers as epitomising all that was best in modern taste. 'I breakfasted with the King's architect who shewed me some civility and made me a present of some valuable, usefull and acceptable modells.'[13] It is possible to trace the influence of Chambers on Boulton's designs, some of which are clearly based on illustrations in Chambers' published works. There is no record of the models that were loaned, apart from a later request from Chambers for the return of two tritons and a griffin.

Boulton was familiar with the work of all the leading architects of the day and his library was well stocked with reference works on antiquities and designs. Among the other influential artists he consulted and whose models he used was the sculptor John Flaxman, perhaps best known for his designs used in Wedgwood's famous jasperware. Boulton also purchased models from his father, also John Flaxman, a competent sculptor, who never achieved the fame of his son. The success or failure of Soho's move into ormolu would depend to a large extent on being able to keep up with the latest changes in fashionable taste. Ultimately it was Boulton who decided which designs were to be used for ornamental objects, based on his wide knowledge of the arts and his connections with fashionable society. He knew what he wanted to achieve and needed the craft skills of others in manufacturing.

The process of manufacture was carried out by the workers in the Manufactory and was a mixture of handcraft and one-off or small batch production. Some items were undoubtedly made almost entirely by hand, but once a successful design had been established, it could be reproduced. For flat items, the original would have been carefully carved and chased and then used as a model for steel dies. The metal, brass or copper, arrived at the works as sheets or ingots and was then rolled out by water-powered machines to create thinner, uniform sheets. It could then be hammered or pressed on to the die to produce the finished articles. Hammering was a straightforward treatment, in which the thin metal sheet was placed over the die and hammered until it assumed exactly the same shape. Pressing was similar, except that the die had two parts: the male and the female. The female was the lower half, held in a rigid frame. The metal was then placed on top, and the male die placed on top, pressure being applied to force it down into the hollow female die in order to achieve the correct shape. Over the years, Boulton improved the processes and in his notes described using stamps, presses and the imposing-sounding Leviathan. A rather more common method of producing the objects was by casting.

Casting in sand had become a familiar manufacturing process by the latter part of the eighteenth century. The first stage was to produce the pattern, which had to be a minutely detailed version of the finished article, but carved out of fine-grained wood. This was placed inside a two-part mould box and then packed closely round with a special casting sand. Then the pattern was carefully removed, leaving a negative image of the pattern. The two parts of the box were tightly fixed together, leaving just a nozzle into which the molten metal was poured. Once the metal had cooled, the box was broken open and the finished piece extracted. An alternative method was the lost wax process. Here the pattern was modelled in wax and the pattern again packed with sand. This time, however, the whole was heated to a high temperature, melting the wax that was allowed to run away. Once again, the space left behind could be filled with molten metal. Using this technique, hollow objects could be cast, which was a saving in metal and, rather more importantly, finer results could be obtained. The benefits of the system are obvious. Once there was a successful design, the same pattern could be used to reproduce it over and over again.

The rough casts still needed finishing, with details added by skilled chasers and by turning on lathes. Once again there was a mixture of old-fashioned craftsmanship and modern technology, with skilled chasers working by hand at the workbench and turners using water-powered lathes. One of the specialities was a product that had contrasting matt and burnished surfaces to give richness and variety of texture. Boulton himself gave the most complete account of the works. In August 1770, he received a suggestion from James Adam that he might co-operate in producing ormolu for the brothers, and possibly open a shop in London to sell the ware:

I think with you and your Brother that an emense Manufacture might be established by improving the designs and taste of plate and other ornamental furniture in Or Moulu and am convinced that no men have greater power than your selves. I like wise know from experience that such a manufacture may be conducted upon much more advantageous terms in a situation like mine than in London, I having seven or eight hundred persons employed in almost all those Arts that are applicable to the manufacturing of all the metals, the semi metals and various combinations of them, also Tortois shell, Stones, glass, Enamels &c., &c.

I have almost every machine that is applicable to those Arts. I have two Water mills employd in rolling, pollishing, grinding & turning various sorts of Laths. I have traind up many and am training up more young plain Country Lads, all of which that betray any genius are taught to draw, from whom I derive many advantages that are not to be found in any manufacture that is or can be establishd in a great & Debauchd Capital.

I have likewise establish'd a Correspondence in almost every mercantile Town in Europe Which regurlary supplies me with orders for the grosser & Current articles which enables me constantly to employ such a number of hands as yields a Choice of Artists for the finer Branches and am thus enabled to errect and employ a more extensive & more convenient aperatus than would be prudent to erect for the finer Articles only – I have Long been convinced that the Shopkeepers in town are the Bane of all improvments as it becomes an imprudent thing for a man to make improvements which are attended with expence when he cannot reap the fruits of his own Labor, and that he cannot do when it passes through the hands of such a race of disingenuous persons as most of 'em are – I must therefore say that a proper connection in London and a commodious situation for Sale wou'd be a very agreeable thing to me: I think no situation superior to the neighbourhood of Durham Yard but my Ideas of a shop or sale room are very different from yours for I wou'd rather choose a large elegant room up Stairs without any other window than a sky light; by this sort of concealment you excite curiosity, more, you preserve your improvements from Street walking pirates: The nobility wou'd like that less publick repository.[14]

Apart from giving some idea of how the works were organised and the imposing scale of the operation, the letter also provides a first insight into the part of the business that occupied a good deal of Boulton's time — marketing. It gives a hint of his approach to selling both himself and his wares. There is not a scrap of false modesty on view, nor any suggestion that his way of doing things was other than the best — and repeated Boulton's favourite mantra that anything London could do, Birmingham could do better. It oozed self-confidence, but however much he played up the efficiency of the works, things did not run nearly as smoothly as this account suggests. For a start, the work did not always reach the high standard that he demanded. He wrote to his partner Fothergill in 1770 in scathing terms about the workshop manager, Richard Bentley:

[I have] one very serious remark to make which if not attended to there will soon be an end of the sale of all vases both great and small and that is, our vases are so nastily turned out of hand, they are so carelessly got up in every particular, that I fear I shall have great difficulty to sell those I have here, and great difficulty to retrieve my character as to clean good work. For all of them are now tarnished and spotted to such a degree as to render them unsaleable — I have sent a pair for you to see — whereas if our manager was a man of care, industry and judgment, the work might be turned out of hand 50 per cent better without more expence, but I am fearfull I shall never be able to succeed with Bentley's management. His mind is not right turned for business, nor any man whose affairs are lying in such confusion as I too often find his warehouse, whilst he is reading newspapers and magazines, or perhaps writeing out a love song and yet I perceive his opinion of his own abilitys is different from mine, I'll venter a wager if you examine his bed chamber you'll find a looking glass, I wish he had one that would not deceive him.[15]

The year 1770 seems to have been one of frustrations. Boulton complained that shops were unwilling to stock the goods because of late deliveries and, even more annoyingly, he noted in an undated letter that he had not received patterns that he had hoped to show to the Queen: 'I am vexed, I am vexed, I am disappointed & there is no remedy!' These represent the two extremes of the techniques used for selling ormolu: the conventional methods of selling through shops; or by direct contact with the aristocracy or, better yet, royalty.

There is no doubt which method Boulton preferred. We have already had his views on the perfidious nature of shopkeepers and his investigation of the possibility of establishing his own showroom in London. This idea never came to fruition. Instead he preferred to hold a number of sales in London auction houses. He was encouraged to do so because he had already built up a reputation among aristocratic patrons, due in good measure to his willingness to entertain at Soho, where many of the visitors purchased vases. This was what he later referred to as 'the agreeable part' of his business. In 1771, Boulton & Fothergill opened their own showroom in a former warehouse at Soho, where the visitors could see vases displayed to the best advantage. It was through these connections that he gained an introduction to the royal family.

Boulton enjoyed mixing with aristocracy, but he was a shrewd enough businessman to realise the importance of keeping up contacts after the visitors had left Birmingham. He made regular trips to London, where he was kept busy, calling on potential customers old and new and displaying the latest wares. He regularly wrote back home to tell his wife about his experiences. In one letter he gave details of his busy round of visits.[16] On the Sunday he called on the Earl of Shelburne, and sat talking in his library. Then they received a message from Lady Shelburne, who said she had a 'putrid sore throat' and was unable to join them, but would like to see some of Boulton's 'pretty things' to keep herself amused. At that, Boulton took a carriage back to his lodgings and 'fetched a load for her and sat with her Ladyship two hours explaining and hearing her criticism'. As in all effective marketing, Boulton sought and did not shy away from critical feedback. The next day he was invited to visit the Duke and Duchess of Northumberland, where he drank coffee with them, discussed art and received a personal tour of the Duke's collection. On the Tuesday he had a call from the Earl of Dartmouth and had an appointment to show his latest *objets d'art* to the Dowager Princess of Wales. The trip culminated in a visit to the royal family, and Boulton sent a chatty account of the visit to his wife and was particularly impressed by the attention he received from the Queen:

> She draws very finely, is a great musician, and works with her needle better than Mrs. Betty. However, without joke, she is extremely sensible, very affable, and a great patroness of English Manufactorys. Of this she gave me a particular instance; for after the King and she had talked to me for nearly three hours, they withdrew, and then the Queen sent for me into her bed chamber, shewed me her chyney [chimney] piece and asked me how many vases it would take to furnish it, for she says all that china shall be taken away.[17]

The visit was not wasted. Boulton asked his wife to arrange for seven or eight good quality Blue John vases to be sent as quickly as possible, as he had promised the Queen she would have them within a fortnight. Ormolu from Soho was to be given an honoured place in both Buckingham House and Windsor Castle. With such illustrious patronage, Boulton felt confident enough to begin his major sales drive in London by arranging an auction at Christie and Ansell's showroom in Pall Mall. He was very excited by the result, but was not very happy with the workmanship; orders were issued to Soho to improve the quality, no matter what the cost. By the following April he was ready to put on a second sale in which he demonstrated that he had listened to the criticisms made of the last show and had made improvements, notably in the gilding. He described it as being halfway between the French style, which was too 'brassy', and the former Soho style, which was too red. He promoted the sale through advertisements in the papers and by personal approaches to the gentry. He was very satisfied with the results, telling his wife, 'I made so great a bussle amongst the Nobility even to such a degree as to stop up Pallmall with Coaches.' The sales became a regular feature, but however much the exhibits were admired, the actual sales too often fell short of expectations, with many remaining unsold and some that were sold fetching lower prices than expected. A third sale, in 1772, fared even worse.

Soho was by now turning out ever more elaborate pieces that were hugely expensive to produce; if they did not sell, it was a serious matter. Boulton was always optimistic, but Fothergill became increasingly gloomy. In March 1773, he wrote to Boulton saying that, given the firm's financial position, the best thing would be to stop work altogether and pay everyone off. Two months later he wrote, not without some justification, that Boulton's emphasis on manufacturing for the nobility was distracting him from the main business of establishing a sound financial footing. 'You undertook the entire management of the Manufactory; it was your desire; it was your delight!'[18] Boulton was already learning the hard lesson that the nobility and royalty might admire his work, but that did not necessarily mean they were prepared to pay for it. Shortly after the 1772 sale he went again to the palace. 'I was with them, ye Queen & all the Children between 2 & 3 hours, there was likewise many others of the Nobility present. Never no man was so much complimented as I have been but I find Compliments don't fill the pocket nor make me fat.'[19]

Among the biggest disappointments of the 1772 sale was that two of his most prized pieces, a magnificent pair of clocks, failed to find a buyer. He blamed the failure on the poor taste of the public:

I find philosophy at a very low ebb in London and I have therefore brought back my two fine clocks which I will send to a market where common sense is not out of fashion. If I had made the clocks play jigs upon bells and a dancing bear keeping time, or if I had made a horse race upon their faces

I believe they would have had better bidders. I shall therefore bring them back to Soho and some time this Summer will send them to the Empress of Russia who, I believe, would be glad of them.[20]

Boulton also found another problem when dealing with the aristocracy: they might purchase expensive items, but it was not always so easy to get them to come up with the cash. Mrs Matthews, who looked after his finances, following the death of her husband, reported in August 1797 that one customer had an outstanding bill for £1,060 18s 2d and his son had asked to defer payment as it would be 'a great accommodation to them'. She noted wryly that he was actually 'well able to make the payment'.

Understandably exasperated by the difficulties he faced in keeping up with all the latest twists and turns of English fashion, Boulton looked increasingly to export markets. He declared ironically that he had a particular interest in America and Germany, as the taste there was so poor he did not have to worry about elegance at all. The same could not be said of the far richer markets of Russia, France and Holland, and he found it necessary to make the occasional European trip, both to sell his own products and to discover the new tastes and fashions that were being developed. He enjoyed being in different countries, but not the business of getting there. In 1779, he left Harwich for Holland on a rough night, for although the winds were high they were favourable and a fast crossing would, it was hoped, keep them out of the hands of French privateers. He described the journey in a notebook:

I soon went to my hammock to prevent sickness but about Midnight the Wind blew hard & I became sick. The Vessell roll'd from one Side to ye other. The Capt. & all hands were upon deck all night managing ye Sails as Violent Squalls often returned. Mr. & Mrs. Cummins were very sick & puked although they declar'd they had crossed the Atlantick 4 times & had been accustomed to ye sea 19 years without ever being sick before, for great Ships have not so much motion as ye packet Boats have.

He was greatly taken with Holland – 'prudence, Industry, decency & seriousness are characteristicks of the Dutch' – and he particularly noticed how clean everything was, even the barges on the canals. But he was not in Europe for sightseeing. He made his usual calls on likely aristocratic customers and even found French ormolu that impressed him: 'It is gilt upon fine German brass & I think keeps its Colour better than ours.'

By the late 1770s, ormolu was selling better on the overseas markets than it was at home. The idea of sending the two clocks to Russia was followed up by a letter to Lord Cathcart, Britain's Ambassador in St Petersburg, to say that a consignment of vases was on its way to Russia and hoping that he would use his influence to see they reached the right hands, going to those who Boulton flatteringly suggested would have 'distinguished taste, like that of your Excellency'. Cathcart responded splendidly and, as a result, the Empress bought the entire consignment. A similar tactic was used with other ambassadors in other countries. Even so, there was no disguising the fact that Boulton & Fothergill were not making money out of ormolu, and a good deal of the blame must be laid at Boulton's door. He was too concerned to attain a reputation as a purveyor of works of fine artistic merit to a discerning public, and too little prepared to attend to the more mundane process of calculating prices and ensuring that what was sold actually brought in more than it cost to produce. In time he became disillusioned with ormolu, discovering that there were never enough customers to make the sort of production runs that could alone reduce costs. James Keir knew this: 'It was too expensive for general command and therefore not a proper object of wholesale manufacture.'[21] Boulton turned instead to another potentially rich market in a material that, like ormolu, was the poor relation of a grander family. He began to look at manufacturing silver plate.

During Boulton's lifetime the proportion of the population that could be called middle class increased and expenditure on luxuries grew as people emulated the upper classes. His father was using silver extensively, in addition to other metals, by the 1750s. But Matthew, with two socially advantageous marriages, was enabled to expand the manufacture of silver goods.

By the mid-1760s Soho was producing silver candlesticks and, by the early 1770s, tableware and other silver items. This was all part of Matthew Boulton's ambition to transform the dingy reputation of Birmingham as a manufacturing town. While small silver goods were not required to be assayed, larger pieces were and this posed a potential difficulty, for the nearest Assay Office was at Chester.

Boulton used the same production technologies and design skills in ormolu, (sterling) silver plate and Sheffield plate, besides other goods made in materials which, although with the appearance of silver, were manufactured in substitutes. This enabled the firm to change from one material to another, unlike London silversmiths who specialised in one material.

Boulton took an interest in a method known as French plating that involved heating a base metal to a high temperature, then cooling it again and cleaning the surface. It was then reheated and quenched to roughen the surface, to provide adhesion for the silver leaf. He began using the technique in a small way in the 1770s and employed a French plater at Soho. It was a task that required a high degree of skill and was not at all suited to the needs of larger-scale production.

A different method of plating was discovered in 1743 by a Sheffield cutler, Thomas Boulsover.[22] The story goes that he was repairing a knife handle made out of copper and silver and he accidentally discovered that they could be fused together by hammering. He developed this into what became known as Sheffield plate. In this process, a sheet of silver was pressed on to a copper ingot, a piece of iron being placed on top to protect the silver, and the assembly being hammered until the copper and silver fused. The fused ingot was then heated in a furnace, when the silver would 'weep' out to the surface of the ingot. It was then allowed to cool, after which it could be rolled into a thin sheet. The silver remained on the surface to give the finished product every appearance of being sterling silver. The process was improved in the 1750s by Joseph Hancock who started producing hollow ware. The appearance was improved by fusing silver on to both sides of the copper, so that both the inside and the outside of a vessel showed a silver surface.

Boulsover began by making small objects, such as boxes, buckles and buttons, just the sort of thing that was bound to catch the eye of a Birmingham toy manufacturer. There is evidence that Boulton went to Sheffield to learn about Sheffield plating in 1764,[23] and he had made Sheffield plate candlesticks by 1765. While Boulton experimented with a variety of other metals, which resembled silver, it was Sheffield plate which achieved pre-eminence in the Manufactory, and plate buttons, which were in production by 1766, were produced in large quantities. Livery buttons were also in demand and a gentleman might have as many as four dozen buttons on one set of clothes, a cartoon of the time showing a lady bending backwards, dazzled by the buttons on a man's coat.[24] By about 1790 Sheffield plate buckles were being made at Soho, although Boulton had declined to make them earlier on. In 1793 he formed a partnership with James Smith specifically to make latchets, a fastening for shoes.[25]

By the early 1770s, Sheffield plate had become a principal element of Boulton's factory production and he was producing a range of tableware;[26] Boulton, not surprisingly, insisted on calling it plated ware, in order to disassociate himself from any perceived connection with Sheffield. As with ormolu, his aim was always to make ware of the highest artistic quality – and, inevitably, of comparatively high cost. One of the problems with plate was that it was possible, with use, to wear away the silver coating to reveal the copper underneath. Boulton regularly made use of another technology, again pioneered in Sheffield, of using silver thread at the edges of articles, such as the lips of vases. These were the areas that were most likely to get worn, hence the need for silver edging, which would never reveal the secret core of base metal. Boulton placed his maker's mark on plated wares, which caused confusion with silver plate until, in 1773, this was prevented by Act of Parliament.

Boulton's plate was so good by the 1770s that even the aristocracy preferred to buy plated candlesticks to the far more expensive sterling silver ones. Only thirty candlesticks in silver were sold in 1781 compared with 2,500 in plate, many of the customers for this work being members of the middle classes.[27] Since tea urns were so large they were generally only sold to the aristocracy and gentry, if made in silver. But Sheffield plate teapots were made in great numbers. By 1780, excluding buttons, plate items comprised 91 per cent of the silver and plate items sold, and it was not long before the London agent was asked to prioritise Sheffield plate orders over silver. By the end of the century, Boulton was quoting prices for ecclesiastical wares in plate, while twenty years previously he had not thought it appropriate. Sheffield plate was half the price of silver plate through the latter part of the eighteenth century, although the cost of making the products was more or less the same. This price differential was due mainly to raw material costs, but also to a tax imposed between 1756 and 1777 for products comprising 100 troy ounces or more. There was no tax on Sheffield plate.

To Boulton, plated ware was no substitute for the real thing. In 1771, he had confided to Lord Shelburne that he wished to become 'a great silver-smith', his aim being to make silver plate services, such as the one he made for Mrs Montague. But production of these was limited to the 1770s.[28] The work was not profitable yet, and James Keir noted in 1809, after Boulton's death, it 'greatly tended to his celebrity and admiration of his various talents, taste and enterprise'.[29]

Boulton and Fothergill's business growth in the 1760s happened at a time when there was a preference for the 'antique taste'. While the Manufactory produced silver and plate decorated with Rococo motives into the 1770s, the new classical taste was pre-eminent from the early 1770s onwards. Boulton was drawn to classical shapes and ornament because his patrons were, as he wrote to Mrs Montagu in 1772:

> Fashion hath much to do in these things, and as that of the present age dis-tinguishes itself by adopting the most elegant ornaments of the most refined Grecian artists, I am satisfyed in conforming thereto, and humbly copying their style, and makeing new combinations of old ornaments without pre-suming to invent new ones.[30]

Boulton acquired volumes of images from antiquity and actively sought publi-cations describing classical sites, especially at Herculaneum and Pompeii. These books were regarded virtually as pattern books by designers and craftspeo-ple all over Europe and their influence can be seen in particular borders or friezes or mounts of Boulton's wares. Some of his designs came direct from architect contemporaries, particularly William Chambers, the royal architect, James Stuart and James Wyatt. Chambers is associated with Palladian influences and, more directly, with objects commissioned for the King and Queen. The longer-term relationship was with the architect James Wyatt, who was involved in work at Soho Manufactory and Soho house, as well as his brother Samuel, architect of Albion Mill. James Wyatt's influence can be seen in elegant sauce boats, for instance, and he was the dominant influence on Soho's in-house designer and partner in plate manufacture, Francis Eginton.[31] Although the Adam brothers seemed to admire Boulton, Nicholas Goodison, in an extensive study, was unable to find any objects from Soho that resulted from coopera-tion with the Adams. Nonetheless, the Adams' work 'at the very least … must have had some effect in training Boulton's eye in the classical repertory'.[32]

But for profit to be made on silver plate or Sheffield plate prompt pay-ment was essential. In 1773, there was a trading deficit of £10,000 and although Boulton managed to negotiate a three-month period of credit with his dealer and resolved to make customers pay more promptly, many failed to do so. An enquiry into the silver plate business concluded that it was unprofitable because the interest on bullion payments was greater than the charge for making the goods. Quickenden points out that, despite Boulton's determination to export silver plate, very little was, and he directed his enthusiasm elsewhere.[33]

Boulton's commitment to silver plate declined with the commencement of his partnership with James Watt from 1775, and the need to conserve capital. From 1777, the silver plate business was run down, Fothergill being adamant that the business must concentrate on Sheffield plate only. After Fothergill's death in 1782, the Matthew Boulton Plate Company was formed, but Boulton was little involved with this, devoting most of his attention to steam engines, and from the mid to late 1780s to the mint.

Boulton was slow to adopt new machinery at the Plate Company and, although a new rolling mill was believed to be essential in 1782, it was not operational until 1786. Also, while Chippendall, the London agent, wanted more fully trained staff to speed up production, Boulton adopted the cheaper alternative of training up apprentices. By the turn of the century, Soho plate was even behind in design terms, and to prove the point, Chippendall took a cup and cover in 1803 to London firms for their opinion, the verdict being 'not entirely encouraging'.[34]

Matthew Boulton had set out his stall to James Adam in 1770 and, while some of the claims should probably be taken with a pinch of salt, his ambitions were clear.

Boulton's silver plate and Sheffield plate businesses brought him to the attention of royalty and government, besides foreign merchants. All of these connections were helpful in seeking to expand toy and silverware sales in Britain, exporting permits for steam engines, defeating potential threats to the engine patent, besides meeting Boulton's desire to have a good table at which he could entertain members of the nobility and overseas guests; a showroom at Soho to which guests on tour would wish to come and buy, besides contributing to his own legacy. It was his silver plate business which prompted Matthew Boulton to lobby for an Assay Office in Birmingham, the tipping point appearing to be an incident in 1771, in which two candlesticks for Lord Shelbourne were damaged in transit. He handled the campaign in a masterly fashion, William Small teasing him gently in writing: 'I hope the King and Royal family, the Nobility and the Ministry and your other friends are well.'[35] The Royal Assent for the Birmingham Assay Office was given in May 1773.

Notes

1   Anthony Burton, *Josiah Wedgwood*, 1976.

2   The prime scholarly study of Boulton's ormolu is Nicholas Goodison, *Ormolu: The Work of Matthew Boulton* (London: Phaidon, 1974) and the newer edition (London: Christie's, 1999).

3   Fiona Tait, 'Coinage, Commerce and Inspired Ideas: The notebooks of Matthew Boulton', in Malcolm Dick (ed.), *Matthew Boulton: A Revolutionary Player*, 2009, pp. 77–91.

4   MB to his wife (AB), 24 November 1765.

5   Wedgwood to Thomas Bentley, 15 March 1768, quoted in Goodison, op. cit., p. 27.

6   Wedgwood to Thomas Bentley, 21 November 1766, quoted in Goodison, op. cit., p. 28.

7   Jeremy Black, *The British Abroad: The Grand Tour in the Eighteenth Century*, 2003.

8   Quoted in Goodison, op. cit., p. 129.

9   Goodison, op. cit., p. 55.

10 MB to John Whitehurst, 28 December 1768, quoted in Goodison, op. cit., p. 30; see also p. 57.

11 Quoted in J. Fleming, *Robert Adam and His Circle in Edinburgh & Rome*, 1962.

12 Goodison, op. cit., pp. 50–55.

13 MB to AB, 6 March 1770, quoted in Goodison, op. cit., p. 5.

14 MB to James Adam, 1 October 1770, quoted in H. W. Dickinson, *Matthew Boulton*, 1937, p. 60.

15 MB to John Fothergill, n.d. 1770, quoted in Goodison, op. cit., pp. 32–33.

16 MB to AB, 6 March 1770, quoted in Goodison, op. cit., p. 84.

17 Quoted in Shena Mason, *The Hardware Man's Daughter: Matthew Boulton and his 'Dear Girl'*, 2005, p. 20.

18 Fothergill to MB, 19 May 1773, quoted in Goodison, op. cit., p. 44.

19 MB to AB, 11 April 1772, quoted in Mason, op. cit., p. 23.

20 Quoted in Dickinson, op. cit., p. 58.

21 Quoted in Goodison, op. cit., p. 44.

22 H. W. Dickinson, *Matthew Boulton*, 1937, pp. 553, 63–71; Kenneth Quickenden, 'Silver and its Substitutes' in Malcolm Dick (ed.), *Matthew Boulton a Revolutionary Player*, 2009, pp. 153–55; Kenneth Quickenden, 'Matthew Boulton's Silver and Sheffield Plate', in Shena Mason (ed.), *Matthew Boulton, Selling What all the World Desires*, 2009, p. 41.

23 Frederick Bradbury, *History of Old Sheffield Plate*, 1968, p. 47.

24 Quickenden in Dick (ed.), *Boulton a Revolutionary Player*, p. 157.

25 George Demidowicz, 'Power at the Soho Manufactory and Mint', in Dick (ed.), *Matthew Boulton*, p. 125.

26 Quickenden in Dick (ed.), *Boulton a Revolutionary Player*, p. 155.

27 Ibid., p. 165.

28 MB to Lord Shelbourne, 7 January 1771, quoted by Quickenden, in Dick (ed.), *Boulton a Revolutionary Player*, p. 169.

29 Keir, 'Memoir to Boulton', printed in Dickinson, op. cit., pp. 70–72.

30 MB to Mrs Montague, 16 January 1772, quoted in Nicholas Goodison, 'The Context of Neo-Classicism', in Shena Mason (ed.), *Matthew Boulton*, selling, p. 32.

31 Ibid., p. 39; Quickenden in ibid., p. 44.

32 Goodison in Mason, op. cit., p. 39.

33 Quickenden in Mason, op. cit., p. 44.

34 Ibid., p. 46.

35 Small to MB, 28 January 1773, quoted in Dickinson, op. cit., p. 68.

7

The Birth of the Steam Engine

On 22 March 1776, James Boswell visited Soho and recorded what are certainly the most famous words ever ascribed to Boulton: 'I sell here, Sir, what all the world desires to have – POWER'.[1] He was talking about the steam engine, but it was not a remark he could have made a decade earlier, for then Boulton was only just beginning to take an interest in the subject, and had little idea that it would become of immense importance not only to his own business but, as he said to Boswell, to the world. To understand what a momentous time this was in his life, we have to step back a short distance in time to look at the early history of steam power.

For centuries, the world had had to rely on natural forces – wind, water or animal – to provide power to work machinery, and these forces had served it well. But an industrial world does not merely require power; it also has to be constantly supplied with raw materials, and here problems were developing. Coal and metal ores were obtained by mining, but as sources close to the surface were gradually used up, miners had to dig ever deeper, and this was where the problem arose. Invariably the mines reached water that had to be removed by pumping, even by using elaborate systems that lifted the water in a series of stages. The old power sources had proved adequate in the past, but limits were being reached where these were no longer able to cope. Something new was required and the first answers began to appear at the end of the seventeenth century.

We now know that the answer would be the steam engine, although the story does not really start with steam but with a new concept – the vacuum.[2] In Germany in the 1670s, Otto von Guericke placed two copper hemispheres together and then exhausted all the air inside the sphere. The two halves now stuck so closely together that a team of sixteen horses could not pull them apart. This was interesting, but no one could see a practical application. Then he did a second experiment. This time he exhausted all the air out of a cylinder fitted with a piston. Fifty strong men tried to stop the air pressure forcing the piston down, but they failed. It was obvious that this could form the basis for some kind of engine, provided a way could be found to form the vacuum over and over again without having to stop the engine. Numerous attempts were made, notably by the Dutch scientist Christiaan Huygens and the Frenchman Denys Papin, but the first practical pump for use in mines was the work of an Englishman, Thomas Savery.

Savery condensed steam in a closed vessel, creating a vacuum.[3] A valve was then opened and water was sucked into the vessel. He then used steam under pressure to force the water out into a second vessel. The vessels were arranged so that while one was being refilled the other was being discharged. He called it 'The Miner's Friend' and in his patent of 1698 referred to it as working by 'the Impellent Force of Fire'. It was successful where water did not have to be raised to any great heights, but Savery had problems getting steam at high pressure. There was an even greater problem when it came to using it in mines, in that the furnace and boiler had to be at the bottom of the shaft. An open fire in a gaseous mine could hardly be described as friendly to miners. A more practical engine was soon to be developed that would rapidly make Savery's engine obsolete.

Thomas Newcomen of Dartmouth had a thriving ironmongery business, providing tools for the tin and copper miners of Devon and Cornwall.[4] He was well aware of the increasing problems with mine drainage, but it is not at all clear whether he knew about Savery's work. In any case, although he too used the creation of a vacuum as the essential part of his engine, he produced a very different design. The traditional pump worked by means of rods moving up and down: like an old-fashioned village pump whereby the job is done by working the handle. This was similar but on a far larger scale. The first part of the engine consisted of pump rods suspended by chains from one end of a massive beam, pivoting at its centre. The rods would drop under their own weight, pulling that end of the beam down and anything attached to the opposite end of the beam would be lifted. To make the engine work, all that was needed was a force to pull that end down again in order to lift the pump rods. Newcomen attached a piston, working in a cylinder to that end of the beam. Steam was then passed into the cylinder, driving out the air. The cylinder was then sprayed with cold water to condense the steam, creating a partial vacuum. Just as in von Guericke's experiment, air pressure forced the piston down, raising the pump rods at the opposite end of the beam. Pressure equalised, the whole cycle could start again.

The Newcomen engine had several advantages over Savery's. There was no need for high-pressure steam, as it was air pressure that did the work – it came to be known as an atmospheric engine. The whole engine could be assembled and installed at the surface, so there was no fire risk, and there was not the same limitation on the height that water could be lifted. The first engine was erected at the Earl of Dudley's colliery in Staffordshire in 1712. It was a huge success and soon the giant beam engines were slowly nodding above mine shafts from Cornwall to Scotland. This was the situation when Boulton began to think about using a steam engine at Soho.

Boulton was interested in all industrial processes, particularly those that impinged on his own business. His notebooks are full of detailed comments on, for example, the local ironworks, and more than once he noted that there were complaints of water shortages for powering machinery, such as slitting mills.[5] Now he faced the same problem himself at Soho, and considered building an engine that would pump water back after it had passed over the waterwheel. He decided to try his own skill at engine design and sent his ideas to Benjamin Franklin, hoping for helpful advice:

My engagements since Christmas have not permitted me to make any further progress with my fire engine but as the thirsty season is approaching, necessity will oblige me to set about it in good earnest. Query which of the steam valves do you like best? Is it better to introduce the jet of cold water at the bottom of the receiver or at the top?[6]

Franklin was unable to offer any useful suggestions, but Boulton went on working at his model, and Darwin, at least, was impressed. 'Your model of a steam engine, I am told, has gained so much approbation in London that I cannot but congratulate you on the mechanical fame you have acquired by it.'[7]

No details about the engine have survived, but the reference to 'the receiver' suggests it might have been based on the Savery model; nor is there any record of it ever being installed. This little flurry of letters does, however, show that Boulton was thinking about steam power and was prepared to consider any practical designs. It is all too easy to think of his role in the story of steam engine development as being no more than that of an entrepreneur, putting up the money, providing facilities for manufacture and selling the end product. This was never the case. He was a practical man, able to think constructively about all aspects of practical engine design. Nevertheless, the huge advance in engine technology was not his, but belonged entirely to James Watt.

Watt was born at Greenock on the Clyde in 1736. His father seems to have been something of a jack-of-all-trades, described at various times as chandler, carpenter, instrument maker and even ship builder. His mother,

Agnes Muirhead, came from a distinguished family and had connections with Glasgow University, which were to play an important part in her son's career. From an early age, the boy showed practical aptitudes and a definite preference for mathematics rather than that other mainstay of eighteenth-century education, the classics. He was physically far from strong and suffered from numerous complaints, and continued to experience poor health for much of his adult life – he was more than a little inclined to hypochondria. He decided on a career as an instrument maker, trained in London and was eventually appointed official Mathematical Instrument Maker to the University of Glasgow. When he arrived he was probably thought of by the academics as no more than a skilled craftsman, but they soon discovered there was a great deal more to him than that. John Robison, who was later to have a distinguished career as a scientist, was still a student when he first met Watt in 1758, an occasion he recalled in 1796:

> I saw a Workman and expected no more – but was surprized to find a philosopher as young as myself; and always ready to instruct me. I had the vanity to think myself a pretty good proficient in my favourite Study and was rather mortfyd at finding Mr. Watt so much my superior.[8]

Watt also met the foremost scientist at Glasgow, Professor Joseph Black, who is perhaps best known for first establishing the principle of latent heat. What is less generally known is that Watt played a major part in establishing the theory by his own experiments. Latent heat is the heat absorbed or radiated when a substance turns from one state to another, for example when water turns to steam at constant temperature and pressure. This might seem to be a piece of arcane scientific knowledge, but it was an understanding of this idea that was to have a profound effect on the development of the steam engine.

During the academic year 1763/64, Watt was sent a model of a Newcomen engine which was not working as it should. Everyone knew that the Newcomen engine was inefficient. In fact, its thermal efficiency was just 1 per cent. In other words, of the energy supplied to the engine, for example by burning coal to create steam, only one-hundredth appears as useful work. But the engine sent to Watt was completely hopeless – not working for more than a few strokes. Watt set out to calculate what the engine should be doing as against its actual performance. He soon discovered that the engine was using more steam than it should, and more water was needed to condense the steam than he had calculated. He realised that the answer was to be found in latent heat; the extra energy was all going into changing the state – water to steam, steam back to water. He recognised that the problem could never be solved while the cylinder was alternately being heated and cooled, but what could be done about it? He described his own Eureka moment:

It was in the Green of Glasgow. I had gone to take a walk on a fine Sabbath afternoon, early in 1765. I had entered the green by the gate at the foot of Charlotte Street and had passed the old washing-house. I was thinking upon the engine at the time, and had gone as far as the herds' house, when the idea came into my mind that as steam was an elastic body it would rush into a vacuum, and if a communication was made between the cylinder and an exhausted vessel it would rush into it, and might there be condensed without cooling the cylinder.[9]

The idea was for a separate condenser, the device that was to revolutionise the development of the steam engine. But it was not the complete answer. Watt would still have to pump air and the water condensed from the steam out of his 'exhausted vessel'. However, that could be achieved by a small pump that could be worked by the engine itself.

Watt had partially solved the problem, but he still needed to keep the cylinder permanently hot. He could wrap it in a wooden jacket, but heat would escape through the open top. He could close the top of the cylinder, but then he would be unable to use atmospheric pressure to force the piston down. Normal atmospheric pressure is just under 15lb per square inch (psi). He realised that it would be possible to produce steam at that pressure to do the same job as air pressure. The atmospheric engine would become a true steam engine.

As many inventors have discovered over the years, it is one thing to have a clear idea of how a new invention would work but quite another to turn it into a practical, manufactured article. That requires time and investment and not a little luck. Watt carried out a number of experiments at the university, encouraged by Black, who then introduced him to the local industrialist Dr John Roebuck. Roebuck had originally been trained as a doctor and practised in Birmingham, where he came into the Boulton circle and was particularly friendly with Dr Small. He was fond of carrying out scientific experiments at home, and soon began to develop these for industrial use. One of his more successful ventures was an improved process for making sulphuric acid, which he began manufacturing in Scotland.[10] There his industrial interests soon spread, and he took an active part in the establishment of the Carron Ironworks. Eventually, this was to prove a hugely profitable concern, but like many ventures with which Roebuck was concerned, suffered from under-capitalisation, made good by short-term and expensive loans. Soon the financial position worsened. Roebuck severed his connections with the ironworks and began a new concern, with coal mines at Kinneil near Bo'ness on the Firth of Forth. Again his ambitions were not totally in line with reality: the coal proved to be of inferior quality and the old Newcomen engine on site struggled to keep the water at bay. He appealed to some of his old Birmingham friends for help with funding and encouragement, including Boulton. He wrote to him, for example, in 1760, complaining about the difficulties of employing miners locally, wanting to know the going rate in the Birmingham area. He was paying 20*d* a ton to move coal from the face to the pit bottom, and 7*d* a ton for inferior slack.[11] But in spite of strong hints, Boulton showed no interest in getting involved in enterprises in Scotland, where he could have no personal control.

Black had already helped Watt with money for experiments but, in 1768, Roebuck offered to pay off Watt's further development debts and to finance Watt in his attempts to gain a patent for his invention. In return, Roebuck was to receive two-thirds of all profits from the enterprise. Watt wrote to him in the November, suggesting that the best plan would be for them to build a small house for Watt at Kinneil where they could carry out their experiments. Here he began the long process of preparing specifications for the patent and making trials with a model engine. He was never a man of huge confidence, and was frequently jollied along by Roebuck, but at the same time others were becoming aware of what was being developed.

Watt had briefly worked as a civil engineer on the Forth & Clyde Canal and had to go to London in 1767 to give evidence before the Select Committee considering the Bill. He made a detour to visit Darwin and Small. Boulton was not at home, but Watt was shown round the works at Soho and the steam engine was discussed. It obviously made a good impression on Small, who talked about it with Boulton on his return to Birmingham. Small wrote to Watt at the beginning of the following year:

> Before I knew your connection with Dr. R my idea was that you should settle here and that Boulton and I would assist you as much as we could, which in any case we will most certainly do. I have no doubt of your success, nor of your acquiring fortune, if you proceed upon a proper plan as to the manner of doing business, which if you do, you will be sole possessor of the affair even after your patent has expired … In a partnership that I liked I should not hesitate to employ any sum of money I can command, & I am certain that it may be managed with only a moderate capital. Whether it would be possible to manage the wheel & reciprocating engines by separate partnerships without their interfering I am not certain. If it is, Boulton & I would engage <u>with you</u> in either, <u>provided you will live here</u>.[12]

The wheel referred to in the letter was Watt's other idea for using steam.[13] He had designed a machine, based on a circular tube, with steam inlets and outlets, and the steam was used to push against free-moving weights inside the wheel. The action would make one side of the wheel heavier than the other, causing it to rotate, much as water falling into the buckets of an overshot waterwheel did.

Small and Boulton were quite taken with the idea, but John Smeaton, arguably the greatest engineer of the age, dismissed it as impractical. He was right, and a good deal of time and effort was wasted on trying to make it work.

Meanwhile, Watt was preparing papers for his patent application (pat. 913, granted in 1769) and once again he made the journey to London. In August 1768, he was back at Soho, this time for a longer visit. He now met Boulton for the first time and the two men found an instant rapport. On his return to Scotland, he told Roebuck that Boulton was still interested in the project. As Roebuck was, as ever, short of funds, he wrote to Boulton to make him an offer:

> Mr. Watt wrote to you some time ago about the New Plan of an Engine. It is some years since a tryal of a very small one was made at Kinneil which convinced me of the justness of the Principals on which it was constructed and encouraged me to take a Burthen of Mr. Watt's hands which his loss of time and numerous expensive experiments had incurred. In a week or two we shall make a more compleat tryal with a larger Engine and if the result is answerable to our expectations I shall with pleasure communicate a share of the Property to yourself in the three Counties in your Neighbourhood Warwickshire Staffords & Derbys: and the terms you and I shall not differ about.[14]

Boulton rejected the offer. His explanation to Watt was forthright and showed a clarity of purpose and breadth of ambition that is quite astonishing.[15] It must have been maddening to Watt to have such a prospect dangled in front of him, when he was unable to do anything about it. This is such an important document that it deserves to be quoted at length:

> The plan [i.e. the Midland counties licence] proposed to me is so very different from that which I had conceived at the time I talked with you upon the subject that I cannot think it is a proper one for me to meddle with as I do not intend turning engineer. I was excited by two motives to offer you my assistance which were love of you and love of a money-getting ingenious project. I presumed that your engine would require money, very accurate workmanship and extensive correspondence to make it turn out to the best advantage and that the best means of keeping up the reputation and doing the invention justice would be to keep the executive part out of the hands of the multitude of empirical engineers who from ignorance, want of experience and want of necessary convenience, would affect the reputation of the invention. To remedy which and produce the most profit, my idea was to settle a Manufactory near to my own by the side of our canal where I would erect all the conveniences necessary for the completion of the engines and from which Manufactory we would serve all the

world with engines of all sizes. By these means and your assistance we could engage and instruct some excellent workmen (with more excellent tools than would be worth any man's while to procure for one single engine) and could execute the invention 20 per cent cheaper than it would be otherwise executed and with as great a difference of accuracy as there is between the blacksmith and the mathematical instrument maker. It would not be worth my while to make for three counties only; but I find it well worth my while to make for all the world.

What led me to drop the hint I did to you was the possessing an idea that you wanted a midwife to ease you of your burthen and to introduce your brat into the world which I should not have thought of if I had known of your pre-engagement; but as I am determined never to embark on any trade that I have not the inspection of myself, and as my engagements here will not permit me to attend any business in Scotland and as the Doctor's engagements in Scotland will not I presume permit his attendance here, and as I am almost saturated with undertakings, I think I must conclude to … No, you shall draw the conclusion; yet nevertheless let my conclusions be what they will, nothing will alter my inclinations for being concerned with you, or for rendering you all the service in my power and although there seem to be some obstruction to our partnership in the engine trade, yet I live in hope that you or I may hit upon some scheme or other that may associate us in this part of the world, which would render it still more agreeable to me than it is, by the acquisition of such a neighbour.

The letter is a testament to the high regard that Boulton had for Watt, even after just a few days' acquaintance. Watt was left working with inadequate resources and was becoming increasingly pessimistic about the future. He wrote to Small, offering him a share in the wheel engine, expressing his disappointment about not being able to reach an agreement with Boulton and his inability to persuade Roebuck to give up any more of his share:

I am resolved unless these things I have brought to some perfection reward me for the time & money I have lost on them If I can resist it to Invent no more. Indeed I am not near as capable as I was once. I find that I am not the same person I was four years ago when I invented the fire engine … I was at that time spurred on by the alluring hope of placing myself above want without being obliged to have much dealing with Mankind to whom I have always been a dupe. The necessary experience in Great was wanting. In acquiring it I have met with many Disappointments. I must have sunk under the burden of them if I had not been supported by the friendship of Dr. Roebuck.

The letter ends with an almost hysterical tirade against other engineers who were working on steam engine development – who were all either incompetent, villains, or both. It is interesting to note that Watt acknowledged his lack of experience in large-scale engineering work and, a recurring theme in his life, his even greater lack of business acumen. His letters to Small became increasingly gloomy. In September he complained about having suffered three months of toothache that had finally been cured by a poultice, but not before 'it had demolished the best of my few grinders'. He was forced to abandon his engine work simply to make some money and accepted a job as engineer for the 13-mile Monkland Canal near Glasgow, which involved working there three to four days a week. Even that proved to be irksome. 'I am certainly very busy as I have about 150 men at work & only one overseer under me, beside the undertakers, who are mere tyros & require constant attention.'[16] He was, however, seriously considering taking on this sort of work full time simply because it ensured a steady income.

The early 1770s were a time of deep depression in all the trades, caused in part at least by troubles with the American colonists, eager for independence, and progress on the engine was inevitably slow. Boulton was luckier than some. He banked with Neale, Fordyce & Downe, but as a result of Fordyce's unwise speculations, the bank failed in 1772. Boulton had heard the news and rushed round, just in time to reclaim £2,000 worth of bills he had lodged there. Others were less fortunate, particularly in Scotland, where virtually all the banks collapsed. Roebuck was among the many affected: he was deep in debt and now had no way of raising more funds. In March 1773, Boulton wrote to Watt, asking him to act for Boulton at a meeting of Roebuck's creditors.[17] Boulton & Fothergill were owed £630 and Boulton had lent Roebuck a similar sum as a personal loan, but as that was not entered into the company books he would not attempt to claim it. Roebuck was desperate and was offering half of his share in the steam engine, but Boulton was not prepared to let him off that lightly. Watt recognised how generous Boulton had been, and wrote to say that if all the creditors had been that kind, Roebuck might have survived. As it was, Watt had stuck by Roebuck, and although, as he said, his heart bled for him, he could do so no longer without injuring his own prospects. By August things had become even worse. Watt wrote to Small to tell him that Roebuck was in a bad state and was prepared to give up the engine business, adding that the terms would have been very agreeable in better times. It was the only hint that Boulton needed. At last, agreement could be reached: Boulton agreed to wipe out all the debts owed to himself and the business and to pay extra if things went well. This was to lead to rather more acrimonious correspondence, but eventually he was paid a further £1,000 – equal to the amount he had already sunk in the venture. In return, Roebuck would give up all his rights to the patent, and Boulton would take over his share of the patent.

The negotiations were complicated by Watt still being in Scotland, while Boulton was equally tied to Birmingham, but their correspondence now had a light-hearted tone, full of optimism for the future. In this letter, Boulton apologised for not having written sooner:

> I have had this summer at the bottom of my Garding a vast crop of Coaches & Post Chaises. I have fancyed my self much hurryed but perhaps it was only for want of health & spirits, however I have some real evils & some bad health. The Lunar doctors have prescribed for me lately 6 purges one bleeding 7 pukes etc. apart of ye purges I consented to & I think myself better for 'em.

He said that he could not possibly come to Scotland, and Matthews, 'who is our money provider', was getting married and going to Brussels on holiday, just when they needed cash and they were behind on button orders – 16,000 gross. 'I have more real difficulties to grapple with than I hope ever to have any other Year of my life!' He ended by saying he would be sending off the partnership agreement: 'I am persuaded that you and I shall not differ whilst we live nor after we are dead, but our Executors may!'

In the midst of what should have been a happy time for Watt, his wife died.[18] He had only one outstanding obligation, another canal survey, for what would eventually become the Caledonian Canal. He would soon be free and eager to leave Scotland for Birmingham. Boulton found a house for him in Newhall Walk, and at last the details of the long-awaited partnership could be negotiated.

Watt was reinvigorated by the move. Now, at last, he would have the facilities and time that he needed to develop a prototype, and he no longer had to think about taking on any other work. There appeared to be only one problem. Boulton was understandably anxious to get a good return on what was already a substantial investment, the £1,000 paid to Roebuck being roughly equivalent to £1 million at today's prices. Unfortunately, because of the long delays in development, the patent now had only eight years left to run, hardly enough time to capitalise on the monopoly position it granted. The decision was taken to apply for an extension that would carry the patent up to the end of the century, and Watt went to London to prepare the necessary documents. There was considerable debate in Parliament, with strong opposition from *laissez-faire* economists who disliked the whole notion of monopolies. But Boulton's connections with influential people proved invaluable. He travelled up to London to carry out some intensive lobbying that proved successful. The extension to the year 1800 was approved on 22 May 1775, providing patent coverage for a further twenty-five years.[19] What the opponents had not perhaps realised was just how all-embracing the patent was. The actual specification was considerably briefer than the lengthy preamble and contained four main clauses: the cylinder was to be kept permanently hot; steam would be condensed in a separate condenser; an air pump would be used; and the engine would make use of the expansive power of steam. In effect, it shut the door against any advances in the new technology that were not either originated by Boulton & Watt or approved by them. In practice, this prevented any major changes in steam engine design being introduced while the patent lasted. This caused serious problems that will be dealt with in the next chapter. There was one other new feature: the patent had originally not covered Scotland and this was now remedied.

There was one sad note to mar the triumph. On 25 February 1775, Small died of 'an ague' at the very young age of 40. He had done so much to advance the partnership but he would never reap the rewards.[20] Engine development, however, was now moving forward at a brisk pace. One of the basic problems had been ensuring a close fit between piston and cylinder. Watt had tried all kinds of different materials without any real success, but it was now Boulton who was in charge of experiments while Watt was in London for the preliminary stages of the patent application. Boulton was very much concerned with practicalities and relished the opportunity to put forward his own ideas, which were not always well received by Watt. Now he found the answer to the cylinder problem at an ironworks in Wales.

John Wilkinson was a more than slightly eccentric ironmaster who had works at Bersham in North Wales.[21] He was known as 'Iron Mad' Wilkinson and lived up to his name, indeed intending to carry it on after life as well, having ordered an iron coffin for himself. He was a great innovator and, in 1774, he developed a new mill for boring gun barrels from blocks of iron. He worked to new standards of accuracy and this was just what was needed for a steam cylinder. Boulton visited Bersham in May 1775. Wilkinson boasted that it took no more time to bore a gun from the solid than it did to cast it hollow, but Boulton soon discovered that it actually took twice as long. The result, however, was well worth the effort. He took notes of everything he saw at Bersham and on visits to other ironworks, altogether filling fifty pages of his notebook. No doubt he had in mind his original idea of one day building his own factory and forge to manufacture engines.

The partnership with Watt was officially sealed in June 1775.[22] Boulton's role was carefully defined, namely to manage the business, while Watt was basically required to make drawings and oversee the engine design and development, for which he was to receive £300 per annum, plus a one-third share of the profits. One of the most famous partnerships in British industrial history was about to go into business.

Notes

1   H.W. Dickinson, *Matthew Boulton*, 1937, p. 73.

2   H.W. Dickinson, *A Short History of the Steam Engine*, 1938, pp. 6–9.

3   Ibid., pp. 18–19.

4   Ibid., pp. 29–37.

5   Fiona Tait, 'Coinage, Commerce and Inspired Ideas: The notebooks of Matthew Boulton', in Malcolm Dick (ed.), *Matthew Boulton: A Revolutionary Player*, 2009, pp. 77–91.

6   Shena Mason, *Matthew Boulton: Selling what all the world desires*, 2009, pp. 5–6.

7   Desmond King-Hele, *Erasmus Darwin, A Life of Unequalled Achievement*, 1999, p. 67.

8   Richard L. Hills, *James Watt*, Vol. 1, 2002, pp. 300–301.

9   Quoted in H.W. Dickinson, *James Watt: Craftsman and Engineer*, 1935.

10   Dickinson, op. cit., p. 38.

11   Roebuck to MB, 4 October 1760.

12   H.W. Dickinson & R. Jenkins, *James Watt and the Steam Engine*, 1927, repr. 1981, p. 38.

13   Hills, op. cit., pp. 428–36.

14   Hills, op. cit., p. 419.

15   Ibid.

16   Dickinson & Jenkins, op. cit., p. 33.

17   Ibid., p. 36.

18   Hills, op. cit., p. 449.

19   15 Geo. III, cap. LXI, p. 1,587.

20   Dickinson, *Matthew Boulton*, p. 85.

21   Dickinson & Jenkins, op. cit., p. 43.

22   Dickinson, *Matthew Boulton*, p. 86.

1 Matthew Boulton, looking every inch the gentleman; an engraving of 1787 from a wax medallion. (Authors)

Matt.w Boulton
24th June 1787
From a Wax Medallion modelled from life, in the possession of
M.r JOHN RABONE JUN.r

JAMES WATT.

2 James Watt, Boulton's partner in the steam engine business. (Authors)

PRIESTLEY.

3 Dr Joseph Priestley, member of the Lunar Society. His house and laboratory were destroyed in the 1791 Birmingham (Priestley) Riots. (Authors)

DR PRIESTLEY'S HOUSE AND LABORATORY, FAIR-HILL, SPARKBROOK.
After the attack by Rioters, July 1791.
Copied from an old Print.

4 Dr Joseph Priestley's house after its destruction by fire in the 1791 Riots. It was clearly one of the sights of the town. (Authors)

5 John Baskerville, printer and friend of Boulton. Baskerville typeface is still used today. (Authors)

Engrav'd for England Display'd.

View of Lord Lyttelton's House at Hagley in Worcestershire.

6 Hagley Hall, Worcestershire, owned by Lord Littleton. Both the architecture and the landscape garden were admired by Boulton and probably influenced him in his aspirations for Soho. (Authors)

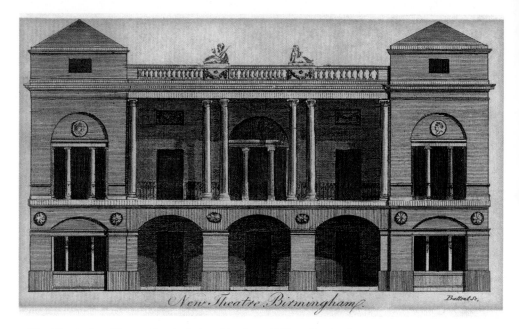

7 The Birmingham Theatre Royal, designed by Samuel Wyatt, Boulton's one-time architect. Boulton also held shares in the theatre. (Authors)

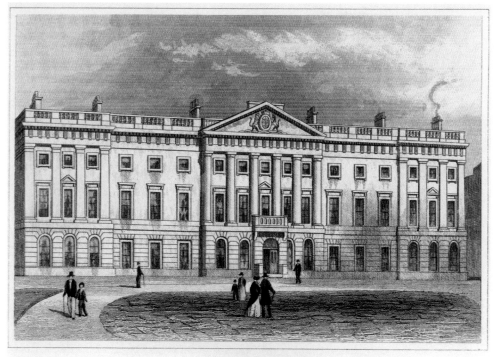

8 Royal Mint, London. Boulton designed the production system and specified the machinery it was to contain. He approved an elegant front elevation but required that he 'design the useful'. (Authors)

9 The old wharf on the Birmingham Canal with the company offices in the background, from a cartouche on an eighteenth-century map. (Authors)

10 Soho Manufactory: the print shows a busy traffic in aristocratic visitors. One coach is leaving; another arriving; and a lady and gentleman stroll in the grounds. (Birmingham City Archives)

11 Soho landscape: the lake provided water power and also served as part of Boulton's landscape garden. The boat emphasises the leisure element. Soho House is shown on the hill overlooking the lake. (Authors)

12 Soho Manufactory and Mint: the Manufactory is on the right; workers lived in the upper floors of the wings, and the workshops and chimneys can clearly be seen to the rear. The mint is the separate building to the left of the picture. (Authors)

13 Cameo portrait of Dr Erasmus Darwin. (Josiah Wedgwood & Sons Ltd)

14 Josiah Wedgwood, potter and prominent Lunar Society member. (Authors)

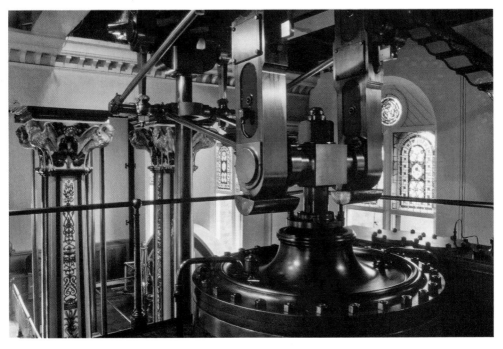

15 James Watt's parallel motion on one of a pair of beam engines installed at Papplewick Pumping Station, Nottingham, in 1884 by James Watt & Co. A century after the device had been invented it was still in use. (Authors)

16 A fine example of Matthew Boulton's silver plate, showing the strong influence of classical architects. (Authors)

17 Ormolu jugs, one of the elegant products of a relatively short-lived business of Boulton's. (Authors)

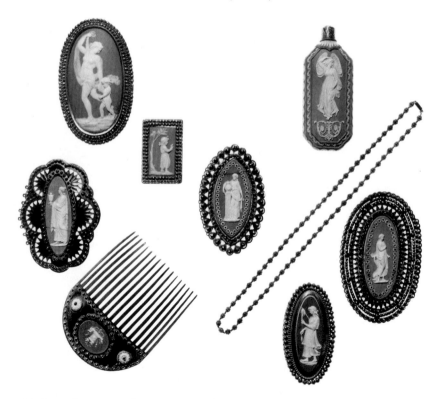

18 Wedgwood cameos with various types of Boulton settings in steel. (Josiah Wedgwood & Sons Ltd)

8

Boulton & Watt

Watt had retained his old engine, with its very modest 18in-diameter cylinder, on which he had worked in Scotland, as part of the settlement with Roebuck, but it was rusty and of little use. He was all for starting at once on new experiments and new models, letting production wait until he felt that he had perfected his masterpiece. This was an area of activity in which he was very comfortable. Boulton, always the pragmatist, argued that they could not sell engines on the basis of a model. They were, after all, not just asking mine owners to buy an engine of an entirely new design but also asking them to scrap their old engines, which, whatever the shortcomings, had kept mines clear of water, until they were made deeper. They needed to have the real thing: a full-scale engine that could be seen to be doing a job of work. He won the argument. The first engine was built for the Bloomfield Colliery at Tipton in the Black Country and started work on 8 March 1776. A second engine for the region, ordered for the Hawkesbury Colliery near Coventry, gave a great deal of trouble, largely due to financial haggling by the owners. At much the same time, Wilkinson ordered an engine for his own works at Broseley in Shropshire. This was a blowing engine, designed to provide an increased draught to the blast furnace – a job that had previously relied mainly on water-powered bellows. It was a strong hint to Boulton that he had to consider different ways in which the steam engines might be used.[1] At this time, most of the effort was concentrated on perfecting the reciprocal engines for pumping. Rotative engines for powering other machines had to take second place and he was still thinking mainly of the steam wheel as the best answer to that problem. It was an idea that would soon be abandoned.

In his initial enthusiastic response to Watt, Boulton had talked about build-ing a specialist factory to make the engines. In the event, he was in no position to do so; the money simply was not there. All the precision parts were made at Soho, and he insisted that all the cylinders should come from Wilkinson. The rest was the responsibility of the suppliers, carefully vetted by Boulton & Watt who insisted on particular suppliers except where distance made this impossible.[2] They specified just how the engine house should be built, for example, and gave details of how to make the overhead beam, which they said should ideally be made from a single log of seasoned oak. Although the partnership provided this full list of instructions for building, running and maintaining the engines, they insisted that their own engineers supervised the whole erection process. The profit was mainly to come from a specially cal-culated premium, based on one-third of the saving between their engine and the equivalent atmospheric engine. Steam engine efficiency was measured by its 'duty', defined as the number of pounds of water raised one foot high by the consumption of one bushel of coal. The first Newcomen engine had a duty of 4.5 million, the much improved version designed by Smeaton did 12.5 million and the first Boulton & Watt engine did 22 million, although later engines improved on that figure.[3] This was a considerable saving in fuel, but not necessarily a big return to the company when they supplied engines to collieries, where coal was inevitably quite cheap. It was a very different matter, however, when the partners turned their attention to the copper and tin mines of Cornwall.

Word of the new engines soon reached the South West, where the situation was becoming desperate. The agent for Wheal Virgin wrote in despair, 'The existing engines at full power and the mine will be forced to stop unless some answer is found … The engines last month used 300 Weys of coal … which sweeps away all the profit.' He was not, however, too keen to go to the expense of replacing his old engines and wondered if he could just add on separate condensers, without making any other changes. Other mine captains were equally sceptical, and one local engineer noted that he could get just as good a vacuum in his old atmospheric engine, proving that he had rather missed the point.[4] The first engine was instead erected in 1777, at Wheal Busy mine at Chacewater near Redruth. It was soon apparent to even to the most diehard of mine owners that this represented a huge cost saving.

Over the years, Cornwall was to be one of Boulton & Watt's most impor-tant customers.[5] Between 1777 and the end of the century, they supplied around fifty engines, varying in size from a very modest 18in cylinder to an imposing 64in version.[6] At first things seemed to be going well. James Keir wrote to Boulton:

It gave great pleasure to hear of the propriety of affairs in Cornwall, & of the reasonable disposition of the Inhabitants. It must make Mr Watt's residence much less disagreeable than if he had found them such a medley of Fools & Knaves as they are at Hawksbury.[7]

This was such an important area of expansion that Boulton felt that he could not entrust the job of winning orders to others; nor, once orders were received, could he regard the job as complete. Agents were appointed to look after the company's affairs, and the first to be appointed was a local man, Thomas Wilson. He was later to be joined by a Scotsman, William Murdoch (who later changed the spelling to Murdock). The story of how he got the job may well be apocryphal, but it is certainly entertaining.[8] Murdoch, impressed by what he had heard about Soho, walked there from his home and presented himself to Boulton as a potential employee. He wore an odd hat made out of wood, which intrigued Boulton who wanted to know more about it. Murdoch explained that he had made it himself, an impressive demonstration of his craftsmanship. He got the job. True or not, Boulton did describe him, in a letter to Watt of 1779, as a 'valuable man' who deserved to be encouraged. Even with good men in place, the partners still found it necessary to make the long journey down to Cornwall.

Boulton was to make many trips to the South West, often accompanied by Watt. Neither of them found the experience particularly agreeable, although on one occasion he was able to persuade Erasmus Darwin to join him, and Boulton was able to mix his hobby of collecting mineral samples with the essential business meetings.

Watt had remarried in 1777, and his wife joined him on his first trip to Cornwall. It was not a happy experience for the new bride, who wrote to Ann Boulton complaining that they had great problems finding accommodation and when they did, it was wretched and the servants worse: 'a set of Laziest Wretches that now Breathes on the Earth to say nothing of their Nastiness.' Although she admired the coastal scenery, she hated the mining area where they were forced to stay.[9] Boulton, while stressing the importance of the Cornish connection, also reminded him to be wary: the Cornish were 'wise as a serpent' and devils to deal with. Boulton had planned to be in Cornwall for the three months before Christmas that year and he must have had a great deal of persuading to do to get his wife to go with him. He succeeded, but the move was not popular. By 1780, he and Watt were finally able to rent a comfortable house near Truro. The landlord had asked for a rent of 150 guineas per annum. Boulton told him to knock the nought off the end and he would take it. Astonishingly he agreed. Even so, Ann Boulton showed little enthusiasm for further Cornish visits.

There was an interesting, and profitable, side product from all these long trips to Cornwall. While he was in the South West, Watt no longer had secretarial help but there was still a need to write business letters. He was faced with the tedious task of personally copying everything he wrote so that he could keep a record. He applied his inventive mind to finding a way out of the problem. He began by changing the ink itself, by mixing it with gum arabic or sugar, so that when, after the ink had dried, a sheet of damp tissue paper was pressed against the original it left an impression, which was, of course, reversed. But by holding the thin sheet to the light it could be read by looking at the back of the sheet. The next stage was to mechanise the process by feeding the sheets through a roller press.[10] The whole copier was then clamped to a table. Watt was very pleased with the result, but it was Boulton who at once saw that this had commercial possibilities. A patent was obtained in 1780 (pat. 1244) and in the same year a new company, James Watt & Co., was set up to manufacture the copying press. In the first year, 630 copying presses were sold at seven guineas each. Although carbon paper was to be invented early in the nineteenth century, it did not come into general use until the invention of the typewriter. Up till then the copying press remained the best means of duplicating handwritten documents. They were practical devices, no bigger than the standard printer now used with computers in homes. Even so, most businesses still preferred to use clerks.

The Cornish business was prospering, but Boulton was very conscious of the fact that it was dangerous to rely on a single market, however profitable, and he was always on the lookout for new markets. Waterworks were an obvious candidate for pumping engines, and the company sold two engines to the Chelsea Water Works, which took its water directly from the Thames. This was such an important contract that Boulton went down personally to conduct experiments to note the engines' efficiency, the results being recorded in his notebook in April 1777. He was also looking overseas for markets. It appears that he received many flattering comments and offers of honours, but his only interest was in getting firm orders for engines:

> I believe the best answer that can be given Van Liender of Rotterdam is to tell him that we are not anxious about the honour of acquiring gold medals nor of making an eclat in philosophical societies; we will not merely talk about the thing but we will actually do it, provided an exclusive privilege could be obtained for us in the united provinces; and in that case we would undertake to raise 500,000 cubic feet of water one foot high with one hundredweight of coal or five feet high with five hundredweight.

There were other markets, but they would require a different type of engine. From Boulton's own experience at Soho he was aware that the developing industrial world was in need of a new power source to turn its machinery. With the steam wheel experiments now abandoned, he began to prod Watt into looking at ways of turning the pumping engine into a rotative engine. There were a number of problems to overcome. The first was that in order to produce rotation, the piston had to push as well as pull, and in the early engines the piston was attached to the beam by a chain – and that could only pull down the end of the beam, not push it back up again. Equally it was not possible to make a simple rigid connection, because the piston was attached to the end of a beam that moved along a circular path. This was solved at first by a ratchet on the cylinder end of the beam. Now there had to be a device that would turn a wheel at the opposite end. The obvious answer was a crank, but that had been patented by James Pickard of Birmingham in 1780 – and the very last thing Boulton & Watt wanted to do was to start challenging patents.[11]

Watt came up with a number of devices. It was the fifth suggested version that was to prove most successful, the 'sun and planet' gear, in which a small cog rotated round a larger one, much as a planet orbits the sun. When Watt submitted the designs for a patent (pat. 1306, granted in 1782) for the new invention, he showed a double-acting engine which both drove pump rods and turned a flywheel. When the first practical rotative engine was introduced, it used the same basic design but without the pumps. Boulton was enthusiastic about the whole project and even sent in suggestions to Watt for mechanical improvements. He received short shrift:

> If you had read the latter part of the specification of the 5th method [sun and planet] you would have found the link you made use of described, and as to the post in front that has also occurred but I wished as much as possible to banish every idea of a crank in the general description and I don't wish for particular reasons any thing to be said or done about the method.[12]

Although, in general, Boulton remained on excellent terms with Watt, the relationship was not without its problems, and Watt was always liable to be less than tactful in his dealings with his partner, as the rather terse note indicates. Boulton never complained, but others were very aware of the situation:

> Your communicating to him your late disquietude was certainly laud- able & would have operated properly had his heart been as susceptible as your own of that rectitude or rule of Action which a candid man should always observe.[13]

Boulton's enthusiasm for the new and exciting world of steam engine construction was understandable, but it was only a part of his business. He had borrowed money on the basis of engine profits to come, but Boulton & Fothergill was languishing. He had already asked his old friend James Keir, who was a managing partner in a Stourbridge glass company, to help run the financial side of things and offered him a partnership. Keir gave up his post, but when he looked into the accounts he declined a partnership, although he agreed to take on the role of financial adviser. He was not impressed by Boulton's involvement in the practical, engineering side of the business:

> My present intention is to call your attention to the General state of your affairs ... For the friendship I have for you obliges me to declare that it is my opinion from what I have been able to collect, that the greatest success that your most sanguine expectations can suggest in the fire-engine business cannot <u>secure</u> you, without a continuance of the most prudent conduct in that & all your affairs, during a series of many years.
>
> The first step is for you to acquire a <u>true state</u> of your affairs. For I cannot think that you have always had a true state of your affairs sufficiently in your mind, otherwise you would not have believed as you did last Summer that the raising of a few thousand could have permanently extricated yourself out of your difficulties.[14]

He went on to list the very large debts, and speculated on likely future income. He painted a gloomy picture, made worse by the fact that Boulton was having to pay a high rate of interest of up to 8 per cent. 'For whatever the great resources the fire-engine business may afford ultimately, the above state, however gross, shews too plainly that the credit of B & F must be in a very precarious state for several years to come.'

He ended by pointing out that Watt did not actually need any help with engineering problems; what he wanted help with was 'the <u>detail</u> of the Manufactory of <u>Engines</u>, Correspondence, Accounts, etc. in all of which your engagements render it impossible to give that constant, regular & daily attention, a service that is wanted'.[15]

There was one major technological advance in 1784, when Watt devised the mechanism of which he was inordinately proud – his parallel motion.[16] Instead of the clumsy ratchet connecting the piston to the beam, he fastened the piston rod to one corner of a shifting parallelogram, to enable the rod to move in a straight line, even though it was connected to a beam moving in the arc of a circle. The rotative engine became a reality when one was sold to Wilkinson to power the hammers of his forge. An even more important sale in terms of future business was the order of an engine by Robinson's of

Papplewick in Nottinghamshire to work their cotton mill.[17] Boulton's success in selling the engine is said to have owed a great deal to the whimsy of the poet Lord Byron. He had been making ornamental lakes in the grounds of his home at nearby Newstead Abbey on which he staged mock naval battles. Unfortunately, the water that was diverted to fill the lakes was the water that had originally turned the waterwheel at Robinson's mill: hence the need for steam power.

Now Boulton had an even more ambitious plan. He took an active part in promoting Albion Mills that were to provide all London with flour.[18] He worked out the possible profits in his notebook, calculating that there were 650,000 people in London, who each ate 1lb of bread a day. A mill with eight-een pairs of stones, working twenty-four hours a day for fifty weeks of the year, could grind roughly 100,000 quarters – the equivalent of 800,000 bush-els – of wheat a year, and that would provide a profit of £31,250 per annum. It sounds a bit too good to be true, but Boulton was convinced and was prepared to appear generous in waiving part of the expected profit – but only because it would ensure long-term advantages:

> Whatever profit the proprietors may be satisfied with less than that sum the publick wd have the advantage of … Then suppose the proprietors were to give up one half of the above profit to the publick it is presumed from the singular advantage of the Mill, arising situation & great Dispatch of Business the proprietors will be enabled to avail themselves of the Rise & fall of the Corn Market greatly to their benefit; probably in some years the advantage may be more than equal to half the above profit.

Not surprisingly, the traditional small millers viewed the arrival of such a monster with alarm and tried to persuade Parliament to stop the scheme. But the mill was authorised and the great building was constructed. The architect was Samuel Wyatt, who became a partner in the venture, and the millwork was entrusted to the Scottish millwright, later to make a name as an engineer, John Rennie. Boulton & Watt were to supply the steam engines. The first engine went to work in 1786 and a second was later added, but on 3 March 1791 the mill burnt to the ground. It could have been a complete disaster, but fortu-nately it was insured and a first payment of £11,000 was made within a few days, with a promise of more to come, although the proceedings were to drag on for years. It might have been a great deal worse. There was undoubtedly financial loss from the destruction of Albion Mills, but there was a huge gain in publicity, and Boulton & Watt had demonstrated the feasibility of powering a corn mill by steam, something which Smeaton had doubted was possible on account of the supposed irregularity of motion. In all, the partners installed eleven engines in corn mills before 1800. The application of steam power to corn milling enabled this industry to relocate at the ports, where grain could be imported and unloaded more cheaply.

The demand for rotative engines more than justified Boulton's enthusiasm: 'I think I understand all the Elements of the horizontal, Elliptical, Eccliptical, Conical, comical, Rotative Mill & a good Mill it is ... the people in London, Manchester & Birmingham be Steam Mill Mad.'[19] Watt's rotative engine had come into its own. The cotton industry was growing fast, although there were initial anxieties about the use of the steam engine: 'We beg to be informed if you are certain [it] will work as steadily as water.' Sixty-one sun and planet engines were ordered for mills in Lancashire and Cheshire, a further nineteen in the Midlands (mainly Derbyshire and the Pennine edge of Staffordshire), seven in Yorkshire and Durham, nine in Scotland, and four in London, the industry being widely distributed at this stage in its development. Sixty-one of the engines were between 8 and 14hp, forty-two engines being larger than this, including one of over 40hp. Initially, the concern regarding steady motion led cotton spinners to use steam power first for preparatory processes rather than spinning.[20]

Many purchasers of the early rotative engines had already been using some other form of power generation in their mills, either horse power, water power, or, in a few cases, another make of steam engine. Even the great cotton spinning entrepreneur Richard Arkwright employed horses in his Nottingham factory. He installed a common engine at Wirksworth in 1780, and one by Hunt in his Manchester mill – but he too changed in the 1790s to a Boulton & Watt one.[21]

Brewers were amongst the earliest users of rotative engines, Whitbread being early on the scene in 1784, and, much to John Rennie's annoyance, 'would not allow his engine to be started but in his presence'. There were few mechanical problems compared with those anticipated in the cotton and worsted industries. Sometimes the engine was directly harnessed to the horse wheel, involving a loss of power but saving on installation costs. The majority of brewery engines were at the large London breweries of Thrale, Goodwyn, Whitbread and Charrington. Some were installed in the larger provincial breweries such as Castle & Ames of Bristol and Green of Nottingham, but country brewers tended to retain horse power for much longer.[22]

Many customers complained about the sun and planet gear: 'The Sun Wheels do their work badly ... scarce a day passes without their breaking or threatening to break.'[23] These problems prompted Boulton & Watt to send a spare set to more remote customers. But the problem was not solely one of design, for the quality of castings was variable and boilers also caused difficulties. However, once Pickard's crank patent had expired, Boulton & Watt were free to use this mechanism which proved to be more reliable, although, in some instances, the customer had to insist on a crank engine. Watt may have been a little reluctant to admit that another mechanism was superior.

The arrival of the rotative engine had an immense impact on British industry. Manufacturers no longer had to look for a site with a water supply to keep their wheels turning but could opt for the convenience of a good transport system instead, such as a canal that would bring in the coal for the furnaces and raw materials and take out finished products. Boulton himself chose just such a site for his own new factory beside the Birmingham Canal. Even today one can see the effect in towns such as Burnley, where the former steam-powered mills line the Leeds & Liverpool Canal.

By the end of the eighteenth century only one-third of the engines that had been sold were pumping engines. Not that the partners rested on their laurels. They were always seeking out improvements. In 1788, Boulton had visited Albion Mills and seen that they had introduced a centrifugal governor as part of the milling apparatus. One of the problems in the conventional water-powered mill or windmill was that the source of power was variable: neither the flow of water nor the blowing of the wind was consistent. Any changes in the flow resulted in changes of speed in the gears, which in turn altered the distance between the grindstones. The governor consisted of a pair of lead balls connected to movable arms. They turned with the wheel, and the faster they turned the more they were forced apart by centrifugal force. The movement activated a spring that automatically adjusted the distance between the stones, keeping it regular. Boulton realised that a similar device could be adapted to regulate the valves of a steam engine, and promptly wrote to Watt to tell him about his discovery.[24] The centrifugal governor was to become a standard fixture on stationary engines.

Not everything was plain sailing in those early years. There were technical problems and customers understandably complained. But complaints were not limited to customers. Wilkinson was always a difficult man to deal with, ready to hand out criticism whenever he felt like it and astonished when anyone objected. Watt had taken offence at something Wilkinson had written and received this reply:

Pray by what authority are you to be exempt from unmerited censure more than others? And why cannot you submit to take the world as it is as well as me or any other of your friends. I thought myself one of the most unfit persons in the world to bear the harangings of inconsiderate men but I am a hero in such circumstances compared with you ... I thought you had been a philosopher but it appears you have got the failings of the clergy that you cannot practise what I have heard you preach.[25]

Letters such as that were not likely to smooth out relationships. There were quarrels about payments that were time-consuming even though they never led to any major breach. There was little that could be done about it. The simple fact was that no ironworks in Britain could turn out engine cylinders to the same degree of accuracy as Wilkinson. And Wilkinson, for his part, was kept busy with orders, even if he grumbled about it, complaining that he received new engine orders with horror rather than joy.

The other major problem that affected Boulton & Watt at that time was the disastrous state of Boulton & Fothergill. Fothergill was particularly hard hit and was demanding a share in the steam engine profits, although he had specifically agreed that the two concerns should be kept entirely separate. But that was at a time when he believed that the engines would never show a profit. Watt was adamant that nothing should be done for Fothergill and it was his opinion that Boulton should spend far more time on Boulton & Watt. Boulton had been doing a juggling act and could no longer keep all the balls in the air, while Fothergill had borrowed heavily to take up his share of the partnership and was not able to repay the debts. There was an acrimonious exchange of letters, in the course of which Fothergill complained, unjustly, of being cheated by Boulton. In such circumstances there was no option but to end the partnership, which took effect at the end of 1781.[26] In some ways, Boulton was probably glad to end the partnership, for Fothergill had a very different temperament from his. Where he was always optimistic, Fothergill was a creature of gloom. In 1777, he had actually proposed that they should simply pay off outstanding debts and give up the business altogether. In spite of their differences, Boulton took a generous line with the Fothergill family, paying over some of his personal share of the engine profits. Watt would have no doubt been infuriated had he taken anything from the company's coffers. For Boulton it was the best of a bad affair:

> I have suffered my pity to predominate over my Judgement & have given him or intend to give him rather more than is consistent with my Stewardship of my own Family: however, peace and happiness cannot be bought too dear.[27]

After Fothergill's death in 1782, and following a long argument, arbitrators ruled that he owed Boulton almost £20,000. There was no hope of recovering the money, but it did result in Boulton now being the sole owner of the Soho Manufactory. Meanwhile, events in Cornwall had been causing fresh concerns and worries.

The problem did not originate in Cornwall itself but on the island of Anglesey where a 500ft-high hill was dignified with the name Parys Mountain. It may not have been much of a mountain, but it was rich in copper ore.

Thomas Williams, a local solicitor, became the controlling force behind the Parys Mine Company in 1778, earning himself the popular nickname 'The Copper King'.[28] By 1780, the 'mountain' was yielding 3,000 tons of ore a year, and soon there were as many as 1,500 workers on the site. They dug shafts and cut levels until the whole hill began to resemble a giant Gruyère cheese. The ore, at least in the early years, was very close to the surface, so that extraction costs were only a fraction of those of the Cornish deep mines. The results of all this work can still be seen today. The hill has been stripped of all its foliage and presents a barren landscape rather like a lunar crater. Boulton & Watt had been asked by their Cornish agent, Thomas Wilson, to consider investing in local mines. Watt made the position brutally clear:

> The greatest objection however is the extravagant rate at which the anglesea company are getting ores, which on any demurr in sales must over stock the markets and infallibly lower the price of copper so much that nothing but loss can be got by it, which indeed makes one tremble for the business in general.[29]

He was right to feel pessimistic. The Cornish tried to make good their profits by increasing the production of tin, but only succeeded in flooding the market. Nicholas Donnithorne, Chairman of the Quarterly Tin Meetings in Cornwall, wrote to the Directors of the East India Company in 1789:

> I am acting in behalf of many thousands who at this time are destitute of even most common necessaries of life. I am lately returned from the mining parishes in Cornwall, where I have been witness to the greatest imaginable poverty and distress, insomuch that I have seen women gathering snails to make broth for the support of their families. It is true that the Cornish tinners have lately been very riotous, and the gentlemen of the county have been obliged to call in the aid of the military, but, when the extremely low price of Tin and the very high price of corn are considered, much may be said in defence of these poor industrious labourers.[30]

In these circumstances, mine owners were looking to make every possible saving they could, simply to remain in business. When the new steam engines had been first installed, they had been welcomed as the saviours of the industry and no one had objected to paying the premium. Now, when they had been running for some years, the novelty had worn off and the premium seemed an unjust burden. It was clearly in Boulton & Watt's interest to keep mines open, and they did in fact take 1/32nd shares in several ventures to help with capital costs, but that was not sufficient to satisfy some mine owners: they wanted the premium either to be reduced or even abandoned. This Boulton & Watt resolutely refused to do. Boulton made his position clear in response to a demand of John Vivian of Poldice, which had been passed on to Birmingham by Wilson:

> JW wrote you last post informing you of the proposition made by Mr Vivian & others that unless the Lords of Poldice & ourselves would agree to give up entirely all manners of dues of premium arising from that mine, until it should have repaid £7,000, which they say new engines will cost, they would vote for stopping the mine entirely. As they did not seem disposed to make the same demand in regard to the merchants profits we look upon the proposal as partial & unjust And even setting that consideration aside we cannot agree to the proposal without receiving a far greater injury than the stopping of the mine can do us, by setting a precedent for demand which must end in the annihilation of our income; & therefore as we must make a stand somewhere it is best that it be understood by every body that we will upon no occasion agree to pay for or contribute towards Engines or those repairs or costs of mines. But in this present case as Poldice mine has not been profitable nor is soon likely to be so, from the current expences of working the mine independent of any new erections, we will make them an abatement of part of our dues untill the mine shall have repaid the losses she has made from the 1st of May last.[31]

Boulton & Watt continued to receive demands for either a reduction or abolition of the premium, and the partners became increasingly irritated by the tone of the demands. They pointed out that everyone else was getting paid, and drew an analogy with the merchants who supplied the coal for the engines. They got paid for doing so and it seemed illogical not to pay a company which had reduced the size of that bill by a considerable amount. In the correspondence that flew backwards and forwards between Birmingham and Cornwall, Boulton generally took a more conciliatory tone than Watt, whose attitude throughout was never to give way on any points at all – and certainly never to reduce premium payments. As a result, the partners who until recently had been perceived to be the saviours of Cornwall were now cast as the arch villains, as Watt wrote to Boulton: 'In short almost the whole country is against us and look upon us as oppressors & tyrants, from whom the Horned imp of Satan [Jonathan Hornblower, see Chapter 9] are to release them!'[32] Things got so bad that there was talk of recalling Wilson and his family to Birmingham for their own safety, and he was advised to keep his bags packed ready for a speedy departure if necessary. In the event, it was never necessary. The slump of the 1780s had been a difficult time, but it is fair to say that Boulton had behaved honourably and shown real compassion for the miners and their families. He had also found another source of the region's problems, which he recorded in 1785:

The late commotions in the Copper Trade have overturned several powerfull and oppulent Houses, some of which have been established for Centuries and although the storm seems now to be subsided, yet there are such a variety of different interests, & such various combinations of them, that in the course of the 7 years *truce* many new plans will be formed. ... However I think I can foresee that the adventurers in Cornish Mines have found it their interest to free themselves from the oppression of the Smelting Cos. They will never become the tools and slaves of such like Cos but will eventually be the smelters of their own ore.[33]

Boulton was ready to invest in a smelting works, provided it did not involve sleeping partners who were unconcerned with the welfare of the mines but only wanted a share of the profits. He was also worried that one of the problems was the lack of competent mine captains, and he gave his own solution:

To *breed up Good Captains* for Mines, a Boy should be set to work at Stamps when he is 10 yrs old & work at them till he is 18 yrs old & then he should be set to work with a pick etc. & do all kinds of work underground. At his leisure hours he should learn to write, & be taught arithmatick.

He was later expected to go on to learn surveying, drawing plans and the like. The ideas for training were very much those he practised at Soho. His plans for a smelting consortium were not quite as straightforward as he might have thought. The smelters may have been making an excessive profit, but there was the inescapable fact that made the project unattractive: a smelter used up to four times as much coal as ore. It was cheaper to take ore to South Wales than it was to bring coal from there to Cornwall. But the notes, which were only intended for his personal use, show very clearly that he had the interests of the region and its mines very much in mind.

Boom times had returned to Cornwall by the early nineteenth century, but by that time the steam agent patent had expired and Boulton sold off all his shares in Cornish mines. Cornwall had been a source of problems which occupied a great deal of Boulton's time, but few were as significant as those involving the protection of the partnership's monopoly on engine construction and experiment, which is the subject of the next chapter.

Notes

1   H. W. Dickinson, *Matthew Boulton*, 1937, pp. 89–90.
2   Jennifer Tann, 'Boulton & Watt's Organisation of Steam Engine Production before the opening of Soho Foundry', *Trans. Newcomen Soc.*, 49, 1977–78.

3   D.B. Barton, *The Cornish Beam Engine*, 1965, pp. 28–30; G.N. von Tunzelmann, *Steam Power and British Industrialization*, 1978, p. 254.

4   H.S. Torrens, 'Some Newly Discovered Letters from Jonathan Hornblower (1753–1815)', *Trans. Newcomen Soc.*, 54, 1982–83.

5   Jennifer Tann, 'Riches from Copper: the Adoption of the Boulton & Watt Engine by Cornish Mine Adventurers', *Trans. Newcomen Soc.*, 67, 1995–96.

6   Ibid.

7   James Keir to MB, 17 October 1778.

8   Dickinson, op. cit., pp. 97–98.

9   Shena Mason, *The Hardware Man's Daughter: Matthew Boulton and his 'Dear Girl'*, 2005, p. 37.

10 H.W. Dickinson & R. Jenkins, *James Watt and the Steam Engine*, 1927, repr. 1981, p. 50.

11 Jennifer Tann (ed.), *The Selected Papers of Boulton & Watt*, Vol. I, 1981, p. 111.

12 JW to MB, 1 February 1779.

13 W. Matthews to MB, 2 April 1782.

14 J. Keir to MB, 1 February 1779.

15 Tann, *Selected Papers*, pp. 174–75.

16 Dickinson and Jenkins, op. cit., p. 141.

17 Richard L. Hills, *Power in the Industrial Revolution*, 1970, pp. 104–5; the mill is illustrated in Jennifer Tann, *The Development of the Factory*, 1970, p. 13.

18 Dickinson, op. cit., pp. 122–25; Hills, op. cit., pp. 142–56.

19 Dickinson & Jenkins, op. cit., p. 159.

20 Tann, *The Development of the Factory*, 1970, pp. 77–85.

21 Jennifer Tann, 'Richard Arkwright and Technology', *History*, LVIII, 1973.

22 Tann, *The Development of the Factory*, 1970, pp. 98–108.

23 Thomas Garton to B&W, 13 June 1788.

24 MB to JW, 28 May 1788.

25 John Wilkinson to JW, 31 August 1779.

26 Dickinson, op. cit., pp. 109–10.

27 MB to JW, 13 November 1781.

28 J.R. Harris, *The Copper King: A Biography of Thomas Williams of Llanidan*, 1964.

29 JW to Thomas Wilson, 27 June 1784.

30 Quoted in A.K. Hamilton Jenkin, *The Cornish Miner*, 1927.

31 MB to Thomas Wilson, 11 July 1786, Cornwall Record Office.

32 JW to MB, 22 May 1782.

33 MB Notebook, Cornwall, 21 November 1785.

9

Patents & Piracy

In principle Boulton & Watt had sole rights to manufacture engines, or to approve others to do so under licence, that incorporated any of the features that were specified in their patent. This was how they could ensure the profits that would pay for their work on development, but it was not quite that simple to keep the monopoly intact. There was the ever-present threat of a challenge to the patent from another engineer and the no less likely possibility of piracy, and there was nothing to stop foreigners in countries not covered by British patent laws simply stealing their ideas, unless the partners could negotiate a separate agreement.

The first possibility of a challenge came from a most unlikely source, a dissenting clergyman by the name of Humphrey Gainsborough, brother of the famous artist.[1] He was an extraordinary man who, apart from his clerical duties, found time to pursue a wide range of other interests. He invented all kinds of machines – from an ingenious fish cart, which kept the fish fresh by blowing air through the containers, to a drill plough. He designed one of the first modern locks to be built on the Thames and worked on a number of improvements to all kinds of timepieces. And, it seems, quite independently of Watt, he invented a condensing steam engine. Who was first, and did either learn from the other? These are questions that were debated at the time and have never been fully resolved. The Cornish engineer Jonathan Hornblower wrote to his uncle in 1789, describing Watt's engines, and then had this to say about Gainsborough:

> Herein is W's great improvement, which was invented by one Gainsbourough [sic] a dissenting minister but secur'd by Mr. Watt, so Mr. G, who is since dead, told my Father, when he visited him at Henley on Thames.[2]

According to Hornblower's account, Gainsborough's engine used both the separate condenser and the air pump, the two key elements of Watt's patent. Gainsborough himself certainly thought he was there first. He applied for a patent of his own at the same time as Watt was asking for an extension of his own patent. Watt suggested that they meet, but Gainsborough was not willing to leave home at that particular time. That he felt deeply aggrieved is very obvious, however, from his reply:

> Those who know both inventions have assured me that mine is totally different from your's. I must therefore leave you to act at your pleasure at the Patent Office, especially as it is impossible for me to be in town at present, and when God only knows, both I and Mrs. Gainsborough being very ill. As you have been ungenteel enough to give me unnecessary trouble, I am only sorry that I did not endeavour to hinder your Bill passing in any form, which I have good reason to believe would have been in my power.[3]

Boulton then joined in the correspondence himself, and although the letter does not seem to have survived, he must have taken a rather more conciliatory tone than Watt, which was often the case. Gainsborough agreed to the meeting, but there is no record of what was said if it did take place, for Gainsborough's health deteriorated again and he was dead just three weeks after writing the letter. No one who knew Gainsborough ever described him as anything other than a scrupulously honest man, so there can be no doubt that he genuinely believed he had a prior claim. It may be that it was simply one of those cases of two talented individuals finding the same satisfactory solution to a familiar problem. Nevertheless, it must have given Boulton a fright, for if Gainsborough could prove to have independently invented the separate condenser then Watt would have been unable to claim his own invention as unique. Hornblower had good reasons for hinting that Watt had stolen another man's ideas: he had his own quarrels with the Birmingham firm, as will appear shortly. Anything that undermined Watt's case could only strengthen his own.

Theft of their ideas by foreigners was a constant possibility and provided something of a dilemma for Boulton. He loved showing off the works, particularly to distinguished visitors, and he must have initially welcomed the arrival of German aristocracy at his door. He soon became suspicious, however:

The German and Prussian barons have been to see all the engines and have
been extreamly inquisitive. They pressed Joseph very much to see the drawings and then would have offered to have bribed him for copies and when
they found they could not succeed with Joseph they tried Cartwright.
Honesty will cover many foibles. I doubt not but he will be properly cau-
tious with these Prussian pimps. If they want engines we shall be glad to
execute their orders as it is the trade by which we profess to get our bread
but if they want to take that bread out of our mouths they must excuse us if
we endeavour to prevent it and I think we should say as much.[4]

Two weeks later, Boulton was in London on business, where he was actually
knocked down by a gentleman's coach when crossing Ludgate Hill after dark.
It could have been very serious, but he only suffered bruising to his hip and
ribs, and the accident did not prevent him thinking about business. He sent
another urgent letter off to Watt:

> I have just received yours of ye 18th and cannot help cautioning you again
> not to consider the Baron as a gentleman and philosopher travelling only
> to perfectionate those characters but consider him as a man that has come
> expressly to England to steal our engine.

In 1787, Boulton was to write to Sir Joseph Banks, setting out what he
called 'A statement of facts' about attempts at industrial espionage.[5] The two
Prussians had bribed a workman to dismantle part of an engine to show them
how it worked, and back in Prussia A. Buckling, who bore the grandiose
title 'Counsellor of Mines of His Prussian Majesty', offered to build a 108hp
engine. His ambition may have been as grand as his title but the result was not.
The engine proved to be a miserable 8hp and failed to work. Other Prussians
came over and tried to discover the secrets of engine construction. They visited Wilkinson in an attempt to get their hands on drawings at a brewery
where an engine was being installed. The erector, Cartwright, accepted money
to correct the drawings they had made, but promptly informed the partners
about what was happening. Boulton praised his honesty – but sacked him
anyway, for taking the money in the first place.

In the event, foreign competition was not to be a major problem, but the
same could not be said of piracy – breaches of the patent. These were to occupy
a great deal of Boulton's time, and much of the firm's money in fighting law-
suits. Problems erupted in those areas where the Watt engine met particular
needs, for example in Cornwall where the deeper mines could not be effectively drained by Newcomen engines; Lancashire, where the rapidly growing

cotton spinning industry was effectively freed from dependence on water-power by Watt's rotative engine; and the Yorkshire worsted spinning industry, which could adapt cotton spinning technologies. And the biggest traitor of all was John Wilkinson, who had insider knowledge of the Watt engine by virtue of having had a monopoly in the supply of bored cylinders, besides having had Boulton & Watt engines for his own use.[6]

By December 1790, piracy had increased to the extent that Boulton directed a legal friend to obtain copies of drawings and specifications for all patents of engines taken out since the beginning of the year, requesting that he 'would not mention our name at all in this business'. With the exception of two pirates, Boulton & Watt avoided becoming embroiled with holders of patents, perhaps because they did not wish to draw attention to Watt's long-term monopolistic coverage.

Whilst the major anti-piracy campaign did not begin until the early 1790s, the activities of two competitors prompted discussion of possible legal action in the 1780s. One was Francis Thompson of Ashover, Derbyshire;[7] the other was Jonathan Hornblower junior who had been granted a patent for a water-raising engine in 1781. Hornblower was in partnership with a Bristol ironfounder, John Winwood, and an engine was installed at Radstock Colliery in Somerset.

Boulton had been having problems with Cornwall from the outset and, in 1782, Watt admitted that the Hornblower engine 'is much more formidable than we may have thought it'. Cornish mines operated on a complex and unique system. At the top of the tree was the landowner, who granted the right to search for and extract minerals on his land. He was paid even if there was no valuable ore and stood to make even more money if there was, and he had no need to invest in the mine. The 'adventurers' put up all the capital for exploration and working the mine. In charge of the mines were the mine captains, normally at least two: one to supervise the underground workings; the other to look after the treatment of the ore once it reached the surface. They were usually men who had come up from the ranks of ordinary workers; they needed to be technically competent and were used to having a high degree of independence. The workers, too, had their own degree of independence – they were not mere wage earners. Groups of men bid to do the work, setting a price on their estimate of how difficult it would prove. If it proved easier than expected then they stood to make a good profit; if they got it wrong, however, they could end up with very little. The men concerned with mining in Cornwall were used to making up their own minds and going their own ways.

When the first Newcomen engines were installed in Cornwall, it was only natural for mine captains to look at them carefully and see whether or not they could be improved. One of these captains was Richard Trevithick senior, father of the more famous inventor of the railway locomotive. He was captain at one of the great mine complexes at Dolcoath in 1775 when a new engine appeared, and at once he saw that the flat-topped boiler was going to be a source of trouble. He promptly redesigned it with a domed top, which proved far more satisfactory. He saw no good reason why he should not take an equal interest in improving on the work of James Watt. Boulton was well aware of the necessity of winning over the mine captains if he wanted orders from Cornwall, and as a first step he invited a group of the leading men, including Trevithick, to Birmingham. The men liked what they saw, but someone thought it would be quite a good idea to take away a set of working drawings. Boulton was not amused:

> It came out that he had been prevailed upon by you to leave the Drawing at the Castle Inn in Birmingham under a promise that it should be returned when you come to Soho the next morning but we find you have take the Drawing with you ... We do not keep a school to teach Fire Engine making but profess the making of them our-selves. When you reflect on this matter you will readily perceive that there was an Impropriety in taking the drawing without our Knowledge & consent and as I am persuaded you would not deviate from the Character of a Gentleman I doubt not that you will return the drawing with every copy that hath been taken of it and which I hear have been exhibited in Cornwall.[8]

There were strong hints that Trevithick was very much involved in this attempt at industrial espionage. Trevithick descended even further in Boulton's estimation when he had the temerity to criticise the new engine, he and his colleagues being branded as the 'Infidels of Dolcoath'. Watt, as ever, went even further after a meeting in 1779: 'During this time I was so confounded with the impudence, ignorance and overbearing manner of the man that I could make no adequate defence, and indeed could scarcely keep my Temper.' But these disagreements were as nothing compared to the trouble Boulton was later to have with Trevithick's son.

Major problems soon arose between the Birmingham partners and Cornish engineers. The latter looked at the new engine and admired it, but some of them had their own ideas for improvements. It seemed to them only sensible that they should be allowed to go ahead and make them. To Boulton this was straightforward piracy if they included any of the elements covered by the patent – and it was virtually impossible to make an effective engine without doing so. Two groups were to prove particularly troublesome: the Hornblower family and Edward Bull.

Just as Trevithick senior had incurred the wrath of both Boulton and Watt, so too did Jonathan Hornblower at the very beginning of their relationship. He had been given the task of installing the very first engine at Ting Tang mine, but had followed the familiar Cornish practice of ignoring the strict instructions laid down for the work whenever he thought he could see a better way of doing things. He was duly ticked off: 'I must once and for all beg that you would not take amiss my insisting upon your strict adherence to my plans & directions even though contrary to common practice.'[9] In the event, the job of installing the engine went instead to Thomas Wilson, who was to become one of the company's most loyal representatives in Cornwall. Soon, however, word was coming back to Soho that Hornblower was now experimenting on his own behalf:

> Jabez Hornblower is trying an Experiment at Wh. Maiden mine which he says will be a Considerable improvement in the Engine branch, in every way preferable to what has been shown in this County but what it is no other yet knows but the greatest part judges it to be the last shift.[10]

In fact, Hornblower was experimenting with a compound engine. In the existing engines, the steam left the cylinder for the condenser but was still under pressure. Hornblower's idea was to pass this steam into a second cylinder to provide extra power. The first results were disappointing for Hornblower, but good news for Soho – the piston moved just 6in on the first trial and then seized. Even so, Boulton was adamant that any such experiments should be stopped in their tracks: 'No man shall use any of these principles in Fire Engines to our prejudice by God.' He then went on to elaborate his thoughts:

> Hence you see a sort of reason for our executing every Idea that may seem plausible to Strangers, such as Putting the Cylinder in the Boiler, such as applying a sinking pipe 35 feet long – Such as using second hand Steam, such as working the Condenser by the least power possible and any other thing that may seem likely in order to shut the mouths of ignorant boasters ... I think all the possabilities of a good Steam Engine lye within a little compass & therefore we should execute all.[11]

Nevertheless, Boulton & Watt did not oppose Hornblower's patent application. Possibly, it was thought that the idea was unlikely to work and would not provide a sufficient challenge to trouble them. There was also another important factor in letting Hornblower continue, as James Watt junior explained when describing the events of those days in a letter of 1834:

It was intended to have proceeded at Law against the Engines he had erected; but another person, of the name of Edward Bull, who had also been employed by Boulton and Watt in the erection of their Engines, having in the meantime made other Steam Engines with the Cylinder inverted (which Mr. Watt had done before) and using the other Inventions of Mr. Watt, it was judged more expedient to proceed in the first instance against him, as his formed a cheaper and better Engine than Hornblowers and was spreading fast.[12]

Bull had arrived from Coventry to erect Boulton & Watt engines in Cornwall in 1781, but he was eager to be rather more than a mere mechanic following instructions. Watt sniffed rebellion in the air, and wrote to Wilson to try and stop the process in its tracks:

In respect to Bull the less we have to do with him the better. If he applies to you on our terms & brings respectable persons as principals you will fix the premium with him & take his order for the size of the engine but we will not be directed how to make it. Had we agreed to let him make one of our Engines in such manner as he pleased, he would have made a bad thing & we should have had our share of the disgrace. As it now stands, his inventions must depend upon their own merit & unless he becomes more knowing than he has been hitherto, the merit will decide in our favour.[13]

Whilst the partners, and especially Boulton, were prepared to listen to new ideas from other engineers, it was axiomatic at Soho that every engineer who tried to act independently, without honouring the patent, was incompetent or fraudulent and usually both. In the meantime, Bull had recruited the young Richard Trevithick to help him with his work. The essence of the Bull engine was that it did away with the cumbersome overhead beam by inverting the steam cylinder directly over the shaft, so that the piston rod could be connected directly to the pump rods. At first, Boulton was content to wait and see; after all, Watt had assured him that Bull was incompetent and that the engine was unlikely to work. But it did work and showed every sign of being popular with the local adventurers.

Boulton & Watt's anxiety about piracy in 1781 and 1782 can be partly explained by the dearth of orders for their own engines – four in 1781 and just two in the following year.[14] But ten orders in 1783 and the figure rising steadily thereafter prompted little further interest in tracking down pirates until the 1790s. In 1792, Bull was telling everyone in the Cornish mining community that his engines were better than Boulton & Watt's and challenged the Birmingham company to a competitive trial. There was no possibility of the

Soho partnership agreeing to that as it would have been an acknowledgement that they were indeed quite different engines. Wilson put the partnership view in a simple demonstration. He put his hat on the table and asked, 'What's that?' When the company agreed it was a hat he turned it upside down. 'What is it now?' Boulton decided the issue would be settled by lawyers not experiments, an action that dismayed many in Cornwall, and there was a good deal of ill will. Anonymous letters were sent and threats made against the agents in Cornwall, but the judge found in favour of Boulton & Watt. It was not all good news for Soho, as the judge indicated that he was not altogether happy that the original patent was clear enough about the specifications – a view that left the door open for future challenges.

The decision that the patent was valid did not deter Bull and Trevithick, who continued to erect engines. The next step was obvious: Boulton went back to law to get an injunction to prevent Bull building any more. Given the previous verdict, the result was inevitable. Bull asked to be allowed to finish the engines already started, although he must have known that it was a lost cause. Now a new problem appeared: they had stopped Bull, but Trevithick was still carrying on and was erecting an engine at Ding Dong mine. It was at a good situation, standing high on windy moorland near Penzance, with good views of any approaching strangers. Nevertheless, an injunction was duly posted and an eyewitness, John Bolitho, described what happened next:

> Boulton and Watt came down with an injunction printed out, and posted it up on the door of the engine-house, and upon the heaps of mine-stuff, and nobody dared to touch them. But Captain Trevithick did not care; he and Bull and William West came and turned the cylinder upside down, right over the pump rods in the shaft; they took off the cylinder top (it was the cylinder bottom before they turned it upside down). [15]

It seems that they were only using steam pressure under the piston for the up-stroke, probably in an attempt to claim a new invention. Although Soho regarded Bull and Trevithick as equal partners, they could not prove the point, as there was no formal agreement between the two men. This meant that the injunction against Bull had no effect on Trevithick, so Boulton & Watt would need to get a separate notice served on him. That proved to be a difficult proposition as Trevithick was something of a local hero. When a bailiff appeared to try and serve a notice, the local miners grabbed him, held him over a mineshaft by his ankles and enquired whether he was quite sure he wanted to carry on with the job. He agreed that, on the whole, he would rather go home. Feelings in Cornwall ran high and relations between the Soho agents and Trevithick deteriorated, but although language got rough, nothing more serious ever resulted.

Bull and Trevithick felt themselves secure, but in 1795 on their way to the ironworks at Coalbrookdale, they decided to stop off in Birmingham to see what was happening in the centre of engine manufacture. Unfortunately for them, they were recognised and the bailiffs were able to reach Trevithick at last. He was furious, but the deed was done.

Bull and Trevithick had not quite given up the fight. Trevithick loudly proclaimed that Watt had not really invented anything of great significance and spread the word that local engineers had wonderful ideas of their own. As one of the Soho agents put it: 'Young Trevithick making way for Bull's horns.'[16] What Trevithick had in mind was to work with high-pressure steam, and injunction or no injunction, he was not about to stop his experiments. There were some willing to keep Soho informed of what was going on. 'Edward Bull hath erected an ingin upon your plan sense hoe wass serve with a enjunction and I ham the pursun that put the ingin twoo gethar by Bulls drawins and is derections.'[17] There remained a strong feeling, however, among most of the Cornish that Boulton and Watt had done very well out of them, and that it was time for local men to be given their chance. That time was soon to arrive when the patent expired in 1800, but in the meantime Boulton was turning his attention once again to the Hornblowers.

In 1791, Jonathan Hornblower junior erected two compound engines in Cornwall and applied for an extension of their existing patent. This time it was contested. Boulton had one great advantage on his side: he was an experienced lobbyist and had friends in the right places. Samuel Garbett helped out with the lobbying process and reported back to Boulton:

Ld. Dartmouth it is to be feared cannot attend but he has many friends … Ld. Aylesford may certainly be of great use, and perhaps Lord Dudley as Baron of Birmingham … & I think Ld. Warwick would have particular pleasure in serving you – you may have some hopes from Lord Coventry & Lord Plymouth – Ld. Lansdowne has been confined with the gout but surely you could call on him – I am afraid his son Ld. Wycombe will not take a part with you but as Minority Men I expect they will be apt to favour Sir Francis Bassett … Lord North would be a great acquisition & he owes you a good turn. If Hornblower's Bill should be committed after the second reading don't forget to beg some of your friends to request the Speaker to appoint them to the Committee, it is a common custom.[18]

Boulton & Watt put out a 'Short Statement' against Hornblower's Bill which began by claiming that they had not opposed the first patent because 'they were willing that Mr. Hornblower should bring his Engine to a fair Trial', which was somewhat economical with the truth. Now, after two engines had been erected, they were convinced that Hornblower had contravened the patent. Their final point makes curious reading:

> That the Two Engines constructed by Mr. Hornblower, are (notwithstanding his having made use of Mr. Watt's Inventions) not superior in any Respect to those erected by Boulton and Watt, but are really inferior; *contrary to the Allegations contained in his Petition and Bill!*[19]

It was part of a recurring pattern, in which rival engineers were branded as hopelessly incompetent, their engines as worthless – but they still had to be brought to see the error of their ways. The Hornblower Bill was thrown out at the second reading.

The anti-piracy campaign had extended to other regions by 1795 and 1796. Bateman & Sherratt of Manchester were well-known makers of high-quality, standard atmospheric engines. Boulton & Watt suspected them of piracy but lacked proof. This came from their customers, Boulton & Watt claiming ten engines all erected in Lancashire in these years. Three engine makers erected pirate engines solely for their own use: Alexander Brodie, in Shropshire; Sturges of Leeds; and, nearer to home, Parker & Co. of Oldbury.

While the partners suspected Matthew Murray of Leeds, they avoided confrontation with him until after 1800, then opposed his patent application. William Symington patented an ingenious engine in 1787, seeking to bypass the separate condenser, and he is known to have produced at least eighteen engines during the 1790s with little interference from Boulton & Watt, probably on account of their seeking to avoid a potentially damaging court case, such as Arkwright's, or gaining adverse newspaper comments.

But John Wilkinson of Bradley, Willey and Brymbo, was the largest single pirate. Between 1787 and 1795, he made Watt engines for his own use, besides selling some, including one to France, whilst still in Boulton & Watt's confidence as a supplier of parts. Eleven pirate engines were erected at Bradley, one at Willey and three at Brymbo, and seven at various lead mines in which he held shares. Seven other engines were sold to British customers and five more exported. Whilst Boulton & Watt suspected piracy, it was not until 1795, when Wilkinson's brother William divulged what had been going on, that the partners were able to compile a 'statement of facts Against J. Wilkinson'. In the face of overwhelming evidence of his piracy, John Wilkinson capitulated, as did other makers and users of pirate engines.

Only J. C. Hornblower and J. A. Maberley refused to submit. This case went to the courts in 1796, judgement being given in favour of Boulton & Watt in the following year. Hornblower and Maberley appealed in 1799, but Watt's patent was upheld.[20]

The costs of pirate chasing were enormous. A document of September 1796 gives the legal bills as standing at £3,313 17s 11d. There is a very real possibility that had Boulton & Watt allowed the competition, they would actually have been financially better off than they were when fighting it. Boulton should perhaps have listened to the advice of his old friend, Erasmus Darwin: 'A lawsuit that pays well to the lawyers goes on like a snail creeping up a pole, which slips down every 2 or 3 inches as he advances until he has beslimed the pole all over.'[21]

Piracy is not the end of the steam engine story. In 1800, Watt's patent finally expired. The way was open for the other engineers to show their worth – which indeed they did, and there is an interesting sidelight to these years. Even before the patent had expired, Richard Trevithick had his mind set on using steam at high pressure, an idea that was anathema to James Watt. Trevithick was not the only one. Watt did not know, however, that one of his most trusted men in Cornwall, William Murdoch, was developing the same heretical ideas: he was planning to build a steam locomotive. He got as far as building a large-scale model and tried it out in secret on a lonely path leading down to the church in Redruth. What happened next was told by a man called Buckle:

> The night was dark, and he alone sallied out with his engine, lighted the fire or lamp under the boiler, and started the Locomotive with the Inventor in full chase after it. Shortly after, he heard distant despair – like shouting; it was too dark to perceive objects, but he soon found that the cries for assistance proceeded from the worthy pastor, who, going into the town on business, was met in the lonely road by the fiery monster, who he subsequently declared he took to be the Evil One in propria persona.[22]

By 1795, Murdoch decided the time had arrived to apply for a patent. Under the pretext of looking for skilled men to work in Cornwall he set off to London. Before he even got there, however, he met Boulton, who made it very clear that he had a straight choice. He could continue with his invention, lose his job and be faced with a lawsuit for breaching Watt's patent, or abandon the enterprise and continue as before in a steady job with good prospects. He sensibly chose the latter course, and turned his inventive mind to new problems. There is some controversy over whether or not his near neighbour Trevithick knew of Murdoch's experiments, but it is absolutely certain that it was the former who built the first practical, full-scale locomotive, which ran on the roads of Camborne in 1801 and was later adapted for use with railways. Ultimately, Trevithick was to fail to profit from his work, mainly because the engines broke the brittle cast-iron rails. Ironically, it was another of the band of pirates, Matthew Murray, who was to build the first locomotive to go into regular use on a working railway. He overcame the rail problem by using a rack and pinion system to provide greater traction with a light engine. He was not, it seems, quite the incompetent that Boulton and Watt had claimed. All that, however, lay in the future, for the Middleton Colliery Railway on which the Murray locomotive ran did not open until 1812. It is, however, part of a continuous story of the great burst of activity that followed the end of the Watt patent – continuous because Murray had to pay for the use of Trevithick's own patent.[23] It is almost irresistible to consider what might have happened if, when Murdoch met Boulton on his way to London, the latter had, instead of parroting Watt's views on high-pressure steam, said that the locomotive sounded an interesting project. One reason Trevithick failed was his almost complete lack of business ability. Murdoch with Boulton behind him could have made a success of his venture and Boulton & Watt might have gone down in history as the first manufacturers of locomotives.

When it came to foreign sales, the partners faced a dilemma. They were anxious to acquire orders but at the same time they did not want to open the door to competition and encourage foreign pirates to join the ranks of those already operating at home. Boulton, who already had extensive business connections with Europe, was the driving force in the search for overseas markets. He began in France and made use of all his connections in both commercial and diplomatic circles to get orders. Much of his effort was concentrated on acquiring an *arrêt du conseil*, a governmental decree that would provide protection similar to a British patent. He managed to acquire three tentative orders: from the Comte d'Hérouville; Joseph Jary, the Inspector of Mines; and the Paris Waterworks. The *arrêt* was granted, subject to a test of the engine's capabilities, and when the aristocratic order failed to materialise, Jary arranged for a trial at a mine in Brittany. It was successful and the *arrêt* was confirmed. As a reward for his part in the process, Jary was granted exclusive rights to act as Boulton & Watt's French agent, controlling sales and erection of engines. Then the Paris order was obtained and Boulton decided that as it was a public works and would establish the superiority of their engine, enabling Jary to acquire far more orders, he could bypass the newly appointed agent.[24] This can hardly have encouraged Jary to act very diligently in securing new orders, and after the initial orders of the 1770s, only one more engine was built for France. In the event, even the *arrêt* proved of little value in preventing piracy. French manufacturers produced their own copies without reprisals. Nevertheless, the partners persisted in trying to acquire monopolies in various countries, including America, but with only limited success. Boulton was equally cavalier in his treatment of the recently appointed Spanish agent. When an order for a large engine for a sawmill appeared, he declared it too big to be covered by the agreement and bypassed the agent entirely. During the years of the British patent, there were a mere twenty-five European orders received, and six of those were later cancelled.

Boulton & Watt fought hard to retain their monopoly and must have had serious concerns about the future when the patent came to an end in 1800. As it turned out it was far from a calamity. Although other engineers competed in the market, Soho continued to innovate, to provide excellent engines, and prospered. These developments will be dealt with in Chapter 12.

Notes

1   Jennifer Tann (ed.), *The Selected Papers of Boulton & Watt*, Vol. I, 1981, pp. 80, 176.

2   H.S. Torrens, 'Some Newly Discovered Letters from Jonathan Hornblower (1753–1815)', *Trans. Newcomen Soc.*, 54, 1982–83.

3   David Tyler, 'Humphrey Gainsborough (1718–76) cleric, engineer and inventor', *Trans. Newcomen Soc.*, 76, No 1, 2006; Jennifer Tann, 'Mr Hornblower and His Crew: Watt Engine Pirates at the end of the 18th century', *Trans. Newcomen Soc.*, 51, 1979–80.

4   MB to JW, 6 January 1779.

5   Tann, *Selected Papers*, pp. 156–57.

6   Tann, 'Mr Hornblower', op. cit.

7   Tann, *Selected Papers*, pp. 107–64.

8   MB to Thomas Innes, 3 July 1776, quoted in Anthony Burton, *Richard Trevithick*, 2000.

9   JW to Jonathan Hornblower, 15 December 1776.

10 Thomas Dudley to JW, 26 February 1778, Cornwall Record Office.

11 MB to JW, 30 July 1781.

12 JW jnr to F. Arago, quoted in Eric Robinson & A.E. Musson, *James Watt and the Steam Revolution*, 1969.

13 JW to Thomas Wilson, 10 October 1791; Robinson & Musson, op. cit., pp. 172–78.

14 Tann, 'Mr Hornblower', op. cit.

15 Francis Trevithick, *Life of Richard Trevithick*, 1872.

16 J. Landor to B&W, 4 May 1797.

17 J. Griffiths to B&W, 7 August 1797.

18 Quoted in Tann, 'Mr Hornblower', op. cit.

19 Quoted in Robinson & Musson, op. cit., p. 160.

20 Tann, 'Mr Hornblower', op. cit.

21 Erasmus Darwin to JW, 9 July 1795.

22 Paper read to the Institution of Mechanical Engineers, 1850.

23 For a full account see Burton, op. cit.

24 Jennifer Tann, 'Marketing Methods in the International Steam Engine Market: The Case of Boulton and Watt', *Journal of Economic History*, June 1978.

10

Birmingham Assay Office

The hallmark is a symbol that a purchaser can be assured of the quality standard of the article or goods being purchased. The best-known 'hallmark' of the 1950s and '60s was the 'little lion' stamped on eggs. But while a really bad egg will smell, certainly when cracked, it is more difficult to determine standards and potentially fraudulent practice in other goods without a technical test. The requirement for assaying and marking sterling silver was instituted by an Act of Edward I in 1300, and Edward III granted a charter in 1377 to the Worshipful Company of Goldsmiths, based at Goldsmiths' Hall, hence the term 'hallmark'.[1] In principle the process of assaying and marking has changed very little over the years. It requires precision and dexterity, together with knowledge of chemistry and metallurgy, as well as a scrupulous attention to detail. Such is the skill of those who collect the samples of metal for assay that they claim they can tell the approximate quality of the metal in even the smallest link of a bracelet simply by the feel of the tool across the metal surface.[2]

The Birmingham Assay Office is the only one of Matthew Boulton's initiatives to survive; indeed it is now the largest assay office in the world. Boulton's part in its establishment has been, in part, eclipsed by those aspects of his life which have captured the public imagination rather more, particularly his partnership with James Watt and his role in the Lunar Society. Nevertheless, without Boulton it is likely that the Birmingham Assay Office would not have come into being. Its story is one of intense rivalry between London and the provinces, 'of conflict between the craftsmen and industrialists, and of tension between the old and the new'.[3]

Boulton had been in the business of manufacturing silverware at Soho Manufactory in partnership with John Fothergill since 1766, and in that year – and surely promoted by Boulton – the Earl of Shelburne noted in his wife's diary, following a visit to Samuel Garbett, 'Another thing they are in a great way of is an assay master which is allowed at Chester and York ... it is very hard on a manufacturer to be obliged to send every piece of plate to Chester to be marked.'[4] By 1773, the need to find a solution to the business of assaying had become compelling. Boulton never did things by halves. He had written to the Earl of Shelburne in 1771, setting out his aspirations: 'I am very desirous of becoming a great Silversmith', adding that he would never be able to pursue this in the intended 'Large Way' unless 'powers can be obtained for a Marking Hall at Birmingham'.[5]

If Boulton was aware that for his silver manufacturing business to succeed, an assay office at Birmingham was necessary then why did he wait so long? This is not altogether clear, but the manufacture of silver plate was only one of his business interests, and his capital base was severely strained. Moreover, there is no record in the archives of Chester Assay Office of any complaint from him about damaged goods. Boulton was an exceptionally able networker and lobbyist, and it seems clear that he was prepared to wait in order to gain the longer term advantage. (He had first heard of James Watt's engine developments in the 1760s, but was not prepared to finalise a partnership until the 1775 Act of Parliament was obtained, granting a twenty-five-year patent.) It is clear that Boulton was exerting some pressure upon the Earl of Shelburne on the matter of an assay office and was not, perhaps, above delaying the dispatch of goods to the Earl or commenting on their damage in transit from Chester, in order to make his point. In 1772, Boulton wrote to another peer of the realm, the Duke of Richmond, informing him that Birmingham was expected to petition Parliament for the establishment of an office for assaying and marking wrought plate.[6]

In January 1773, Boulton was in London, deeply involved in parliamentary lobbying. This was a skill to be further honed in the early years of his partnership with James Watt, particularly in seeking overseas privileges/patents for their steam engine. While Boulton would probably have preferred for Birmingham to go it alone, this was not to be. His activities in London had come to the notice of the Sheffield Cutlers' Company and its clerk contacted Boulton to ask if Birmingham manufacturers would permit the workers in plate from Sheffield to join them, 'so as to go hand-in-hand with you to Parliament, and to be both comprehended in the same act of Parliament, only to be separate Companies and separate Offices'.[7] Boulton was well aware that neither Birmingham nor Sheffield was a corporate town. They both represented the business expansion and urban growth of the Industrial Revolution.

There was no mayor before whom an Assay Master could be sworn in, nor were there magistrates. Other English provincial towns which had (or had previously had) assay offices – York, Chester, Exeter, Bristol, Norwich and Newcastle-upon-Tyne – had corporate status.[8]

Boulton & Fothergill's response referred to conversations held with the King as well as their many contacts with the nobility and many current ministers 'who all seemed persuaded of the justness and propriety of the establishing of such an office at Birmingham'.[9] Boulton sought to assure the cutlers of Sheffield that he wished them to be on an equal footing with Birmingham, but he was not prepared to alter his plans without consulting friends and patrons, adding, as if to placate them, that 'there is not the least doubt that if Parliament make such an Act in favour of Birmingham it will not be refused to Sheffield'.[10] Recognising that the Goldsmiths' Company of London was likely to be strongly opposed to the plan, Boulton had some concern that he might be seen to be asking for too much at once. And he seems, at first, to have believed that a positive outcome was more likely to be arrived at if the manufacturers of Birmingham and Sheffield, whether separately or together, should press ahead with all speed. By 18 January 1773, the Sheffield cutlers had prepared their petition and applied to the nobility of the county who had approved of their intended bid to Parliament. Boulton set out for London, having purchased a new hat and gloves especially for the occasion.

It was not long before interest groups in London, in particular the Goldsmiths' Company, began to gather support in opposition to the Birmingham and Sheffield petitions. Boulton had friends behind the scenes, including the Earl of Dartmouth, who was at the time Colonial Secretary and had spoken on Boulton's behalf with Treasury officials earlier in January. Boulton pushed aside London concerns with the comment, 'Were we less accustomed to their want of veracity, I might have been surprised to see so much written on the subject of which I had said so little, and that only to members of Parliament.'[11] Boulton's preference was for the promotion of a general Bill for the whole country which would allow the establishment of assay offices in any town where the manufacture of gold and silverware was sufficient to justify it. This would prompt the closure of offices in towns which no longer had an extensive gold or silver manufacturing industry. However, this would have provoked an even greater outcry than the proposal to establish assay offices in Birmingham and Sheffield (with the requirement that all silver made in those towns, or within 20 miles of them, be submitted for assay and hallmarking).[12]

Petitions were sent from Sheffield and Birmingham to the House of Commons on successive days: Sheffield on 1 February, and Birmingham on 2 February 1773. The Birmingham petition referred to the inconvenience that manufacturers laboured under in sending their goods to Chester some

70 miles distant, for not only was there delay and expense but also hazards such as theft and damage to the goods. The petition implied that Birmingham was being held back by this inconvenience. Boulton had initially thought that the best way would be to obtain a Motion in the House, but following behind-the-scenes advice from the Prime Minister, Lord North, which was given to Boulton by Lord Dartmouth, a petition was deemed to be the more appropriate route.

Both petitions were referred to a Committee of the House of Commons, and Boulton left nothing to chance. He circulated a 'Memorial' to members of the House who would have to vote in due course. This set out the context of the Birmingham petition, emphasising that the main purpose of assaying and hallmarking was consumer protection. Boulton also argued that it was hard to protect new designs when these could be seen by rivals 'before the Inventors have reaped Benefit from them'.[13] He concluded by asserting that silver goods manufacturers in any town threatened by the Birmingham proposal should compete on price and quality rather than privilege. But Boulton, depending upon the case in hand, was perfectly capable of arguing for either free trade or protection, as the situation warranted, and frequently did. His skills as a parliamentary lobbyist were never as stretched, however, nor as effectively used, as in the bid to establish an assay office in Birmingham.

By February the opposition had marshalled its forces and the Goldsmiths' Company presented a petition to the House of Commons on the 17th of the month. They implied that since neither Birmingham nor Sheffield was an ancient corporate town, they had no ancient guilds of goldsmiths and the establishment of assay offices in those places might 'open the door to deceit and uncertainty … and tend to destroy that credit and reputation which the Goldsmiths Manufactory in these Kingdoms has justly acquired'.[14] This petition was also referred to the House of Commons Committee that was considering the Birmingham and Sheffield petitions. Only one person was called as witness for Birmingham and this was Samuel Garbett, manufacturer, friend of Boulton's and a fine parliamentary lobbyist.[15] The Goldsmiths' Company of London and its supporters produced thirty-three witnesses, while the Sheffield case was supported by six. However, Boulton remained in the background in London and was far from idle. In a letter to his wife, he suggested that the battle might take so long that 'I shall not have patience to stay'. Feelings ran high, with accusation and counter-accusation, the London Goldsmiths at one point claiming that Birmingham manufacturers plated goods of steel and other metals with silver to make them look like plate. The Chester Assay Master, interrogated by the Committee, when asked if Boulton & Fothergill had ever sent any plate to be assayed in Chester that was above or under standard, replied, 'It has generally been 2 or 3dwts [pennyweights] above standard.'[16]

It was also suggested that certain of Boulton's former employees, then in London, had been offered bribes to blacken Boulton's name by alleging that they had been paid in counterfeit money. That their paymasters had sought to fill 'Counsel's mouths to be a blot on Mr Boulton's character' cannot have helped the London cause.[17] The local newspaper was quick to defend Birmingham manufacturers, pointing out that there were more manufacturers in gold and silver in the town that anywhere else in the kingdom, and 'in this town there is neither Beggar nor a Justice of Peace'.[18] The argument was so eloquently put that the reader might be forgiven for wondering whether Boulton had a hand in it.

The House of Commons Committee presented its report in March and leave was given for a Bill to be presented. It may come as no surprise that this had already been drafted and submitted to Lord North with a covering letter from Boulton. He made clear that he was prepared to accept 'any amendment' which would enable the desired end to be achieved.[19] The Bill received its first reading on 26 March and its second on 7 April. In the meantime, an inquiry into the conduct of existing assay offices had been instituted and this Committee reported on 29 April, alluding to abuses and impositions that had been committed, stating that further checks and regulations were necessary and that these should be introduced into the new Assay Bill then before Parliament.

Sensing defeat, the Goldsmiths' Company, together with the Goldsmiths and Silversmiths of London, presented further petitions on 6 May, alluding to 'certain abuses' committed in Birmingham and Sheffield. Once more, these were roundly countered in the Birmingham newspaper in a statement by Samuel Garbett, who wrote of the 'Most infamous Reflections' which had been printed in newspapers and handbills, and assured the readers that 'Noblemen and Gentlemen' of eminent rank had agreed to become members of the Birmingham Assay Office when it was allowed to come into being.[20]

With his eyes on victory, Boulton gathered his forces for a final assault on the opposition in mid-May. He addressed the accusations of London Goldsmiths point by point in two handbills, while taking the Goldsmiths and Silversmiths of London to task for producing work of lower value, poorer design and workmanship and yet more highly priced than that of the provinces, suggesting that the petitioners from Birmingham and Sheffield, being distant from some of the main markets, would be particularly concerned that the intrinsic value of their products was incontestable. He also challenged the assertion that the manufacturers of plate in Birmingham and Sheffield had combined, claiming that they were rival towns and had never formed an association.

He showed no mercy in taking the evidence given before the two Committees, demonstrating that the standard of silver produced in London was lower than the legal standard of silver produced in Birmingham by nearly

1 per cent. Moreover, neither the men at Goldsmiths' Hall appointed to scrape specimens from the plate sent, nor the assayer, on whose authority the mark was stamped on plate, received any control or oversight to detect fraudulent practice.[21]

The Committee Stage Report, due to have been presented on 11 May, was delayed as members of the House had sat until 11 p.m. on the previous evening. Whilst the London case was being made by counsel, Boulton, who had 'taken great pains to make a proper impression upon ye members ... [decided to] submit ye case simply to their decision'. However, not one to leave anything to chance, he commented to his partner that were his plans to go awry, he had twice the interest in the House of Lords to that in the House of Commons. Boulton did not stop at senior members of the aristocracy; he had laid his case before the King himself. His personal physician and friend Dr William Small, knowing his technique only too well, had written earlier in the year, 'I hope the King and Royal family, the Nobility and the Ministry and your other friends are well.'[22] And by this stage Boulton seems to have taken on responsibility for promoting Sheffield as well as the Birmingham interest. Several amendments were made to the Bill and, on 17 May, these were considered and agreed by the House, the final reading taking place the following day. On 28 May 1773, the Lords agreed to the Bill without amendment and the Royal Assent, authorising the establishment of assay offices in Birmingham and Sheffield, was given that same day. Boulton returned home triumphantly to the pealing of the Handsworth church bells.

It remained to Boulton to thank the Earl of Dartmouth on his own behalf and that of his neighbours for the very considerable help that had been received. And, since much of the business in London had been transacted at the Crown & Anchor Tavern, a hostelry in the Strand frequented by politicians, it is likely that this is the reason that Birmingham and Sheffield employed the sign of the tavern in their assay office marks. How it was decided is unknown, but ever since 1773, Birmingham's mark has been the anchor, and Sheffield's the crown.[23] In 1904, Sheffield adopted the mark of the Yorkshire rose on gold and, in 1975, also on silver, but the Birmingham Assay Office still uses the anchor.

On 31 August, three months after the Royal Assent had been given, the Birmingham Assay Office opened for business in three rooms above the King's Head Inn, New Street. Boulton & Fothergill were not only the first to register their sponsor mark and to submit work for assaying and hallmarking but they also contributed financially to the setting up of the office.

In Samuel Garbett the Birmingham silversmiths had an advocate with a very considerable knowledge of refining. In his letters to Boulton during the petitions and counter-petitions, the Birmingham case was supported by both knowledge and expertise in the science of metals. Garbett at one stage sent 50oz of silver to Boulton, urging secrecy: 'When you have obtained the Law I suppose you and I shall be made acquainted with their most sacred Art and Mistery – but don't let us give any of them our Real knowledge in exchange for their Shabby Occult Misteries.'[24] As Sally Baggott puts it, science had become the real knowledge and the sacred mystery was shabby and occult, completely reversing the implications of provincial backwardness which had formed the basis of the London case. Garbett asked, 'What must we Country Folks think of the Insolence of such Pretenders to Accuracy?'[25]

Birmingham's assay office contributed to the great expansion of the Jewellery Quarter in the years after 1773, and Birmingham has since then been the home of leading silversmiths whose work is held in international collections and collected worldwide. Boulton's own plate business, while clearly the source of delight to him – with its opportunities to mix with eminent architects and designers on the one hand and aristocratic customers on the other – was not particularly successful in a financial sense. It has been suggested that he overestimated the potential cost reduction of die stamping and had to pay London wage rates to workers he imported to Birmingham, finding himself competing in the London market at London prices.[26]

The 1773 Act permitted the Birmingham Assay Office to assay and mark goods of silver plate, but in 1824 it was granted powers for both gold and silver made in Birmingham or within 30 miles of the town. Makers of gold or silver plate within this radius were required to send their goods to Birmingham for assaying and marking until 1854. The Act specified that the manufacturer had to mark each article with his own mark, the punch having been registered at the assay office, before sending it the article for assay.

The maker's mark consists of the first letters of the first name and surname, or the name of the firm – Boulton's silver plate is marked MB or MB/IF for Boulton & Fothergill. For silver the assay office makes three more marks: the anchor (Birmingham's own mark), the mark which denotes the standard of silver, and the letter of the alphabet denoting the year in which the article is hallmarked. The original Act identified two standards of silver: Sterling Silver (11oz 2dwt per Troy pound – 12oz) and Britannia standard (11oz 10dwt). Prior to 1875, most of the date letter cycles consisted of twenty-five letters, the second and fourth cycle comprising all twenty-six letters of the alphabet. (Assay offices had their own practices with regard to date letters; year letters were not harmonised until 1975.)

Strict and clear procedures were established by the 1773 Act for validating the quality assured by the Birmingham Assay Office. A set of trial plates of silver, deposited at Goldsmiths' Hall, was to be the ultimate standard against which the Birmingham standard would be tested annually, a process known as the trial. At the sampling stage in the process of assaying, the scrapings from each article were divided into two. Half was for the assay and the other half was reserved for the trial, being put into a locked box with three different locks, which was known as the Assayer's Box. The half of the scrapings which were to be assayed were sent forward to be processed. The trial scrapings were sent once a year to the Royal Mint, and the Master of the Mint was required to prepare a memorial to the Lords of the Treasury. If the trial scrapings passed, the material was returned to Birmingham for sale; if the silver was found to be of insufficient quality, the assayer was fined £200 and lost his job. The fine has never been levied.

Birmingham Assay Office was, from the beginning, governed and managed by the Guardians of the Standard of Wrought Plate, who were elected for life. The organisation of the assay office changed little from 1773 to the mid-nineteenth century: thirty-six Guardians were appointed, four of whom were chosen to be Wardens of the Company. The role of Guardian was not oner-ous – Guardians were appointed for their standing in the region or for their knowledge of wrought plate and met just once a year. The first Guardians included members of the aristocracy and gentry, amongst them being the Earl of Dartmouth, Lord Archer, Sir John Wrottesley and Sir Henry Bridgeman. Representatives of the mercantile community included Samuel Garbett, Sampson Lloyd junior and Isaac Spooner. At no time were there to be more than nine or fewer than six trade Guardians, a deliberate decision to ensure the independence for the management of the office. Boulton was one of the first trade Guardians. James Watt became a Guardian in 1789, taking the place of a deceased member, and Matthew Robinson Boulton, Boulton's son was elected in 1792 to take the place of another deceased Guardian. New Wardens were elected each year, Boulton being one of the first four.

The original Act specified that two Wardens were to be present on assaying days and, together with the Assay Master, to inspect plate brought to the office for hallmarking. Wardens were required to supervise the weighing of scrapings into the requisite boxes and were responsible for keeping the register contain-ing the names and marks of all makers within a 20-mile radius of Birmingham. It soon became clear that the position of Warden was not avidly sought and, in 1786, some Guardians sought to resign. Matthew Boulton and Samuel Garbett were appointed to enquire whether, without expense, it would be possible to remove the clause regarding being a Guardian for life in the Act and also to seek to discover whether it would be possible for only one Warden to be present on assaying days. The Guardians' Minutes contain nothing further on this issue and it must be presumed that Boulton and Garbett were advised that it would be better not to raise the issue of the Birmingham Assay Office in Parliament so soon after obtaining their Act.

As with the appointment of Guardians, the Assay Master – someone 'experienced in the assaying of silver' – was appointed for life unless he was found to be neglectful. James Jackson was the first Assay Master and by 1788 the business of the office had increased so much that he requested the appointment of an assistant. In 1789, Thomas Phipson was appointed, succeeding to the post of Assay Master on Jackson's death in 1792. Thus began the dynastic element in the management of Birmingham Assay Office, members of the Phipson and later the Westwood families continuing as Assay Master through to 1971.

The duties of the Assay Master included keeping in touch with other offices, particularly Sheffield and, on occasion, Chester, as well as attendance at special meetings in London to conduct business at Goldsmiths' Hall. If the assay office had to initiate the prosecution of offenders for fraud, the Assay Master played a leading role in collecting evidence for the case.

The by-laws of the Birmingham Assay Office were agreed by the Guardians in November 1773. The office was to be opened up for assaying and marking every Tuesday, plate being required to be brought to the premises from 7 to 9 a.m. between March and September, and from 8 to 10 a.m. between September and March. Manufacturers were required to sort their articles into categories before they were weighed, attaching a note with the date and details to each, and it was established from the outset that no employee was allowed to take 'Box Money Fee Perquisite or Reward' other than his fixed salary or wages. It was also resolved that 'no embosser, worker or chaser in Gold or Silver shall in future be employed in the Assay Office'. It is not clear whether this ruling was made to prevent this happening in the future or whether there was a case behind the ruling.[27]

The Guardians paid attention to enforcing the assay office monopoly for hallmarking in the region and, in 1775, ordered a list of silversmiths and plate workers who had registered their marks at the office to be published in the Birmingham newspapers, together with a warning of the penalties to be incurred by those who did not register. For this to be effective the office had to be able to respond to requests for assaying and hallmarking in reasonable time, and this caused a problem, for the business fluctuated with the state of the market for wrought plate and the toy trades, posing a problem for office administration and the wages bill. With a low level of demand, a modest increase could exert considerable pressure on the system. By 1778, business had increased and it was decided to have two marking days per week – Tuesday and Friday – but by 1785, this was felt to be too frequent and the first Tuesday in every month and every Friday were assigned as assaying and marking days, although, with three days' notice to the Assay Master, extraordinary assay days could be agreed on. The question of the frequency of opening in response to demand which fluctuated with the trade cycle was a major problem for the administration of the office for a number of years.

A regional anomaly emerged at the outset of the assay office's operations, one which in retrospect might have been anticipated. It concerned the respective quality of wares marked in Birmingham and London, some silversmiths complaining in 1775 that they suffered a competitive disadvantage in that silverware marked in London could be of 2 to 2½ pennyweights lower in quality than that marked in Birmingham. The Sheffield office was also discussing 'substandard' London articles and had resolved to put the matter in the hands of one of their MPs if the London practice did not cease. Birmingham Assay Office believed the fault to lie with the London Assay Office rather than the workers in silver or the sellers of the finished article, and thought the only feasible action was that both the assays and the Diet of the Goldsmiths' Company be checked in the same manner as they were at Birmingham and Sheffield. Sheffield claimed that they could not bear any more expenses if a solicitor were to have to be employed to further the case. In 1784, Samuel Garbett produced a draft Bill for the amendment of the 1773 Act, and a special meeting resolved that the Assay Master should apply to the Goldsmiths' Company seeking its opinion. To obtain wider support, the Guardians resolved to ask members of the Birmingham Commercial Committee, an early forerunner of the Chamber of Commerce, to consider the best ways of proceeding. No record survives of the discussions and the question of equality of silver standards between Birmingham and Sheffield and the other assay offices, particularly Goldsmiths' Hall, was not resolved, and neither was Garbett's Bill presented.

The complexity of the Birmingham toy trade and the traditional interdependence of small masters and workmen, as well as the great variety of wares produced, posed particular problems for the regulation and management of Birmingham's assay office compared with those in other towns. While the 1773 Act set out, in some detail, the organisation structure and system of assaying, it did not specify categories of goods which were exempt. These had been covered to some extent by the Act of 1738 and, later, that of 1790, although the question was always a complex one. Many manufacturers sent goods which were not required to be assayed and marked. And wares which consisted of several distinct parts, such as watches, were problematic, manufacturers sometimes altering them after hallmarking. Where a manufacturer believed there to be a less rigorous service, he might send wares to another office illegally. Some Coventry watchmakers, for example, sent wares to Chester for marking and when, at Birmingham's invitation, the Chester Assay Master sent samples to the Birmingham Assay Office it was found that pendants 'of a very inferior standard' had been attached to the watch cases. Some manufacturers intent on cost-cutting resorted to ingenious ways of, for example, filling in hollow goods with solder after they had been hallmarked.

When John Fothergill, Boulton's silver manufacturing partner, died suddenly in 1782, Boulton continued to make silver under his own name, marking it as MB. But, despite the renown of these wares at the time and their lasting significance in collections, Boulton's greater legacy was the Birmingham Assay Office. Established in the teeth of considerable London opposition, it represents the challenge of the provinces to the capital, the new to the old.

Notes

1. The practice of hallmarking seeks to prevent fraud. But this too can be the subject of fraud. In the mid-nineteenth century the practice of faking an antique by employing older designs and faked hallmarks emerged, one which has continued to the present day.

2. Jennifer Tann, *Birmingham Assay Office 1773–1993*, 1993, p. 35.

3. Sally Baggott, 'Real Knowledge and Occult Misteries: Matthew Boulton and the Birmingham Assay Office', in Malcolm Dick (ed.), *Matthew Boulton: A Revolutionary Player*, 2009, p. 202.

4. Sally Baggott, 'I am very desirous of Becoming a Great Silversmith: Matthew Boulton and the Birmingham Assay Office', in Shena Mason (ed.), *Matthew Boulton, Selling what all the world desires*, 2009, p. 47.

5. Ibid., p. 201.

6. Ibid., p. 203.

7. Tann, op. cit., p. 8.

8. Exeter closed in 1883, Chester in 1961, Glasgow in 1964, Newcastle in 1884, Norwich in 1702, York in 1857.

9. Tann, op. cit., p. 18.

10. Ibid.

11. Ibid.

12. It was not until 1854 that wares could be sent to an assay office of the manufacturer's choice, Tann, op. cit., p. 40.

13. Tann, op. cit., p. 20.

14. Ibid., p. 20.

15. 'Samuel Garbett and the Early Development of Parliamentary Lobbying, in Great Britain', *Economic History Review*, 10, 3, 1958.

16. Baggott, 'Real Knowledge and Occult Misteries: Matthew Boulton and the Birmingham Assay Office', quoted in Mason, op. cit., p. 49.

17. Ibid., p. 51.

18. Tann, op. cit., p. 21.

19. Ibid., p. 22.

20. Ibid.

21. Ibid., p. 23.

22 Ibid., p. 24.

23 Ibid., p. 26.

24 Baggott, 'Real Knowledge and Occult Misteries: Matthew Boulton and the Birmingham Assay Office', p. 214.

25 Ibid.

26 Ibid., p. 215.

27 Tann, op. cit., pp. 61–62.

11

Money & Medals

Matthew Boulton, ever a man with an eye to the main chance, was quick to recognise that some of the technologies employed in the button trade could be transferred to the making of coins and medals. This recognition coincided with an emerging market for substitutes for small denomination coinage. The Royal Mint, the place of manufacture of coins on Government instruction, had struck relatively little copper coin since 1754 – a small amount being minted in 1762–63, rather more in 1770–75, and none at all for the two subsequent decades. Inevitably, counterfeiting flourished, and had been a growing problem since the 1720s.

Unfortunately for Birmingham's reputation, many of the small backstreet workshops with screw presses employed for legitimate purposes were also employed in making counterfeit coinage. And although not all counterfeit half-pennies were made in Birmingham, a large proportion was. Until mid-century they were usually cast in moulds, but screw presses became more frequently used from then onwards. Essentially, all that was required was a knowledge of the basic techniques, a safe place to make the counterfeits, and the know-how to get rid of them as quickly as possible.[1] A London magistrate estimated that two or three people could produce between 96,000 and 144,000 counterfeit halfpennies in the matter of a week. Some Birmingham counterfeiters were sufficiently blatant to practise their craft more or less openly, selling on to the wholesale dealers, who then sold to the end users. Boulton noted that some Birmingham makers advertised what they were doing, putting up signs in the street advertising that copper coins were made there:

> You can have no Idea of the immense quantity of bad ½ pence that are
> made in London & Birmingham, many of our Knights of the Sadle [*sic*]
> Bag take out upon their Journeys pattern cards of half pence as regularly as
> the two of Buttons to get orders & some Manufacturers of them have the
> audacity to hang up Signs in the Street ALL SORT OF COPPER COINS
> MADE HERE.[2]

It is clear that Birmingham's reputation for shoddy goods (Brummagem
wares) was widely recognised; one commentator was clear that counterfeit
halfpennies emanated from 'shabby dishonest button makers in the dark lanes
of Birmingham'.[3]

Traditionally, money had been made by 'hammering'. The imprints on the
face and reverse of the coins were made in two moulds called dies, one die
with the face and the other with the back. A 'blank' – a piece of copper, silver
or gold of the requisite thickness – was placed between the dies, which were
held together by clips. The dies were then hit by brute force. This was not only
a time- and energy-consuming, as well as expensive, way to make coinage, but
the resulting coins were inconsistent in appearance and easy to counterfeit. It
was estimated in the mid-eighteenth century that half of the copper coinage
in circulation was counterfeit. Silver and gold coins were also copied.

Boulton's first mechanical innovation in coining was the use of the screw
or fly press, a heavy machine requiring two or three men with ropes attached
to the heavy ball on the lever fixed to the screw, which they activated by a
rapid jerk. The screw press had been invented in the seventeenth century and
Boulton already used it in his toy business. Its application to minting enabled
the two faces of the coin to be lined up, permitting greater accuracy and consistency of image. James Watt recorded that he and Boulton had had numerous
conversations in about 1774 on the application of steam power to coining.
Boulton proposed that the coin be struck in a collar which would keep the
diameter exact and permit the border of the coin to be raised, the better to
take wear and tear. Each coin was to be of a specified thickness.

The process of coining involved rolling the metal to the required thickness,
cutting out the blanks to the required diameter, putting the blanks into the
dies and collar, and feeding them into the screw press. The coins were subsequently cleaned and polished. Some of Boulton's minting equipment was
retained at Birmingham Mint until its closure.

Boulton's first step towards becoming a coin manufacturer was taken in
1787, when he contracted to supply the East India Company with copper
coins for Bencoolen (Benkulen), the company supplying the copper to Soho
Manufactory, where the blanks were made, being subsequently converted
into coins on hand presses which Boulton installed in a London warehouse.

Convoluted this may have been, but it demonstrated Boulton's capability to mint, besides being an incentive to establish a mint at Soho. He did not manage to deliver the coins on schedule – transporting the blanks to London being partly to blame – but, as Boulton reflected, 'in all new manufactures & new establishments there will be both losses in time & money at first setting out'.[4] The East India Company was annoyed at the delay but, nevertheless, gave a second order, this time for Sumatran coins.

The Royal Mint was slow to act to prevent counterfeiting. Within the knowledge of existing technology, it could have increased the weight of coins, marked the edges to make copying more difficult, and reproduced dies mechanically so that each was identical. Moreover, the standard of engraving was not high and because the mint did not call in its copper coinage it remained in circulation, becoming so worn that it would have been difficult to distinguish the genuine product from a fake.

A further complication, and also an opportunity, was presented by the appearance of trade tokens from 1787 onwards. These were produced by manufacturers and tradespeople in response to the dire national shortage of coin of small denominations. The first token was issued by Thomas Williams, 'The Copper King', who, as we have seen, had more or less cornered the market for copper from his vast Parys Mine on Anglesey, and trade tokens were soon issued by a number of businesses, their name being on the face of the token. While some tokens had a purely local value, others, such as those issued by Thomas Williams and some other major manufacturers and merchants, were widely trusted and came into more general circulation. Many of these tokens were produced in Birmingham, some by Boulton.

The growth of counterfeit coinage prompted business optimism to get the better of Boulton and he convinced himself that a Government contract for copper coinage would soon be in hand. Samuel Garbett campaigned for Boulton, pointing out that the coinage 'must be considered as a manufacture by which reasonable profit may be made'.[5] In 1788, anticipating that a Government order for coinage was imminent, and having been to discuss a new copper coinage with Prime Minister Pitt and the Privy Council, Boulton began to build 'a Mint & new Manufactory for it in my Farm Yard behind the Menagery at Soho'.[6]

Boulton and Watt had visited Paris in 1786 at the invitation and expense of the French Government, the reason being to observe the ancient system by which water was raised from the River Seine at Marly to supply the royal palaces. These waterwheels and pumps had been in existence for some long time and there was the possibility of an order for a steam engine to replace them. Boulton, interested as he was in supplying a steam engine to replace the wheels at Marly, had other interests too. One of these was to visit and learn from French expertise at the Paris Mint. In this way, he was able to meet with able men, including Jean-Pierre Droz, a talented die-sinker (one who designed and engraved the image on the die). Droz had a personal agenda to gain employment from France's First Minister, Calonne. It seems likely that Droz thought two agendas could be met by showing the hand of friendship to Boulton. However, three months after Boulton and Watt had returned to Soho, Calonne had fallen from power. Not only did it seem likely that the best laid plans for exporting to France had fallen on bad ground, but George III's illness had put paid, for the time being, to plans for a British Regal copper coinage. Even by 1789, it was unclear whether Prime Minister Pitt would address the issue of currency when he had other major concerns. And by this time Boulton had employed Droz, who had intimated that he could improve Boulton's coining technology.

The success of the first Soho Mint was dependent in some considerable measure on the employment of skilled die-sinkers. Boulton persuaded himself that Droz was a key figure, and from the beginning of 1787 he worked to bring him to Soho. He then had the problem of trying to get Droz to do things once he had arrived. Boulton began correspondence with him in March 1787, at a time when he had no firm orders for any large-scale minting. Droz was commissioned to work on a die with the head of George III. Boulton sent several representations of the King to help him in this task, and Droz was then to strike silver pieces from it and send them to Britain. But Droz did not bother to reply for some five weeks and then complained about the quality of the portraits of the King that he had been sent. He also stated that he had devised a new way of marking his coin edges in a collar. And, as Droz's prospects for a French coinage diminished with his patron's fall, he offered to come to England if that were Boulton's wish. Through the spring and summer of 1787, Boulton entreated, wheedled and sought to persuade, to little effect. Finally, he offered to pay Droz £100 for the drawings and £100 for every press built on Droz's model. Each time Boulton asked for something more, Droz raised the price. Droz finally came to Britain in early September 1787, returning to Paris in October, apparently fired with enthusiasm. But he appears to have had to be played like a fish – one that, at the time, appeared to be worth catching. Boulton assigned a house for Droz and made it clear that the work on the structure of the mint had been completed. He finally arrived at Soho and it fairly quickly dawned on Boulton that Droz was no more likely to deliver the goods in Birmingham than he had in France; every way he turned, Boulton was given half promises or rewarded with complaints.[7]

Boulton began to have serious doubts about the wisdom of bringing Droz to England, for he continued to raise the stakes and failed to deliver what he promised. Boulton therefore started a search for a successor, and in a letter to a possible replacement in France he referred to Droz as 'the Great Artist ... who can do everything with his Tongue (except speak English).'[8] Moreover, the hoped-for contract for a copper coinage order for Britain failed to materialise. (Doty suggests that this was due to behind-the-scenes opposition from the Royal Mint, which could not match Boulton's production in either quality or speed.)[9] Droz, who had arrived with an entourage of a hairdresser, an artisan and a mistress, was lazy and secretive. The medal for the King's recovery, produced in 1789, was just about the only work Boulton ever got out of him. He would not share his craft skills, his non-performance was spectacular, and the success of the first mint, seemingly against all odds, was due in large measure to the people whom Boulton employed from the local population, besides trusted associates from the engine business.

Zacchaeus Walker, Boulton's brother-in-law and business associate, did not pull his punches:

> I can not conceive Mr Droz, either honest in Principal, or good in disposition – Honesty in Principal will not warrant one man in taking another's Money without performing what he promises and rendering the agreed value of the money.[10]

Boulton agreed to give Droz one final chance and, in November 1789, an agreement was drawn up, but he was pretty sure that Droz would fail to keep his side of the agreement and, in this event, Boulton would not have to pay. Indeed, in the same month, Boulton was writing to Paris to find a new assistant who could turn portraits on a lathe in order to produce the images for dies. The man in question was Rambert Dumarest. He stayed at Soho less than a year but produced designs for a number of coins and tokens. Finally, Boulton went to arbitration with Droz, which found in the former's favour, Droz being required to deliver his models, dies and puncheons, besides teaching Boulton or his nominee how to complete a coining press expertly and to teach employees at Soho all he knew about die making. Droz finally departed, but not before another French medallist, Noel Alexandre Pouthon, signalled his wish to resign because of what he saw as preference being given to Droz. He added that the English seemed to prefer a highly finished work to a work of art.[11]

Boulton had invested heavily in Soho Mint between 1786 and 1789, during which he needed to find uses for his presses, in the absence of the hoped-for Government coinage contract, while increasing and improving his knowledge and techniques of manufacturing coins. In his communications with the Privy Council in 1789, Boulton pointed out that 'though I must unashamedly lament the derangement of our beloved Sovereign's health and the probable fall of the prosperity which this Country so recently and eminently enjoyed, yet amid the calamities, I cannot help turning my thoughts to the loss I am likely to sustain by the probability of the copper coinage falling to the ground'.[12] Boulton reminded their Lordships that he had perfected his apparatus which was now capable of making coin 'superior in Beauty & Workmanship', besides which it effectively prevented counterfeiting. In this latter claim he severely underestimated the capabilities of some of his competitors in the market. As David Symons remarks, it was the quality of the preparation and the use of the collar in striking that enabled Boulton to mint more rapidly and consistently than others and, while he could not eliminate counterfeiting, he raised the stakes against the back-street copiers.[13]

Complaints about the state of the national currency were made in many quarters; meetings were held and petitions raised. It was the workers who suffered most by being paid in counterfeit or token coinage which might only be accepted at a discount. Boulton found it difficult to pay his own workforce and, with his usual energy, set about reform. In 1789, he wrote to the Privy Council, pointing out that small manufacturers and traders purchased counterfeit halfpence at little more than their nominal value, and their labourers suffered. But it was not to be. Indeed, it was not until 1797 that Lord Liverpool invited Boulton to London to discuss a new coinage.

In the absence of the Government contract, Boulton had to justify the mint's existence by undertaking other contract work. One of his first, in 1789, was as subcontractor to John Westwood for Roe & Co. of Macclesfield and an Irish mining company, as well as undertaking a total mintage of over 29½ tons of coinage for Thomas Williams' Anglesey company. In December 1790, Boulton received advice that there was a contract for Bombay coinage which could be his. However, the East India Company had previously agreed that Thomas Williams would supply the copper. When Williams heard that a business rival had been given the minting contract, he delayed and only delivered the copper under pressure. A year later, Boulton could proudly report that he had delivered all the 100 tons of coinage ordered by the company. In nine months he had struck over 17 million coins for Bombay.[14]

With orders for medals and tokens being irregular and generally small-scale, the coinage order from Monneron Brothers in 1791 must have seemed like a gift from the gods (see below). Boulton and, indeed, Wedgwood had been sending goods to France in the wake of a commercial treaty between Britain and France. There was a huge demand for military buttons for national guardsmen in France. All looked set fair. Boulton's aspirations in the French market involved three main alternatives. First, he could supply one or more complete steam-powered mints and install them; alternatively he could supply coin blanks to France where they could be struck; and, third, if all else failed, he could produce unofficial token currency and medals to order.[15]

Boulton's first two aspirations were not fulfilled and, in time, it was clear that the third was destined to founder too. First, Minister Calonne had committed considerable resources to the visit by Boulton and Watt to France in 1786. Boulton's decision to work with the Monneron brothers was undertaken in the knowledge that he had failed to influence the politicians then in power to accede to either of his first two proposals. Boulton's agent in Paris endorsed the respectability of the Monnerons and, by the summer of 1791, he was buying quantities of cake copper, with the intention of providing the brothers with commercial token coinage, sending over specimen coins of different weights and sizes for his partners to inspect. But, while tokens were widespread in Britain and reasonably officially tolerated, this was not the case in France. There were few token producers compared with the large number in Britain, and it has been suggested that the quality of their output was poor.[16] The first of the tokens to be issued featured a reference to an article of the Declaration of the Rights of Man, and, to begin with, these tokens were popular and met a need for low-value coinage. But by the spring of 1792, it was becoming clear that token coinage would not be permitted for much longer; accordingly, Boulton and the Monnerons turned their attention to commemorative medallions, which were safer. But this required fundamental re-tooling in the mint and could not be undertaken immediately, Boulton promising to make as many as 'my Button guilders can do, without stopping my Button Manufactory'.[17] The Monnerons had originally envisaged a series of commemorative medallions celebrating people and events of the Revolution. One of the key people to be so commemorated was Lafayette. But, in August, he defected and it became clear that the position of the Monneron brothers was somewhat precarious. Boulton told his daughter Anne that he had received two letters from one of the brothers, who took his leave, intimating 'that before the letter comes to my hand he will be no more'.[18] Boulton finally ceased his dealings with the brothers in March 1794 and, in the process, suffered considerable financial loss. Nonetheless, what this episode provided was a demonstration of the capability of the Soho Mint, for he had struck well over 7 million 2 and 5 sol copper tokens for France, besides several thousand medallions and tokens and medals in silver and gilt.

Early in 1791, a large order arrived for coinage for Bombay. And then in March, Albion Mills burned down, costing Boulton several thousand pounds, which he could ill afford, besides losing a major showcase for the steam engine and for an integrated manufacturing unit.[19] The combination of a lack of orders, the Droz affair and the mills burning led to lost tempers in the mint; James Lawson, a trusted middle-ranking Soho employee, was so severely tried in the early hours one morning that he came to blows with another employee. Boulton needed to focus on Soho to calm things down. During the period of coining for the Monnerons, there was the additional pressure of designs being changed, besides the strain on production and machinery occasioned by the size and weight of the largest tokens. These were a cause of two quite serious industrial accidents in which one of the bars of the press broke and hurt first one workman and, a few days later, a second. The Monneron tokens were tearing the mint apart.

In September 1792, Boulton asked one of his clerks to compile a statement of the profits and losses of Soho Mint, from the beginning of the coinage to the present time. The costs on coinage before 1791 amounted to nearly £6,500 and, with the cost of presses and other expenses for the buildings, the total came to £7,780. Against these debits was 321 tons of copper made into coin and tokens, which generated a little over £5,000. Boulton had struck almost three-quarters of a million pounds of copper and was £2,500 in the red.[20] Soho Mint did not become a fully viable business until Boulton gained the first Regal coining contract in 1797. Soho Mint was subject to periods of little activity, interspersed with feverish work to accomplish orders. And Boulton was concerned for the well-being of his employees. In lean times workmen had to be laid off. Boulton did his best to solicit orders and continued to agitate for a British coinage, while looking out for opportunities overseas. He appealed to Robert Wissett at East India House, asking if there was any likelihood of a new coinage for the company. An American industrial spy, Thomas Digges, reported to Thomas Jefferson in 1793 that Boulton was 'by far the neatest & best Coiner & has a more excellent apparatus for Coining than any in Europe'.[21]

Meanwhile, Boulton continued to mint private tokens. There were four issues for different customers in 1795 and 1796, and in 1796 he received an order for the Gold Coast. Unfortunately the three largest denominations contained a misspelling: 'PARLIMENT'. The error was not detected until the coins were in circulation, but in 1801 a new shipment was requested and the error corrected. In 1797, he received an order for American commemorative medals, including one of the President, but was concerned that they were required to be somewhat larger than a dollar and the thickness of a half-dollar, 'which is something like asking for a small pocket Bible in a very large print'.[22]

In March 1797, Boulton received communication from the Earl of Liverpool that the Government was considering a new coinage. 'There is no Man who can better judge of the Propriety of this measure and of the plan that ought to be adopted.' Boulton was asked to go to London to meet the Earl and Prime Minister Pitt. The new British coinage order was for pennies and twopenny pieces. There would be no raised, lettered edge; they would be struck in a simple rather than a segmented collar, the designs being less artistic than had been envisaged ten years previously. The Government made a decision in March 1797, but Boulton did not receive a formal contract until June, although, in the meantime, he had to take the risk of acquiring copper, consulting on the details for the reverse of the coin and getting confirmation as to which engraving of the King's head the monarch preferred. Boulton began to coin for the British Government on 19 June 1797. But Soho had to contend with an imposed inspector/controller in the form of one Joseph Sage, the senior moneyer at the Tower, someone who quickly became an enemy. By the time the dies were destroyed, in conformance with the contract under the scrutiny of Sage, on 26 July 1799, Soho Mint had coined nearly 43 million pennies and some 700,000 twopenny pieces, although Boulton had to chivvy for payment: 'A man of large landed Property may put off from time to time, the day after payment, but a Merchant must pay his acceptances to an hour or he falls.'[23]

Soho Mint was coining not only British currency. An order for Sumatra was undertaken in 1798, and one for the Isle of Man in 1799. In the late summer of 1799, Boulton had once more to authorise the discharge of some of the mint operatives in view of the lack of forthcoming business. But, in 1802, he was asked to undertake coinage for Madras – it was a large order – and this was followed by orders for Bombay and Ceylon. Thus began what Richard Doty calls 'Soho Mint's greatest days', which lasted from the autumn of 1802 until the spring of 1811, some two years after Boulton's death.[24] Since 1797, there had been a proposal and two attempts to countermark Spanish Pieces of Eight for the Bank of England. Both attempts had failed (and had been widely forged) but, in 1804, Boulton came up with the idea of striking an image as large as the coin itself in a one-piece collar. He observed that he would not be able to obliterate completely the Spanish markings on the coins, but argued that some retention of the original image might be a safeguard against forgery.[25] He always referred to these as 'regenerated dollars'. This, too, was a means of demonstrating the superiority of Soho Mint technology, for the re-struck coins would have far greater clarity and precision in the making than the originals. Every day, 40,000 dollars were re-struck; by late June 1804, over a million coins had been over-struck. Soon after this he was producing a new copper coinage for Ireland. Ever alert to the possibility of new orders, he told Sir Joseph Banks, 'Please to remember that in the year 1802 I coin'd 80 million of small pieces of copper money ... My best coining customer is the East India Co. from whom I have two considerable orders in hand.'[26]

Boulton mainly produced coins in copper, but there are examples in white metal, gilt, copper, silver and gold. He never invaded the Royal Mint's privilege with respect to gold coinage, although he did use gold for specialised medals and he struck silver coinage for Sierra Leone, as well as over-striking the silver tokens for the Bank of England and Bank of Ireland.

Celebratory medals continued to be minted and, after the Battle of Trafalgar in October 1805, Boulton determined on a medal of Nelson. One fan wrote ecstatically from London:

> When Britons, ages hence, shall fondly trace
> Their Hero's features on the Medal's face
> And while they glory in their Nelson's fame
> They'll not forget the patriotic Boulton's name.[27]

Lady Hamilton was, however, less impressed, finding not much resemblance to Nelson – no more than in the two earlier attempts at a likeness.[28] In the autumn of 1803, Boulton commissioned his own medal; on the one side was his portrait and on the other a brief history of Soho Mint, with the number of coins of various sizes which could be produced per minute. What better way to counteract threats of piracy and dubious claims than to show the capability of Soho Mint and its creator in an outstanding product of the mint.

Notes

1   David Symons, 'Matthew Boulton and the Forgers', in Richard Clay & Sue Tungate (eds), *Matthew Boulton and the Art of Making Money*, 2009, p. 3.

2   MB to Sir G. Shuckburgh-Evelyn, March 1797.

3   George Selgin, *Good Money: Birmingham Button Makers, the Royal Mint, and the Beginnings of Modern Coinage, 1775–1821*, 2008, p. 30.

4   MB to John Motteux, 19 April 1787, quoted in Richard Doty, *The Soho Mint & the Industrialization of Money*, 1998, p. 300.

5   S. Garbett to MB, 31 March 1787.

6   For a description of Boulton's Mint in the landscape see Ballard et al., *A Lost Landscape: Matthew Boulton's Gardens at Soho*, 2009, pp. 13–15, 21.

7   Doty, op. cit., p. 38.

8   MB to Duperat, March 1790, quoted ibid., p. 41.

9   Ibid., pp. 145–51.

10 Z. Walker to MB.

11 Noel A. Pouthon to MB, September 1791.

12 MB to Lord Hawkesbury, 12 January 1789.

13 Symons, op. cit., p. 10.

14 Sue Tungate, 'Technology, Art and Design in the Work of Matthew Boulton ...', in M. Dick (ed.), *Matthew Boulton, A Revolutionary Player*, 2009, pp. 185–86.

15 Peter Jones, 'Trading in Liberté: the commercial token and medal coinage of the Monneron Frères', in Clay & Tungate, op. cit., p. 28.

16 Ibid., p. 29.

17 MB to Monnerons.

18 MB to AB, 8 April 1792, M. Boulton Papers, Boulton Family, 71. MB later learned that Monneron had survived.

19 Albion Mills at Blackfriars, London, was a showcase for B&W, both of whom were partners in the business.

20 Selgin, op. cit., p. 119.

21 Jones, op. cit., p. 38.

22 MB to Rufus King, 29 January 1797.

23 MB to Lord Liverpool, 9 June 1799.

24 Doty, op. cit., p. 61.

25 M. Boulton Papers, RSD, 7.

26 MB to Sir Joseph Banks, 30 January 1804.

27 W.T. Fitzgerald to MB, January 1807.

28 J.I. Tuffin to MRB, 26 February 1806.

12

Mints

Matthew Boulton's first major coining undertaking (for the East India Company) was accomplished using traditional technologies and without steam power. The major process improvement, until then, had been the adoption of the fly press. With this machine the two faces of the coin – the obverse and reverse – could be struck at the same time. The fly press, in use in the Birmingham toy trade from the late sixteenth century, was a heavy piece of equipment and required two or three men to operate it.

Soho Mints

James Watt recalled that he and Boulton had had many conversations from around 1774 on the subject of steam power and its application to coining in rolling metal strip and operating presses.[1] With the prospect of obtaining a contract for a new British currency, Boulton had determined to erect a purpose-built mint at Soho, incorporating new presses and a steam engine to drive them. He experimented in January 1788 with aligning the coining presses into rows, linked to the engine by sliding rods. By November, the presses were arranged in a circle, being powered by bars from a horizontal wheel turning above. By the end of 1788, six presses had been fitted up and set to work, together with plant to roll copper to a consistent thickness, cutting out blanks, as well as forging and multiplying the dies. At this stage, Boulton was employing known methods for minting, albeit with an attention to detail and incremental improvements which ensured greater consistency of product

and speed in execution. His major innovation at this stage was an organisa-
tional one, in that each machine was located in a logical relationship to the
others, the materials being fed from one machine to another through shoots
into boxes in order to minimise handling. This is the origin of flow production
which has characterised efficient factories ever since and was the technology
that he used for the copper coinage for the American colonies and the silver
coinage for Sierra Leone.

Good quality metal was essential for blanks, copper being delivered as sheet
or cake. The metal was rolled a number of times in order to achieve the precise
desired thickness. Then a steam-powered press punched the discs to a specific size and weight, the blanks being smoothed in shaking banks which were
powered by steam. The blanks were cleaned again, sometimes with sulphuric
acid or lime, and dried with sawdust. Peter Ewart, a millwright and later a
cotton spinner, who was a friend of James Watt junior, devised an improved
method of burnishing blanks by putting them between brushes at an angle
so that the pieces came out perfectly well brushed.[2] The polished blanks were
then ready to be struck in the mint's coining presses, being fed by gravity into
a vertical tube attached to the press. After the pieces had been struck, they
were checked, counted, weighed and packaged.

To be able to mint coins or tokens consistently and speedily was not sufficient for Boulton. He wanted to demonstrate his capability as a producer of
goods with a strong aesthetic and this depended on the quality of the images
on the obverse and reverse of the medals and tokens. He therefore directed his
attention to die making. Two dies were necessary and in order to speed the
whole process up, dies needed to be made with shallower images which gave
them a longer life, less force being needed in striking. Boulton introduced the
collar, a ring-shaped piece of metal which surrounded the blank and ensured
that the edges of the coins were straight, vertical and consistent in size.

On returning from attending the Privy Council Committee on Coinage
in London in 1788, Boulton received a message from the French engraver and
die-sinker, Jean-Pierre Droz in Paris, asserting that everything so far done on
the first coining press at Soho was wrong but, nonetheless, he would prepare
a model of the correct coining press – as if Boulton had not been trying to
get such information from him for some time. Boulton needed patterns for
halfpennies as a demonstration of Soho Mint's capabilities and Droz complained about the trouble this caused him. The Lords had given Boulton until
1 June to have his mint up and running, and he needed eight cutting-out
presses and six coining presses to be ready within five months, in addition to
several new buildings and a steam engine to power the apparatus. None of
this would be done by 1 June 1788, but some of the small presses were ready
and employees recruited.

The number of coining presses to be powered by the overhead wheel was increased from six to eight. Boulton and his employees had a head start in practical learning as to what worked and what did not, and Soho Mint is an example of more or less continuous technical innovation. James Lawson, John Southern, Busch and Peploe and other employees created the mint in spite of Droz (who had been expected to contribute so much) rather than with his help. A spirit of invention pervaded the mint. In accessing the skills of men employed in the engine business, Boulton was able to transfer expertise from one business to another and accelerate the transfer of technical ideas and practices.

In 1790, concerned that Droz might claim the steam coining press as his own invention, Boulton took out a patent (pat. 1757) for the 'application of motive power to Stamping and Coining'. His coining patent covered eight coining presses connected to a steam engine, the specification describing two alternative means for producing powered coinage, both of which Boulton claimed to have invented. The method for connecting the engine to the coining presses used at the first Soho Mint was serviceable, and Lawson later commented that so much money had been sunk in this that Boulton should not abandon it for a supposed preferable design without a compelling need.

Boulton, with some degree of well-deserved pride, described what Soho Mint could do:

> Each machine is capable of being adjusted in a few minutes, so as to strike any number of pieces of money from fifty to one hundred and twenty per minute in proportion to their diameter and degree of relief ... The whole of the eight presses are capable of coining, at the same time, eight different sizes of money.[3]

He went on to describe how each machine required only a 12-year-old boy to supervise a press. And because the blows of the machine were more uniform than when operated by manual power, the dies were far less liable to break. In a communication to Garbett, he added:

> Of all the mechanical subjects I have ever entered into in my life there is none in which I ever engaged with so much ardour as in the perfecting of the coin in the reign of G ye 3rd ... I have succeeded in all my mechanical attempts to the extent of my wishes.[4]

When, at last, there seemed every prospect of obtaining a Government coinage contract, in 1797, Boulton began thinking about constructing a new Soho Mint embodying the learning achieved from the first 1788 one, and in May he wrote to John Southern, 'I hope you have not lost sight of the new Mint for I am perswaded that it will be far more compleat & harmonious than the present one, & the more I think about it the more I am pleased'.[5] Southern, a trusted engineer and head of the drawing office at Soho, persuaded him to adopt an entirely new method of conveying power to the coining presses. Boulton encouraged Southern to construct the mechanism and, if it worked, undertook to pay him £500 for the idea, making him superintendent of the mint machinery. It did, and Boulton paid up.[6]

No longer was there a circular arrangement of presses but a linear one. When the new coining room was built, Boulton wrote detailed instructions about the arrangement of the rooms, how the metal should be rolled and cleaned, and how the dies should be forged. His intention was a form of flow production in which raw metal entered one part of the building and finished coinage exited from the other. When the steam-powered presses were working optimally, they were capable of coining rapidly. And, as so often happened in the early Industrial Revolution, this innovation created a bottleneck upstream in the production system and fast-acting blank feeder machines had to be designed to match the speed of the presses. The new mint was completed in spring 1799, and in May, Southern reported that 'all the eight presses have been at work together for a considerable time this morning'.[7] The old mint could now be demolished.

Joshua Gilpin, an American Quaker, visited the new Soho Mint in August 1799 and noted in detail the processes of coining manufacture. He described the steam engine located in the room above that contained the presses. A boy, aged about 12, wearing a blue and red uniform, attended each press, his task being to put the blanks into the hopper, which fed the die and put the coins in an iron box when minted. Boulton used a single rolling mill to produce all the metal required at Soho, both for coinage and all other uses.[8]

The second Soho Mint was Boulton's showcase. As William Murdoch later said, it was 'the favourite and nearly the sole object of the last 20 years of the active part of Mr Bolton's life'.[9]

Russian Mint

The possibility of a mint order being made on behalf of the Empress of Russia was highly prestigious; one which, like the proverbial hooked fish, Boulton had to play over a number of years. Discussions began in 1795, but the Napoleonic Wars adversely affected the project. This was not the only reason for it taking far longer than expected to come to fruition. Some of the delay was due to Boulton and his colleagues having to learn how to design and implement a major initiative thousands of miles distant from Birmingham.

The Russian Mint was not fully operational for twelve years. It is likely that serious discussion began in 1795, and Boulton was approached by Alexander Baxter in May 1796, then acting as Russian Consul-General in London, who wrote on behalf of Empress Catherine the Great, concerning the purchase of all necessary apparatus and machinery for striking coinage and 'some masterly hands to engrave dies'. Baxter suggested that the mint should be capable of producing coin worth £1 million each year. Boulton drew up an estimate for the mint comprising eight presses, especially created to strike heavy Russian coins, together with eight cutting-out presses, three edge-marking machines, four apparatuses for drying blanks, one or two turning lathes and the requisite connecting mechanisms, together with a steam engine and oak beams to fix the machinery in place. The total amounted to £6,520. A rolling mill not originally included in the quote was added later. Boulton was asked to go to Russia to superintend the mint construction or to substitute two British engineers of his choice. There were concerns about the requisite permission for export being given, but he was assured that this could be obtained.[10]

Many difficulties lay ahead; the Empress died of apoplexy and it was by no means clear whether her son, Tsar Paul I, would favour the project. A Russian delegation of five set out for Birmingham to learn about coining, arriving in January 1797. The new Tsar proposed to construct a minting facility quickly, stating that the Alexandrovsky Machine Works would supply the coining presses and steam engine, while for the management of this new Bank Mint, he would rely on Charles Gascoigne, a former acquaintance – and an untrustworthy one at that – of Boulton's.

After two years of wrangling to obtain the necessary permissions to export the mint, Boulton was informed in February 1797 that the order was cancelled and the Russian associates were required to leave for home. It is likely that Gascoigne had managed to persuade the Tsar of his abilities. Boulton, undeterred, continued to draw up plans. The mint included a more automated system of transferring work between departments than at Soho, coinage passing from one section of the works to another by tubes. Five months after having been told that he had lost the contract, Boulton received news that it was to be reinstated. One reason may have been the fact that Gascoigne's plans failed to deliver. Indeed, some coins were struck by his machinery, but it is unlikely that they were produced by steam power. Six Russians arrived at Soho in early 1798, including Alexander Deriabin, who was to be taught the metallurgical aspects of minting. Another colleague learned how to sink dies, a father and son learned how to direct and maintain machinery, and two men were to be trained in instrument making. A contract between the Russian Government and Soho was drawn up. Boulton had imagined that the coining arrangement would be the same as at Soho – powered by an overhead steam-driven wheel. But the Russian Government required coining to be done in separate departments for gold, silver and copper, and this would not have been possible under Boulton's original plan. After having given this some thought, he wrote:

> I have now invented the means of working any Number of Presses, placed almost in any direction in different rooms & at the same time to strike very large Money with 1 Press & very small money with another ... Before I attempt to erect any Part of it in Russia, it shall be erected & tried here.[11]

Boulton proposed a coining room for each metal: two presses for gold, four for silver and six for copper, later changing the plan to one press for gold, three for silver and four for copper. He set out his approach to flow production involving separate departments for each process or operation, never allowing those who worked in one apartment to enter another, arranging the rooms 'in such an order that the Metal & the money shall go forward progressively from one room to another'. And these consecutive processes were to be undertaken at the same level on the ground floor '& never be carried up & down, that being expensive'.[12] A model of the proposed mint was dispatched to Russia in October 1798, and Boulton recommended an architect by the name of Dixon, whom he knew 'to be a man of character and abilities'.[13] John Rennie was to undertake the millwork and rolling mill, as he would do later at the Royal Mint in London (see below). In response to the request for a timetable, Boulton replied that the machinery and steam engine could be ready to sail in April or May 1799, and that the whole could be installed in 1799.[14] As Doty remarks, 'Of all the optimistic pronouncements of Matthew Boulton, none would be more breathtakingly inaccurate than this.'[15]

In the summer of 1799, an Act of Parliament was passed allowing Boulton to export the mint and enabling skilled craftsmen to travel to Russia to set it up. This was not achieved without protest. Mechanics were worried that the export of technology would lead to Britain being undercut in world markets. Recalling the fateful Birmingham riots of 1791, in which public anger was violently expressed against dissenters, some of whom were known to support the French Revolution, Boulton was anxious. On 1 May 1800, disturbances and protest meetings took place in Birmingham and, the following month, forty-seven merchants signed a 'Memorial', which discussed the anticipated effects of the export of machinery and personnel. In response, Boulton did what he did so well, writing to people in high places to refute the arguments point by point, even going to London in case Lord Liverpool required him to contest the claims.

But Boulton had over-extended himself; he was coining copper for Britain, holding initial talks with Denmark for a mint, sending blanks to America, and rebuilding his own Soho Mint. Nonetheless, most of the machinery had been finished between the end of 1799 and early 1800, the coining presses, cutting-out machines and steam engine, together with the rolling mill, being dispatched to Hull for St Petersburg in April 1800. At this point, Boulton had no clear instructions as to how it would be housed. Finally, in late July 1800, he received detailed plans (which he had been requesting for two years) learning that the mint was intended for the Fortress of St Peter and St Paul. The second shipment of machinery left Hull in early October 1802, and four Britons – James Duncan, James Walker, James Harley and William Speedyman – set out for Russia, the first two being on loan from the Rennies. So far so good; but who would oversee the operation? There was the possibility of Matthew Robinson Boulton going, but instead Zacchaeus Walker junior, Boulton's nephew, went in 1803.

Upon their arrival in St Petersburg the four Soho men set about inspecting the mint building and rapidly came to the conclusion that it was not adequate, 'being an old building and all cracked and rent'. It was almost 100 years old and too small, so the men decided that it must be demolished and another erected in its place. But this would take time, and the machinery could not even be removed from the crates until there was somewhere dry in which to work. The mint project suffered both from the harsh Russian climate and from Russian officials who seemed unwilling to take decisions.[16] The men quickly realised that their wages, whilst adequate in Birmingham, did not meet their needs in St Petersburg. And there were rivalries between the four men.

Zacchaeus Walker was granted full power to act on Matthew Boulton's behalf and to control the workmen employed. When he arrived in Russia, Walker was not impressed by the 'endless list of shabby Secretaries & Servants who obstruct every Avenue & render it next to an impossibility to proceed beyond the first ante-chamber for anyone not wearing ½ doz Stars, Crosses & Ribbands'.[17] Walker's dealings with Russian officials got no easier, for he was required to attend numerous meetings which achieved little. After a particularly frustrating episode, during which he was told that the layout of machinery must be changed, he lost his temper and stated that the mint must 'either be erected according to our Plans and Directions or not at all'. This appears to have done the trick, achieving a reduction in meddling that allowed work to progress on the building through the summer and early autumn of 1803. The new mint was surrounded by old buildings and a high wall and, notwithstanding the necessity for good light for coining, the Russians insisted on heavy gratings being placed at the windows. The building was nearly complete by the winter of 1803, but it was damp. Renewed activity in 1804 enabled steam engines and rolling mill machinery to be moved to their respective places, but they could not be set up as the building was still damp. In the autumn of 1804, Boulton sent dies in various stages, together with pieces struck from them, as a teaching aid for those who would become responsible for the mint. And, at the end of the year, he was clear that he had to bring his 'Mintaneers'[18] home, the reason being that he had two other minting projects on hand – the Danish Mint and the British Royal Mint – and he hoped to be able to send one or more men to Copenhagen.

The assembly and testing of the machinery was almost complete by the middle of 1806, and the boilers were fired up and the first trial coins produced in June 1807. By this time, Boulton was concerned to receive the balance of the sum due to him for the mint. Zacchaeus Walker called on the Russian Minister Count Vasiliev, seeking to hand the mint over, order passports for the returning Soho workmen, and name the day when payment would be received. Just when everything seemed likely to be settled, the Minister died suddenly in the night. However, a successor was appointed more rapidly than experience would have suggested was likely, and Boulton received the outstanding sum, plus interest, in December 1807, together with a ring, a token from Tsar Alexander I. James Duncan stayed in St Petersburg – he had learnt Russian and became foreman at the mint. James Harley remained in Russia, too, but James Walker and William Speedyman returned to Britain in late 1807. Zacchaeus Walker left in October 1808 and, perhaps, the last word on the Russian Mint should go to him:

> The Russians in general may with propriety be still considered as great Babies, who, when they hear of a novel & pretty thing cry after it & must have [it] … whilst the fit lasts, but it is seldom of long duration & as soon as the attention is diverted by some fresh object, the former is totally forgotten.[19]

Royal Mint

In August 1804, Sir Joseph Banks visited Soho Mint. Boulton wrote to him shortly afterwards:

> It is of little import to argue upon the philosophical principles of the machine; & as to its original cost being Expensive I consider that an advantage, in as much as it is a bulwark against counterfeiters & moreover will coin a far greater quantity in less time & at less expense than ever has been done in this or any other country … No man upon earth has expended so much of his own money to improve the art of coining or made so many

experiments or improvements or coined so many millions of pieces as I have done.[20]

Later in the year, Boulton was approached with an enquiry on behalf of Lord Liverpool, asking how long it would take to set up 'a compleat System of Machinery for coining gold and silver' in London, together with the requisite buildings.[21] By October it had been decided that two steam engines would be needed for the rolling mill and presses, together with a small one for several purposes.[22] John Rennie was asked to inspect the existing Royal Mint premises and report on what would be required to establish a mint on an improved plan, co-operating with Boulton on its construction.[23] Boulton favoured building the new mint at Somerset House on land adjacent to the Thames, since coal would be required for the three steam engines and 'there is a certain prison-like gloom within the walls of the Tower ... A new mint could be erected without stopping the old and would be cleaner and more orderly and light.'[24]

There was much to-ing and fro-ing; the Duke of Montrose was said to be delighted that the mint was to be built on a new site, the architect James Wyatt having said that it was more expensive to modify the present building than to build afresh. Montrose recognised that Boulton would be able to coin copper better and more economically than the Royal Mint. 'However, as any generation cannot expect to have a Boulton, it is well to leave them room to do what may then be found necessary.'[25] Boulton was clear where the different responsibilities lay:

> The buildings in general should be plain, simple & strong & all the operative buildings need not be more than two stories high, many of them one at most, except the front which may be simply elegant in the Wyattistic style ... Mr Wyatt may design the ornamental part but I must sketch the useful.[26]

This point was emphasised by Rennie, who told Boulton's son that the buildings were 'to be done in a magnificent style'.[27]

By January 1805, the division of work between Soho and John Rennie had been clarified, Rennie being responsible for 'the general disposition of the whole', the great rolling mill, some wheels by the cutting-out mill and such applications of the small engine that were unconnected with the mint.[28] The rolls, frames and screws for the great rolling mill were 'better to be made at Soho, because I intend new machinery for making more perfect rolls'.[29] Wyatt was not to be the architect but James Johnson, who estimated the overall costs: the mint buildings, including houses for principal offices and strong defensive wall £95,330; Boulton's machinery £14,790; Rennie's machinery £15,770;

and wells for the steam engines £600.[30] The building was being staked out in July; by November, James Lawson reported, 'I was at the foundation of the Mint two days ago & they are going on clearing & preparing for beginning to build with all expedition. Mr Rolles seems very anxious that everything in the building may be done well.'[31] The building and machinery installation took place between 1805 and 1810. For much of this period and until his death in 1809, Matthew Boulton was ill, for some of the time being bedridden, working with an amanuensis who both took letter dictation and made drawings under his supervision. James Lawson was released from Soho, at the request of Sir Joseph Banks, to become superintendent of machinery and the principal workman of the Royal Mint.[32]

Danish Mint

At one level, the Danish Mint should have been one of the more simple and straightforward Soho operations. The country of destination was much nearer than Russia, and the mint required was smaller. Moreover, it was to be constructed from scratch, so there were no problems over the proposed site. Boulton could advise what was required and the Danes could implement. But that was in principle. Instead, it proved to be the most drawn out of all. Indeed, Soho foundry did not receive the second half of the payment due until ten years after Matthew Boulton's death. The reality was that Boulton was fully extended in meeting a coinage order as well as supplying the Russian Mint, and he delayed. In so doing, the enterprise was adversely affected by the Napoleonic Wars.

The first contact was made in 1796 by an official of the Danish Government, one Baron Gustavus Buchwald who, on being given samples of Boulton's coins, probably when visiting Soho, recommended him for the work. The London agents of the Danish Government, Wolffs & Dorville, were the intermediaries and quickly became irritated by Boulton's seemingly relaxed attitude to time. In a particularly optimistic frame of mind, Boulton assured the Danish Government that their new mint could be supplied in 1798. This, however, did not satisfy them, Count Schimmelmann reminding him that if Soho postponed the construction of their mint, the Danes might look elsewhere. But they requested permission to send a visitor to Soho, a businessman with scientific curiosity, one Professor Olaus Warberg, to whom Boulton took an immediate liking.[33] This was fortunate, for the delays would have been enough to try a saint. In March 1798, a jointly composed document consisting of a series of questions, together with Boulton's answers, was sent to Denmark. Boulton did not do himself any favours when he admitted that he could not complete the Danish machinery until spring 1799, on account of his other minting engagements. And then, curiously, he offered to provide coinage instead of a mint, probably recognising that he needed to try to keep his customer happy. This offer was never taken up and, by early 1800, Warberg had returned home. But in June of that year, he wrote to inform Boulton that the Danish Ambassador to London was to apply to the British Government for an Act of Parliament to enable Boulton to export a mint to Denmark.

By then, however, Britain and Denmark were in a naval stand-off. Tsar Paul of Russia, having been a British ally, had arranged a League of Armed Neutrality of Denmark-Norway, Sweden, Prussia and Russia to enforce free trade with France, and this was hostile to British interests. Tactically planning an attack before the Baltic Sea had thawed, the Royal Navy, with Nelson at the helm, severely damaged the Danish-Norwegian fleet and achieved a truce. In these circumstances it is hardly surprising that plans for the supply of the Danish Mint were placed on hold. Negotiations between Soho and the Danish Government recommenced in 1803, and Warberg returned to Britain to discuss the revived project. In January 1804, he was authorised to come to a business agreement with Boulton to provide for coining presses, cutting-out machinery and other apparatus, together with a rolling mill. But patience was wearing thin and Warberg was summoned home in June. This time the delays were occasioned largely by the British Government which had other concerns, including a further breakdown in George III's mental health. And once more, Boulton encountered opposition in Birmingham, 'with an intent to prevent the passing of the Act of Parliament'.[34] The Act was finally passed, permitting the export of machinery and authorising workmen to travel to Copenhagen. And it was this latter point which caused further headaches for Boulton, for the Soho employees in St Petersburg had not yet returned. Boulton had banked on being able to persuade at least one of them to go to Copenhagen. In the meantime, he set about training a Danish contingent, including Warberg, who would become the superintendent of the mint, once it was ready.

By February 1806, the machinery – four coining presses, six cutting-out presses, two milling machines, a dye multiplying press, a turning lathe, and a shaking machine, together with a 14hp engine, a rolling mill with spare rolls and millwork – was completed and dispatched to Hull for transport to Copenhagen.[35]

Boulton received the first half of the payment due in August 1806, but the firm was going to have to wait a long time for the second half. The Danish Government agents in London argued that Boulton had not met the full contract by failing to dispatch trained operatives to install and train those who would be responsible for operating the mint. In the event, the Danish Mint was built and put in working order by Olaus Warberg, Friedrich Holst and John Gillespie, and it is likely that the first coins were struck in 1809.

However, a combination of events, including Britain and Denmark being at war and Boulton's death in 1809, meant that it was not until 1814 that finally Boulton, Watt & Co. sought payment of the second half of the contract, including interest on the unpaid sum. Warberg, by now unsurprisingly alienated from Soho, was no help, but the new British envoy to Copenhagen, coupled with the help of a Danish national, enabled Matthew Robinson Boulton to be paid the principal sum and a reduced amount of interest. The matter was finally settled in 1816.

Whilst the British, Russian and Danish Mints were constructed during Boulton's lifetime, there were other minting possibilities, some of which – such as the abortive Paris Mint project – ran for several years and were ultimately unfulfilled.

Abortive Mints

When he was in Paris, Boulton was reminded by Baron Bretoul that the French 'commenced their projects with more rapidity than the English but ... the latter accomplished the End sooner', a point reiterated by Boulton, who claimed, 'I know a man at Paris that would erect a Coining & a Rolling Mill with his tongue in One month but I am sure it would not work with effect in a year',[36] although he, too, could be carried away when it came to projected schedules for the delivery of coins or mints.

The first of Boulton's three proposals for supplying France with coinage was the provision of a complete mint for Paris:

It certainly would be a proper & desirous thing for so great a Kingdome as France to have one Compleat Hotel de Monneis at Paris & if it were not larger than the one which I have built in my Garden, it would be sufficient to coin more than 300,000 Louis d'Ors Pr Jour or near 3 million pr Week & consequently do as much or more than all the 18 Hotel de Monnies which are now established in different parts of France.[37]

Mindful of the cost of transporting coal, Boulton had favoured siting the rolling mill, with a 60hp engine, near Rouen 'exactly upon a spot where an English vessel may discharge its loading either of Coals or Copper into the Mill and where a Paris boat can be charged out of the same mill'.[38] The mint was proposed to be located in Paris, operated by a less powerful engine for cutting out blanks and coining, with rooms for cleaning, drying and packing, all one storey high. Boulton suggested leaving the present Paris Mint site, to build a cheaper 'not Magnificent' one nearby, and offered to talk with the

Minister, provided he was paid 100 guineas expenses – an offer which was not taken up.[39]

But neither a mint nor the minting of French currency at Soho was to be fulfilled, for the French Revolution and the subsequent French Wars intervened. Zacchaeus Walker, on his way to Russia in 1802 to represent Boulton at the St Petersburg Mint project, stopped off in Paris and sent his uncle a précis of the situation. Jean-Antoine Chaptal, French chemist and statesman, had suggested that even if there did exist at Soho some 'important philosophical principle unknown or un-practised here, that France possessed Men of Genius enough to discover it, or to obtain it by some means or other ere long, & apply it if advantageous'. It was thought that the French were determined to adopt the most perfect machinery possible, and 'will discover or steal the best plan if practicable so that it may pass for their own, no matter at what expense, provided they need not appear to have condescended to borrow ideas from England, of which their jealousy increases daily'.[40] French engravers, Walker added in another letter, seem to consider work in England 'as only a few Degrees preferable to that of slaves under a Jamaica planter' besides being deprived of artist comrades, the Louvre and their mistresses.[41]

In 1798, Boulton received a request made on behalf of a Portuguese minister asking for details of his coining apparatus, whether it was for sale to foreign kingdoms and, if so, what was the cost? He was also asked the conditions upon which he would undertake to produce coin for foreign governments.[42] Another letter was received four months later, the author begging an appointment with Boulton before setting out for Lisbon, in order to receive instructions concerning the establishment of a Portuguese Mint.[43] A further enquiry was received in 1802, but no order materialised.[44]

Sir John Robison, son of the late Professor Robison of Glasgow, friend and supporter of James Watt, wrote to James Watt junior from Hyderabad in 1805, having suggested to 'a minister of the court' that 'considerable advantages' might be gained by importing a small mint from England, capable of coining 10,000 to 20,000 rupees per day.[45] Three years later, Matthew Robinson Boulton was in contact with John Rennie concerning the supply of millwork and a rolling mill for a projected mint in Bombay. Rennie suggested that it would cost the same as the work he had recently undertaken for the Royal Mint – £11,060. Since the patterns already existed this would enable a saving to be made. A note on the back of the letter in Robinson Boulton's hand identified a 30hp engine at £2,160 and mint machinery at £16,990.[46] No order was forthcoming, but Robinson Boulton sold Soho Mint in 1823 and it was dispatched to Bombay in 1824.[47]

In 1808, Boulton & Watt had received a letter from one Manoel Antonio de Paiva, then in London, regarding the possibility of a mint for Rio de Janeiro, together with British coiners who could instruct local men to undertake the task. De Paiva was adventurous enough to suggest that it might be a good idea to consider sending two or three mints to different parts of the country, asking whether there would be any accommodation on price.[48] He was invited to Birmingham and was much impressed by what he saw. The proposed mint, larger than that in Denmark but smaller than the Russian Mint, comprised six coining presses, four cutting-out presses and other machinery, and was to be powered by a 10hp engine. Official permission to export the mint was obtained in 1810. The machinery and engine were eventually shipped in 1811, Thomas White having left earlier in order to make ready for the installation. There then ensued a row over whether the existing building which had been chosen to house the machinery was appropriate, and then the vessel carrying the machinery and engine was shipwrecked, fortunately with no loss of life. In the event, the machinery was retrieved, but Robinson Boulton, having been informed of the ship's loss, was not reassured for a year, on account of the Portuguese Government's desire to make an insurance claim for all the machinery. Meanwhile, White somehow managed to bring all the equipment some 2,000 miles over land and water, eventually 'triumphantly appearing at the gates of the capital like a water-logged phoenix, his machinery in tow'.[49] Eventually, in 1813, White was paid off and reappeared at Soho in mid-July. The mint, by then rusty and corroded, was not erected.

After Matthew Boulton's death there were some other projects for overseas Mints (and minting), but Matthew Robinson Boulton did not address the business with his father's passion. In his memoir of Boulton, James Watt wrote, 'Had Mr B done nothing more in the world than what he has done in improving the coinage, his fame would have deserved to be immortalised ... He has conducted the whole more like a sovereign than a private manufacturer.'[50] Pun probably not intended.

Notes

1   H. W. Dickinson, *Matthew Boulton*, 1937, p. 135.

2   Richard Doty, *The Soho Mint & the Industrialization of Money*, 1998, p. 38.

3   1792, M. Boulton Papers, Soho Mint.

4   MB to Garbett, 29 March 1790.

5   MB to Southern, 15 May 1797.

6   After Boulton's death a dispute arose as to who had devised the method of connecting the engine to the presses. Southern had claimed the invention and, since he was paid by Boulton for it, this would seem to have been justified. But Matthew Robinson Boulton challenged this and a conference was held at Soho with Southern, James Lawson, Peter

Ewart and Robinson Boulton present. The matter was amicably concluded with Southern apparently being able to prove his point. M. Boulton Papers, Soho Mint.

7   Doty, op. cit., p. 56. The new Soho Mint was a two-storey building of functional appearance, Jennifer Tann, *The Development of the Factory*, 1970, p. 90.

8   Doty, op. cit., pp. 58–59.

9   Dickinson, op. cit., p. 148. This mint was taken down and dispatched to Bombay in 1824 (see below) and MRB constructed a third Soho Mint between 1824 and 1826 (Doty, op. cit., p. 66).

10   A. Baxter to MB, 27 May 1796; MB to A. Baxter, 21 July 1796.

11   Memorandum … Of the Mint in Russia, 6 February 1798.

12   MB to James Smirnove, 20 February 1798.

13   MB to Smirnove, 3 October 1798; MB to Smirnove, 4 October 1798.

14   A detailed plan exists (dated 1800), Tann, op. cit., p. 92 (pf. 713).

15   Doty, op. cit., p. 88.

16   Ibid., p. 99.

17   Ibid., p. 108.

18   The term is Boulton's.

19   Z. Walker to MB, 15 February 1804.

20   MB to Sir Joseph Banks, 12 August 1804.

21   T. Lack to MB, 21 October 1804.

22   John Rennie to MB, 14 October 1804.

23   W. Fawkener to MB, 26 October 1804.

24   MB to Rennie, 12 November 1804; Rennie to MB, 3 November 1804: Rennie, mindful of his debt to the older man – Boulton having assisted him earlier in his career – wrote, 'Your plan came safe to hand – it would be presumption in me to say anything in it is wrong but I trust you will give me credit when I say it meets my entire approbation.'

25   Rennie to MB, 10 November 1804.

26   MB to Rennie, 15 November 1804.

27   Rennie to MRB, 31 July 1805. A plan and section of the Mint (1806) is illustrated in Tann, op. cit., p. 88 (pf. 716).

28   James Lawson to MB, 22 November 1805.

29   MB to Rennie, 20 January 1805.

30   Rennie to W. Fawkener, 26 June 1805.

31   Doty, op. cit., pp. 156–57.

32   M. Boulton Papers, Rennie.

33   Doty, op. cit., pp. 131–37.

34   Ibid., p. 133; MB to Warberg, 3 July 1804.

35   A plan (dated 1805) is reproduced in Tann, op. cit., p. 93 (pfs 709–10).

36   MB to Monneron, 24 May 1792.

37   MB to A. Monneron, 7 June, 1792.

38   MB to Monneron, 29 December 1791.

39 MB to Monneron, 7 June 1792.

40 Z. Walker jnr, Paris, to MB, 24 November 1802.

41 Z. Walker jnr, Paris, to MB, 6 December 1802.

42 J. J. & J. Stephens, Lisbon, to MB, 9 May 1798.

43 Henry Moller, Birmingham, to MB, 24 September 1798.

44 Manoel de Souza to MB, October 1802.

45 Sir John Robison, Hyderabad, to JW jnr, 23 July 1805.

46 Rennie to MRB, 8 February 1808. Another engine estimate of around the same time provided a lower figure: '30H. Engine, including carriage to London £1,808; if, however, Wood
    was to be used a 40H. boiler would be necessary, raising the cost to £1,881.' Estimates for
    the East India Mint engines, 12 February 1808.

47 Doty, op. cit., p. 65.

48 Ibid., pp. 166–67.

49 Ibid., p. 176.

50 Dickinson, op. cit., p. 156.

13

The Final Years

By the 1790s, Boulton had many worrying factors to contend with. The unexpected declaration of war by France in 1793 had led to a trade depression that affected every manufacturer and merchant in Britain, but he also had more specific worries of his own. In particular, he was keenly aware that Watt's patent on the separate condenser would expire by the end of the century, and he had no very high hopes that it, or any other steam engine patents, would be renewed. The portents were not good. Arguably the most important patents in the industrial world, and the only ones that could be compared with Watt's for their huge influence, had been awarded to Richard Arkwright for a carding engine used in the preparation of cotton for spinning, and for his water frame for spinning. The carding engine patent was the first to go, in 1781. It was based on dubious claims of originality, and rival manufacturers in Lancashire made out an excellent case for its overthrow. Boulton was not particularly sympathetic, as he wrote to Watt:

> He swears … he will ruin those Manchester rascals he has been the making of. It is agreed by all who know him that he is a Tyrant more absolute than a Bashaw, & tis thought that his disappointment will kill him. If he had been a man of sense and reason he would not have lost his patent.[1]

Boulton may have had a low opinion of Arkwright, but as Darwin pointed out when the next patent was challenged in 1785, it was important to lend him his support:

He had a trial last year, & it was in my opinion unjustly given against him. He has made many improvements in the machine since … I believe some shyness has existed between you & Mr. Arkwright but is it not in your interest to assist him with your evidence on his trial? Which also may make good humour between you, & you make fire-engines for cotton-works in future.[2]

Darwin was quite right in thinking that if one industrialist lost a patent others might soon follow. In the event, the patent was lost, one of the problems being that Arkwright's originality lay in the production system as a whole rather than an individual machine.[3] The following year Boulton was to suffer a similar fate. He had acquired the rights to manufacture the Argand lamp under a patent of 1784. Two years later it was being challenged in the courts on the grounds that it had already been described in Britain before the patent application was made. Boulton reported the result in a letter to Watt:

The Judge & jury have this day given all the Merit of the Lamp to Argand but at the same time have given a Verdict against him in consequence of Maggelan & another proving that ye invention was introduced into Engld a few days before ye date of his patent … some of the Jury express'd their reluctance to giving an Evidence against Argand but bow'd obedience to the letter of the Law. The Verdict was most certainly not just.[4]

Argand was devastated by the verdict, which now gave him no rights to any income from lamps manufactured in Britain, his own factory being one of the many that suffered during the French Revolution. He contracted malaria and died in poverty. Boulton put the blame for the débâcle mainly on the shoulders of the glass manufacturer William Parker, who was also a partner in the enterprise. It appeared that Parker had tried to monopolise the trade in the lamps and exacerbated the position by overpricing them. It was the traders who had been unable to join in this profitable new invention who had brought the case. Boulton likened Parker to Arkwright, as a man who had abused his monopoly. As he wrote in a later letter to Watt, 'If he had been a more civilized being & had understood mankind better he would now have enjoyed his patent.' The lesson to Boulton was obvious: whatever the moral merits of an inventor's claim to patent protection, what mattered was the interpretation of the law.[5]

The market for Boulton & Watt's engine business after 1800 was dramatically changed. The actions of the steam engine pirates had shown that there were engineers in Cornwall, Yorkshire and Lancashire ready to go into production. There was a very real possibility that if that happened, the sale of engines to the Cornish mines would come to a halt, as indeed it did.

No Boulton & Watt engines were sold there after 1801. The demand for engines did not disappear, but orders went instead to local foundries, such as Harvey's of Hayle. Fortunately for the fortunes of the Birmingham company, a new market had developed as the demand for steam engines to power textile mills and other industries grew. But these new customers did not necessarily have the expertise of the Cornish engineers, who were quite ready to assemble an engine themselves and rely on local foundries to provide parts that were not sent down from Soho. There was also a problem with John Wilkinson, who had always bored the cylinders for the steam engines. He had disagreed with his brother William, who was partner in the Bersham works, and was threatening to close the whole operation down. This was a very serious matter, and what made it doubly serious was the fact the Boulton had become increasingly concerned about the profitability of his silver and ormolu businesses and needed the income from the engines even more than before. He was determined to give up 'such branches as depend upon the Fashion of the Day; the whim, tast, caprice & fancy of Nobility & persons of Fashion are never profitable in the end & often ruinous to the undertaker'.[6]

Steam engines were not about to go out of fashion. There was only one reason to defer making major changes in the business and that was the state of the economy. In May 1794, Boulton wrote to Watt, 'My Treasury and Ministerial friends seem much alarm'd and low spirited as the evil spirit of sedition, anarchy and war are likely to blast the blooming prosperity of Britain.' But he decided that he needed to act regardless of the political and economic climate. The time had come to consider making good the prospect that Boulton had first set out to tempt Watt into a partnership – to create a specialist factory that would turn out complete engines, ready for use.

There was another issue that influenced Boulton. His son, Matthew Robinson Boulton, was reaching an age where he was ready to take his place in the family business. He had been given a good all-round education and had proved a reasonably diligent scholar, even if he had shown a somewhat frivolous interest in fashion. Boulton was proud of his efforts and brought him into the firm to learn the rudiments of business in the 1790s. The younger of the two Watt boys, Gregory, was highly gifted but took little part in the business, dying of consumption in his twenty-seventh year. James junior, having finished his formal education, was learning business practice in the textile industry in Manchester, and began to take an interest in radical politics. The older generation had always been careful to avoid anything that had even a sniff of controversy about it, unless it was a cause with direct implications for their business. James, however, joined the Constitutional Society of Manchester, a body founded by cotton merchant Thomas Walker and barrister Thomas Cooper to press for parliamentary reform. This was the age of rotten boroughs, when a virtually non-existent settlement such as Old Sarum could send two representatives to Parliament but the great manufacturing towns sent none. Young James Watt was obviously not only an active member of the Society but must have been highly regarded, as he was sent by them as a delegate to revolutionary France in 1792. Edmund Burke, who was in favour of slow, moderate reform but an outspoken opponent of the French Revolution, denounced young Watt in Parliament. This was not the sort of publicity the family firm courted. As a dedicated reformer, James might have expected a warm welcome in France, but by this time anyone from England was regarded with deep suspicion. Instead of being treated as a fraternal delegate, word began to be spread that he was actually a British Government spy. He only escaped the country in safety by not taking the obvious route home to England but heading south for Italy. He returned eventually in 1794. His elders decided that this was a salutary lesson and that now perhaps was the time for him to settle down to serious work. He was now to join his old friend Matt at Soho. The next generation was about to be taken into the family business.

Watt's copying machine patent was due to run out, so the two young men – Matt Boulton and James Watt junior – were permitted to run the manufacturing company James Watt & Co. to see what they would make of the challenge. Whatever faults James might have had, he soon showed that he had inherited something of his father's engineering abilities. The original press had been quite cumbersome, so he set about devising a portable version that could double up as a writing desk or secretaire. It had special compartments for paper, sponges for damping, ink powder and writing implements. It also had a damping box, and there were elaborate instructions given on just how much water to add to each sheet of paper, and a drying book. The top opened out to form a convenient writing desk. The instructions for use ran to a rather daunting fifteen pages, but it was a commercial success. The young men had shown their worth and were now ready to move on to greater things. A new company was formed in 1794, Boulton, Watt & Sons. Now it was time to think about providing new premises for the construction of steam engines.

The first requirement was to find an appropriate site. This was a time when Britain was in the grip of what became known as 'canal mania'. In the three years from 1792 to 1795, Parliament passed no fewer than thirty-nine Acts authorising canal construction, and among these were several that would have been of considerable interest to a Birmingham manufacturer of steam engines. The connections south to London were to be greatly improved, largely thanks to the construction of a new direct link, the Grand Junction, which Boulton, together with other Birmingham industrialists, had lobbied for. There were also new connections being made to the northern canals, serving the burgeoning textile industry. Boulton had always supported canal construction and had bought shares in the Birmingham Canal, begun in 1768. It had proved a good investment – the value of the shares had more than doubled – and now it was time to make more than just a monetary profit on his shares. He would look for a canalside site from which he could send engines all over England.

The Birmingham Canal was one of the earliest to be built, and was laid out by the pioneer canal engineer James Brindley. His policy was to avoid obstacles rather than confront them, so he kept his canal on the level as much as possible. The result was a waterway that wandered across the countryside and it was on one of the extravagant curves that Boulton decided to build the new factory, south of the original Soho works near Smethwick. It was called Soho Foundry and was built with its own dock, leading off from the main canal, so that up to four boats could be loaded and unloaded within the factory walls at the same time. In the early years of the nineteenth century, the wriggles of the old canal became a severe nuisance, slowing down traffic, and the Scottish engineer Thomas Telford was given the job of constructing a new, straight main line. Using cuttings and embankments, it carved through Brindley's original canal, but the latter was not simply abandoned: there were too many important businesses on its banks, which were among the canal's best customers. So the sweeping bends were retained as loops off the new main line, and one of these is still known as the Soho Loop.[7]

James Watt junior was now sufficiently back in favour to be given a large degree of responsibility for overseeing the construction of the new works, and he tackled the task with enthusiasm. Work began late in 1795 and soon James was recording excellent progress. By September eight bricklayers had been at work on the main building that was to be 46ft wide and 100ft long – and he might be forgiven for being a little self-satisfied when he wrote to his father:

> We hope that with this specimen you will give us some credit for activity and that you will not be angry with us, if the success of our past exertions induces us to go beyond the line originally proposed and to finish the foundry this year.[8]

He made good his promise and Boulton himself conducted the official opening ceremony on 30 January 1796. It was a grand affair with all the workmen present and began with a splendid feast:

> Two fat sheep (the first fruits of the newly cultivated land at Soho) were sacrificed at the Altar of Vulcan. ...These two great dishes were garnished with rumps and rounds of beef, legs of veal, and gammons of bacon, with innumerable meat pieces and plumb puddings, accompanied by a good band of Martial Music. When dinner was over, the Founder of Soho entered, and

consecrated this new branch of it, by sprinkling the wall with wine, and then, in the name of *Vulcan*, and all the Gods & Goddesses of *Fire* and *Water*, pronounced the name of it SOHO FOUNDRY, and all the people cried *Amen*.[9]

The name may have been the Soho Foundry, but that does not give an indication of its true nature: it was very much more than that. It could reasonably be described as the world's first purpose-built engineering works. There were nine separate departments, each one specialising in making one specific component or set of components. The most impressive contained the new boring mill. It was unlike Wilkinson's in that it was vertical instead of horizontal, designed by Manchester millwright Peter Ewart, who had been a pupil of John Rennie. The actual construction of the machine was overseen by William Murdoch, who had now left Cornwall for good to take up a new appointment at Soho. The continuing troubles at Bersham were to prove a benefit after all, as James reported in July of that year that all Wilkinson's moulders had left Bersham and been taken on at Soho. It would not have been a difficult decision to make: no one in Britain had more experience of casting steam cylinders than Wilkinson's key workers. When completed and fully operational, the foundry was capable of turning out twenty complete engines a year.[10]

There was, however, a rival on the scene. The Soho manufacturers had been very scornful of the abilities of Matthew Murray of Leeds (see pp. 120–22) and, although the partners were ambivalent as to whether he was infringing the Watt patent, he was producing castings to a very high standard and, it was said, better than anything produced at Soho. Murray, too, had a new works, with a circular erection shop, giving it the name of the Round Foundry. He seems to have been willing to make an amicable arrangement with Birmingham, and invited Murdoch to Leeds to see what he was doing. He obviously expected a reciprocal arrangement, but when he asked for permission to visit Soho he was refused. James soon showed that he had a ruthless streak when it came to business rivals. He hit on a novel, if expensive, way to prevent Murray expanding his business. He went up to Leeds himself to look at land adjoining the Round Foundry 'with a view to seeing whether we could purchase anything under their very nose'. In the event, they paid something in the region of £1,000 simply to keep land out of the hands of Murray.[11]

Matt was also very busy in the new business. He described his new life to Zacchaeus Walker, the son of Boulton's agent:

In a word all are well & busily driving our separate wheelbarrows. You will be not a little surprised to find that I am a very regular attender in the counting house & immersed in business. Like a person hesitating on the brink of a cold bath I found that the only means of conquering my aversion was to plunge in: my experiment has so far succeeded."[12]

The young men were settling into their new lives. The foundry was to prove highly successful and Boulton's original urging of Watt to work on rotative engines was more than justified. By 1800, Boulton & Watt had supplied 164 pumping engines and, although the rotative engines were developed later, by that date 308 of them had been built, the original sun and planet gear having been gradually replaced by the more functional crank. Cornwall had provided a rich field in the early years, but according to figures supplied by the local agent Thomas Wilson, the company had never received the full premium due. In a document dated 22 February 1799, he gave these figures:

Total amount of fuel saved	£803,869 19s 8d
One third part due for premium	£267,956 13s 0d
Amount recd by Boulton & Watt	£105,904 9s 5d
Short	£162,052 3s 7d[13]

In spite of the apparent accuracy of the figures, recorded down to the nearest penny, it is fair to say that they would have been disputed by the majority of Cornish mine owners. Even allowing for that, it shows both a considerable shortfall and, in spite of the discrepancy, a very healthy profit. It would be over £3 million at today's prices. The other interesting figure is the price of a new engine delivered, complete with boiler, from the foundry in 1800. This ranged from £327 for a modest 10hp engine to £1,727 for a 50hp. Taking an average figure of £1,000 per engine, which is admittedly not very reliable, it would suggest that the sale of rotative engines brought an income of over £300,000. When the partnership of Boulton & Watt ended, to be replaced by Boulton, Watt & Sons, Watt effectively retired altogether. He had never been an enthusiast for the business life. Boulton remained nominally an active partner, but it was not long before the younger generation were effectively in complete control of the steam engine business.

Boulton, having got a taste for building, now decided that it was time to modernise and extend his own home, Soho House.[14] It was not a new idea. As we have seen, he had already spent a good deal of time and money on improving the grounds, erecting small buildings, including the Temple of Flora and the Cascade Library, as well as planting more shrubs and flower beds. He had also discussed alterations with the architect Samuel Wyatt. The plans called for wings to be added to either side of the existing building, which was to be given a new Classical front. Boulton did not make up his mind to go ahead with such an ambitious plan, but he did get an interesting new addition.

This was a wooden extension with a dressing room and the very latest in toiletry. It included a Joseph Bramah water closet, one of the very first flushing toilets that he had patented in 1778. The main glory, however, was the immense steam-heated bath, over 8ft long, nearly 6ft wide and 5ft 6in deep. But there the alterations came to a halt for a few years.

When James Wyatt took over the Soho House project, Boulton did have one idea of his own that he would definitely go ahead with:

> It is absolutely necessary that the stables & coach houses should not join nor appear to be a part of the same building as the kitchen etc. ... because of those being of different materials & I think stucco is very improper for stables, kicking horses & rolling carriages.

His other big idea was to have a rear entrance for the family, to avoid them having to step out on to the carriageway at the front. Soho House was still one of the places on the aristocratic tourist itinerary, and there was a regular procession of carriages to the front door. The rear entrance enabled the family to keep clear of the busy traffic and to keep their feet out of the dung that is an unavoidable accompaniment to the passage of so many horses. It also gave him a chance to redesign that side of the house and to bring his monstrous bath into the main building. Plans were constantly changing, but eventually it was decided to have just one new wing, and instead of replacing the original frontage it was covered in slate, stuccoed and embellished with a new portico. In 1796, Wyatt sent in his bill for £78 15s for 'elevation etc of venetian window, entablature for house, details of Mr. Boulton a room and capital for ionic column to portico'.[15]

Wyatt, however, had become a very fashionable architect and could not spend very much of his time supervising work at Soho. Things were often in a state of considerable chaos. In a letter to Sir Joseph Banks in the summer of 1797, Boulton apologised for not writing sooner because of pressures of work:

> To which I should add the uncomfortable estate I am in respecting my home having been driven out of it for this fortnight past by the taking off the whole of the Roof, pulling down the Stairs & in every respect indeed perfectly uninhabitable, however I flatter myself that it will be recovered before the 21st at least as far that we may eat & drink in it without danger.[16]

Meanwhile, there was a flurry of orders for new furniture, carpets and everything from chimney glass from the Albion Plate Glass Co. to commodes, in spite of the new toilet being installed. One of the most important innovations was a central heating system. Air was heated by a coal-fired furnace in the basement and then led through ducts in the wall and under the floors. Holes in the risers of the main staircase allowed the hot air to circulate through the house. It was one of the earliest domestic central heating systems of this type to be installed in Britain since the Romans built their villas and hypocausts.

When completed, Boulton finally got his much-enlarged library in the new wing, and he eventually spent over £500 on new fixtures and fittings. Just as in his factory he had produced goods in ormolu and plate to simulate gold and silver, in his house he also went for materials that imitated grander originals. Wooden columns were painted to look exactly like marble and the floors were covered with varnished cloths that resembled decorative stone. The effect was of a very grand house indeed, incorporating all the latest ideas, but not quite what it purported to be. It was, however, unmistakably the house of a gentleman of taste.

Boulton moved easily between the London intelligentsia, aristocracy, royalty and leading entrepreneurial manufacturers. He inherited land as part of his wedding settlement, but it was in the 1790s that he began acquiring property in his own right. It all started with his desire to acquire the freehold of the land at Soho from the landlord Wyrley Birch of nearby Hamstead Hall. This possible purchase was tied to a wider scheme for an Enclosure Act to take in common land on Handsworth Heath. Enclosures were common throughout the eighteenth century as a means of improving poor ground and making it more productive, a process that seemed eminently sensible to the landowners and was ultimately to prove very successful in its main aims. It looked very different, however, to the cottagers who had no legal rights to the common land they had been living on for centuries and which they had been using to feed their livestock and to gather fuel. A popular rhyme of the time put it succinctly:

> The fault is great in man or woman
> Who steals a goose from off the common.
> But what can plead that man's excuse
> Who steals the common from the goose?

The enclosure of the common was pursued by Birch and Boulton, and Watt was also involved as he planned to build a house for himself on the land. The plans, however, involved evicting several of the cottagers. 'There is no news here except about the common. The cottagers are extremely enraged at you Mr. Birch Mr. Whately and myself & I hear there is a petition from the Parish to Mr Birch not to turn them out.'[17]

The petition failed and Boulton eventually acquired around 113 acres of land on the heath. He could claim the traditional rights of a landowner when it came to evicting the cottagers, but he was less enthusiastic about one of the landowner's traditional obligations: the payment of tithes to the parish church. He had already had one run-in with the local vicar over an enclosure of 1773:

> Could you imagine that your new Inclosure on ye Common was Tithe free? Or are you the only Occupier of land in the Parish who does not know yt; whoever carries off his Crop, before he has set out his Tithe, or acquainted the parson of it, forfeits treble the value.[18]

In 1795, he was no more enthusiastic about tithes. He wrote to complain to the President of the Board of Agriculture that he had bought 100 acres of 'the very poorest land'; it was 'all sand and gravel' but he had managed to improve 17 acres and grew potatoes 'at the loss of a few Hundred pounds to myself but with a <u>profit</u> of 25£ to the parson that being the sum he charges in lieu of Tithe. So much for the Encouragement of Agriculture and parochial Harmony.'[19] Nevertheless, his distaste for the tithe system did not prevent him from investing in land throughout the 1790s, even if he decided occasionally that the times were not favourable. In times of war, land was always seen as the safest investment, but with what he described as 'the unexpected burst of peace' in 1802 he lost interest – it 'bated my ardour for buying of <u>land</u>'. When war returned the following year, he reversed his opinion and started once again looking for suitable properties. In 1803, he wrote, when making enquiries, 'I do not want a place of Residence but mearly an improvable estate for money.' In other words, he was still looking for land that could be enclosed and improved. By 1808, Matt was doing most of the negotiations and was looking to purchase an estate in Herefordshire. The old theme was repeated. Matt, he wrote, 'has appointed to meet a gentleman in Herefordshire to finally conclude upon the purchase of an estate of some importance ... land in these plundering times seems the only secure property'.[20]

Boulton was following the ideas of agriculturists such as Arthur Young, who saw commons and heaths as no more than unproductive and misused land that could be transformed only by men with enthusiasm and the necessary capital – men such as himself. He used economic arguments in favour of enclosures, particularly pointing to the large amount of money being spent on importing grain, which could be grown at home once the land was improved. There was another motive involved in his purchases of land round Soho: it kept others at bay. Birmingham was expanding rapidly and developers were on the look-out for suitable building land. One landowner, Isaac Riddell, offered Boulton land on Birmingham Heath and tempted him with the suggestion that if he made an investment, he and his friends would 'form a Building Society on a large scale ... Perhaps in the course of a few years, not only the said land but

also Birmingham Heath – the chief part of Handsworth – will be nearly covered with buildings.'[21] He even suggested that the new development should
be called Boulton Town, with an appropriate statue in the middle. Boulton
bought the land, but had no interest in the development. He had no wish to
see his house and its beautiful parkland enveloped by cheap housing. It is perhaps as well that he could never have guessed how densely Handsworth would
be built up in the nineteenth and twentieth centuries.

One factor must certainly have crossed Boulton's mind. The ownership of
land conveyed status. When he was appointed Sheriff of Staffordshire, a post
that incurred him considerable expense, he had to provide livery for himself
and his retinue of twelve javelin men and a trumpeter. As his daughter noted,
he 'no doubt will make a great splash'. But he probably thought the expense
well worth it, for his post also gave him the right to have a coat of arms. The
arms he chose feature two leopard heads and an anchor. It was conventional to
have an arrow rather than an anchor, but he wanted to incorporate the mark
of the Birmingham Assay Office. Boulton was unquestionably proud of his
arms, but he was equally proud of the achievements that had brought him the
honours he now enjoyed. Visitors were expected to be suitably impressed if
they came to tea – the arms featured on his fine silver tea urn.[22]

Throughout the period when the new businesses of minting coins and
building steam engines seemed to dominate Boulton's working life, it is easy
to forget that the business with which it had all started was still flourish-
ing. There had not been very many major changes at the works, although
a new engine had been added in 1788 to drive the lap machinery, used for
polishing metal; hence it was generally known as the 'Lap Engine'. It was a
sun and planet engine and the very first to be fitted with a centrifugal governor. (It is now preserved and on show in the Energy Hall at the Science
Museum in London.) By this date there were around 1,000 workmen at the
Soho Manufactory. When Boswell had visited the works in March 1776, he
had described Boulton as 'an *iron chieftain* and he seemed to be a father to his
tribe'. He recounted how one of the workmen had asked for help because
his landlord was about to distrain all his goods for non-payment of rent, at
which point Boulton offered to pay half the arrears if the man could raise
the rest of the cash. In this respect he was typical of many of the more pater-
nalistic employers of the age, who prided themselves on looking after their
workforce. Boulton was certainly a good employer in many respects, hand-
ing out Christmas presents to the workforce every year. But he went much
further than the vast majority of his contemporaries when he established 'The
Insurance Society belonging to the Soho Manufactory' in 1792.

This was a mutual benefit society open to all workers at the Soho factory who
earned more than 2s 6d a week, and the scheme was later extended to the foundry.

Payments were on a sliding scale, starting at ½*d* a week for the lowest earners to a top rate of 4*d* for those earning 20*s* or more. Payments for sickness
or injury were also scaled, between 1*s* and 8*s* per week. There was also help
available for funeral expenses. Money was paid into 'the box' and the scheme
was run by a committee, overseen by elders appointed by Boulton. The committee members were required to visit the sick every week, for which they
were allowed half a day. This was not so much a concern for the unfortunates'
welfare as to make sure no one was cheating. The rules were strict. Article IX
begins: 'If the committee can make it appear that any member feigns himself
ill, he shall forfeit five shillings to the box, besides being publicly exposed.' If
the illness could be shown to be due to 'any intemperance, such as drunken-
ness, debauchery, quarrelling, or fighting' then there was a ten-day delay before
the first payment was made. The worst offence was being seen in the alehouse
while supposedly off sick – all payments were then forfeit. There is no mention of payment into the fund by the employers.[23]

The rules cast an interesting light on some aspects of work at Soho. There
was a concern for health and cleanliness that was by no means the norm at that
time. Article XXIV begins: 'As it is for the health, interest, and credit of the
men as well as the masters to keep this MANUFACTORY clean and decent,
it shall be claimed a forfeit of one shilling to the box for any one found guilty
of any indecencies, or keeping dirty shops.' Article XXIII notes, 'It has been
a frequent custom for workpeople to ask money of the gentry' visiting the
works, and that too called for a minimum fine of 1*s*. It is clear, however, that
the gentry were expected to tip their guides, but that the money should be put
straight into the insurance fund; anyone pocketing it for themselves got a 5*s*
fine. It seems obvious that there was no let-up in the number of gentry asking
to be shown round Soho, nor it seems was there much less enthusiasm on
Boulton's part for entertaining them. Some visitors got far more lavish treatment than others.

Although most of Boulton's aristocratic connections were on the basis of
merchant and customer, there were some who became personal friends. Among
them were the Russian Ambassador, Count Woronzow, and his two children,
Mikhail and Ekaterina – their mother had died at a young age. In August 1799,
the family, together with the chaplain James Smirnove and Ekaterina's governess Miss Jardine, came to stay with Boulton at Soho House.[24] Boulton laid on
some extravagant entertainment. He had arranged a visit to the Theatre Royal,
only recently rebuilt after a major fire, a very handsome building with a façade
by Wyatt that had survived the blaze. The theatre was a great source of pride,
as Boulton had been one of the group of local businessmen who had put up
the money and arranged a licence for the original theatre in the 1770s. This
was not a provincial performance. The London theatres were closed for the

season, so the Drury Lane stars were shining in Birmingham. They saw one of the most famous actors of the day, John Philip Kemble, in *Hamlet*, and enjoyed it so much that they returned for a second visit to see a double bill of *The Clandestine Marriage* and *Blue Beard*. This time Boulton arranged a small surprise. As the Count and the rest of the party entered their box, the band struck up *God Save the King* and at the end of the performances, the cast assembled to perform a specially arranged patriotic Russian song. The result could hardly have been more gratifying to Boulton:

> The Count was devastated by delight & turned to shake hands with me every moment saying he was sure this was my doing but which he considered as the highest & most acceptable Compliment that could be made him. It also pleased the house & was encored and joined in the Chorus by the audience.[25]

There were other surprises in store. Boulton had arranged a canal trip for the party as part of the essential tour of the various works. The first port of call was the foundry, where Boulton had arranged for a wind band to be hidden from view. As soon as the boat appeared they began to play, to the Count's delight. The journey also included a visit to a tunnel, part of the Dudley Canal that linked the Birmingham Canal to the Staffordshire & Worcestershire Canal. Tunnels were still a novelty – the first canal tunnel in Britain had been opened only in 1766 – but Dudley was, and is, particularly remarkable. This is no simple through route but a system that links a complex of limestone quarries and mines. So, while in places it is so narrow that a boat scarcely seems to have room to fit inside, at others it opens out to echoing caverns. The party entered the tunnel, lit by a hundred torches, with the band still playing and the music 'beautifully echoed from the Salons of Erebus'. It must have been a quite extraordinary occasion. The whole visit was a huge success, and the Count wrote an effusive thank you letter:

> My dear and respectable friend, it is impossible for me to express (as I told you before) how very thankful I am for the friendship and the confidence you shew to me. I am flattered and honoured by it, and I may say that I deserve it by what I feel for you. – The Hospitality with which you have received & treated us during the very happy 6 days that we have spent in so cheerful manner at the House of the most worthy of men and in the most agreeable society has completely spoiled the remainder of our journey. The great and beautiful things conceived and executed by men of sublime genius, the amiable society where entertainment was always accompanied by interesting instruction – all this is finished for us.

We now shall only see fine parks, gardens and houses which are also to be found in all countries.[26]

The exchange of letters shows very clearly that Boulton was perfectly capable of appearing in the most aristocratic of company with no sense of inferiority, and that he was, in turn, treated as an equal by others. Watt was never so enamoured of showing visitors around Soho. He may have considered it a waste of time, but he was also concerned, for good reason in some instances, about industrial espionage. However much Boulton may have enjoyed showing off the works and however profitable it might have been to have the wealthy visit Soho to see the goods on offer, in 1802 a surprising announcement appeared:

SOHO MANUFACTORY

THE PUBLIC are requested to observe that this MANUFACTORY cannot be SHEWN in consequence of any Application or Recommendation whatever. Motives, both of a public and private Nature have induced the Proprietors to adopt this Measure and they hope their Friends will spare them the painful Task of a Refusal.

SOHO, May 20 1802.

There could be many reasons for the change. Boulton was now in his seventies and his enthusiasm for entertaining may have lessened. In the previous year he seems to have flirted with the idea of retiring altogether. His friends realised that his life was actually centred round his business as much as anything. Mrs Matthews, who had taken over management of his financial affairs following the death of her husband, wrote to him, regretting that he was in low spirits. 'But the Idea you suggest of giving all up to your Children retaining only an annuity for yourself – & retiring to a Cottage – would make them both miserable, so that I entreat you will instantly discard such an Idea!'[27]

The younger generation may well not have shared Boulton's enthusiasm for entertaining. In a letter to Lady Blackwood, who had applied to visit Soho in 1803, Boulton had to turn down the request, noting that 'he has given offence to … Many princes, Nobles & Persons of High rank yet daily experience has convinced my young Partners of the Necessity'. There was also an increasing awareness of the need for security, which was difficult to maintain when strangers were constantly wandering about the works. There had been one scare at Christmas 1800, when Boulton was warned that there had been an attempt to bribe the night watchman to let men into the Manufactory and that they had duplicate keys for the counting house. At that time of year there was not just the usual cash for wages, but extra funds for Christmas bonuses. On the night of 23 December, Boulton joined his son and James Watt junior as well as trusted staff, well armed, to await the intruders. The would-be thieves arrived but were unable to make the keys work, leaving empty-handed. The watching party did nothing. They were sure they would return and were keen to catch them red-handed. They duly appeared the following night and, this time, were able to take the money, but as soon as it was in their hands Boulton sounded the alarm, torches were lit and four of the men were grabbed; a fifth, William Foulds, who had planned the whole enterprise, got away, only to be caught later. Boulton wrote to his daughter, who was staying in London, to reassure her that all was well, but that the only result so far was that he had developed 'a troublesome cough'. But he clearly enjoyed the adventure that he described as 'the agreeable employment of thief watching'.[28]

Everyone in the household was jumpy, and when there was a disturbance in the night a little later on, one of the staff fired his blunderbuss in the direction of the noise. It was only on the next morning that Boulton discovered what had actually happened. As he told Anne, 'In the morning I found our gray pony had been graseing under the windows & had been more frightened than I was. We have examined her but find she is not hurt.'[29] Boulton may have been contemplating retirement, but he had clearly lost none of his old spirit.

With the end of the steam engine patent drawing near, Boulton & Watt began to withdraw their key men from Cornwall, William Murdoch among them. He had been an exemplary servant of the company and a stalwart in the war against the steam pirates. Although he must have been sadly disappointed not to have been able to pursue his interest in steam locomotives, he was not a man simply to give up the search for new ideas and settle for a familiar routine. Forced to leave the development of the railways to Trevithick and his successors, he developed a new interest – gas lighting. He began a series of experiments on the destructive distillation of different fuels, including wood, peat and coal, and eventually decided to try and use the gases produced from coal as a new light source.

The technique was not in itself new, in that heating coal in iron retorts to drive off the gases was a process already in use to make coke, a vital ingredient for smelting iron. Up to then, however, the gases had simply been allowed to escape into the atmosphere. Murdoch's first success came when he lit his own house in Redruth. He had a retort out in the yard, and the gas was led through a pipe that passed through a hole in the window frame and was led up to the ceiling. When he returned to Soho in 1798, he was able to work on a larger scale. He described his apparatus in a letter to Sir Joseph Banks in 1808:

My apparatus consists of an iron retort, with tinned copper and iron tubes through which the gas was conducted to a considerable distance; and there, as well as at intermediate points, was burned through apertures of varied forms and dimensions ... the gas was also washed with water, and other means were used to purify it.[30]

He was not alone in working on gas lighting. The Frenchman Philippe Lebon, working quite independently, took out a patent in his own country. It is unlikely that Murdoch knew anything about it, since the two countries were at war. The Peace of Amiens of 1802 gave Boulton the opportunity to do what he loved doing – make a spectacular demonstration of his latest interest. The Manufactory was specially illuminated by gaslights, set at each end of the main building, making a splendid show and a fine advertisement. It was not, however, a first, for Lebon had put on a similar demonstration at the Hôtel Seignelay slightly earlier. The Manchester industrialist George Lee, a friend of James Watt junior, was sufficiently impressed by what he saw to arrange for his own house to be lit by gas, which he declared was very efficient but a little smelly. He saw, however, that gas lighting would be just the thing for his factory to be able to keep it open for as long as he liked, regardless of seasonal changes. Boulton & Watt developed Murdoch's work, for a while, seventeen factories in the north being lit by gas.[31] Murdoch became fully involved in running the foundry, where he made a number of important innovations.

During the last decade of the eighteenth century, Boulton was keen to show his patriotism. It might perhaps have been the 'Church and King' riots in mind when he had been spoken of as a potential supporter of revolutionary France, but it is more likely that it was a genuine wish to contribute to his country. He applied in 1797 to the Marquis of Stafford for permission to raise a 200-strong militia – an early version of the Home Guard of the Second World War. They were to be equipped with a variety of muskets and old blunderbusses, but as the threatened invasion from France failed to materialise the militia was never needed. In 1800, he contributed to the Birmingham Light Horse Volunteers and the Birmingham Loyalty Association. He had another chance to show his patriotic fervour when he acted as master of ceremonies at a concert to mark the British fleet's victory over the Dutch at the Battle of Camperdown. Inevitably, if Boulton was concerned, there was a good deal of Handel on the programme and, equally inevitably, a performance of Arne's *Rule, Britannia*.

In his later years, he took a very active part in public affairs in his home town. He was a supporter of the Birmingham Dispensary, a note of 1794 recording that he chaired the annual general meeting, and he was consulted about approving a vaccination programme in 1800. The idea of deliberately infecting patients with an infection, cowpox, in order to prevent them suffering from a far more virulent infection, smallpox, was revolutionary. It was, however, based on careful scientific research and experiment, and was eventually to result in the almost complete annihilation of the disease. But it is typical of the age that equal credence was given to other therapies with considerably less basis in scientific work. Thomas Beddoes first began experimental treatments for tuberculosis based on his observation that butchers seldom seemed to catch it. He decided that a sensible treatment was to have a clinic with cows kept next door that were encouraged to breathe over the patients. His next work involved the study of the effects of breathing in different gases, other than bovine breath, to treat disease. He set up the Pneumatic Institution at Hotwells, Bristol, in 1799.[32] Richard Lovell Edgeworth was a keen supporter, Boulton contributed to the costs, and Watt helped with setting up the apparatus. The first superintendent was Humphry Davy and among the gases he investigated was nitrous oxide, but he failed to recognise its anaesthetic properties. Boulton's interest in science never diminished; in 1801, he campaigned in favour of forming a society to study botany and establish a botanic garden. His idea was eventually to be realised, but not in his lifetime. He also subscribed to a society for building a new library for Birmingham.

As the new century began, deteriorating health forced him to take life a little easier. In 1802, he became seriously ill. It is always difficult to assess exactly what was wrong with him, given the state of diagnostic medicine at the time, but we do know that shortly afterwards he was found to be suffering from kidney stones. He received practical help not so much from his doctor as from the dentist Charles Dumergue, who had transplanted Anne's teeth. There could be no better example of the strength of Boulton's aristocratic connections than what happened next. He was sent the Prince of Wales' own wheelchair with a note from Maria Fitzherbert who had famously married the future George IV, even though the wedding was illegal – a fact that did not prevent her continuing the relationship as his mistress. 'The Prince,' she wrote, 'would feel great pleasure if his Chair contributed to your comfort in the smallest degree.'[33] Over the years, the best relief he could find was visiting Cheltenham for the waters.

Boulton was not the only family member to suffer from bad health. Anne had learned to live with her birth defect and to make an active life for herself, but she had fallen from a horse in 1794, damaging her knee, and had followed that with a second fall, slipping on steps and exacerbating the injury. Various treatments were tried – at one time she was having her leg sprayed with cold water every hour and treated with leeches. The next attempt at a cure involved a trip to Brighton to bathe in the sea, but that only seemed to make things worse. She was understandably reported as being in low spirits, a condition not helped by one eminent doctor recommending amputation. It was, he declared, a question of losing her leg or losing her life. Fortunately this drastic remedy was resisted. She went to convalesce for a time with the Dumergue family in London, where more remedies were tried, but with only occasional relief from the pain. She stayed away from Soho for a total of three months, with her anxious father receiving regular news of her progress or, more frequently, lack of it. Her return, in January 1801, delighted Boulton, who wrote to thank the Dumergues and told them of his 'unspeakable Joy' at having her back home, reporting that although she was tired by the journey, she was soon 'chatty and cheerfull'.

One of Boulton's preoccupations was to see his children happily married. At one time it seemed likely that Matt might marry the daughter of John Fothergill, but that came to nothing. Other possible matches for both Anne and Matt were mooted, and each time a new prospect appeared, Boulton sat down to work out the financial implications of the match. It had seemed at one stage that Anne would be the first to settle down, when a marriage was planned with her doctor, John Carmichael, and Boulton even went as far as purchasing a house for the pair. It, too, came to nothing. Anne was never to marry, but Matt eventually chose a bride when he was in his mid-forties. She was 19-year-old Mary Anne Wilkinson, related to both the Priestley family and John Wilkinson of Bersham. His father, who had done his best at matchmaking, never lived to see the event.[34]

Boulton's health continued to deteriorate, and even the prospect of a visit by George III and Queen Charlotte to Soho was not enough to rouse him. Of all the visitors who had walked through the doors of the Soho Manufactory, these would have been the grandest, and he must have been very ill indeed to pass over the position of host to his son. News was sent from London that even if it was Matt who was to show the royal party around the works, the King was determined to call on Boulton, but even that did not fully compensate for the disappointment. Then, at the last moment, it was the King himself who became ill and the visit was cancelled.

With the prospect of Anne never marrying, Boulton began to make provision for her future. He wanted her to be quite independent and to have sufficient funds to maintain her home and keep her carriage, which he knew to be essential given her continuing poor health. He also wanted to make sure that she never had to rely on her brother for funds. Although still making allowances for the possibility of a husband appearing in the future, he was not relying on it. Boulton set up a deed that gave Anne assets of £34,000, a considerable fortune. It was now time for him to make his will; the pain from his kidney stones was getting worse. Friends noticed the change and began to think that even with his famously robust constitution he was unlikely to survive.

In March 1809, Anne was staying in Bath when she received a letter from her father, sounding a note of despair that had never appeared in any earlier letters:

It is with difficulty that I write this which you cannot be assured that I shall not be hapy until I clasp you in my arms for I am now very misable & therefore beg you will return to Birmingham where I hope to receive you in 7 or 8 days if you wish to see me alive. Pray come soon for I am very ill.[35]

He survived but lingered on in pain until he died peacefully on 17 August of that year, just before reaching his eighty-first birthday. A post-mortem revealed some damage to the prostate and bladder, but the cause of death and the pain from which he had suffered for so long was found to be stones in both kidneys. The funeral took place a week later at Handsworth Parish Church. James Watt and his wife were in Glasgow at the time and unable to get back, and it was left to James junior to represent the family. The ceremony was, he reported to his father, 'awful and impressive'. The coffin was carried from Soho House to the church by some of the oldest of the Soho workmen, taking it in turns to bear the load. They were followed by more than 500 of his old employees, family and friends, and thousands lined the route. There were many tributes paid, but few were more heartfelt than that of his old friend and partner James Watt, never a man to wear his heart on his sleeve. He sent a letter of condolence that perhaps expressed the views of many who had had the pleasure and privilege of knowing the great manufacturer:

We may lament our own loss, but we must consider on the other side his relief from the torturing pain he has so long endured & console ourselves with the remembrance of his virtues & eminent qualifications. Few men have had his abilities & still fewer have exerted them as he has done and if to them we add his urbanity, his generosity and his affection to his friends, we shall make up a character rarely to be equalled. Such was the Friend we have lost and of whose affection we have reason to be proud, as you have to be the son of such a Father![36]

Notes

1   Quoted in Anthony Burton, *Remains of a Revolution*, 1975; R.S. Fitton, *The Arkwrights: Spinners of Fortune*, 1989, p. 98.

2   R.S. Fitton, op. cit., p. 106.

3   Jennifer Tann, 'Richard Arkwright and Technology', History, LVIII, 1973.

4   MB to JW, 24 February 1786, quoted in H.W. Dickinson, *Matthew Boulton*, 1937, p. 128.

5   Ibid., pp. 128–29.

6   MB to Eckhardt, 1796.

7   Dickinson, op. cit., p. 167.

8   J. Watt jnr to J. Watt, 15 September 1795.

9   *Aris's Birmingham Gazette*, 1 February 1796.

10 Sir Eric Roll, *An Early Experiment in Industrial Organisation: Being a History of the Firm of Boulton & Watt, 1775–1805*, 1930, repr. 1968, pp. 166–71.

11 Ibid., p. 167; J. Watt jnr to MRB, 14 June 1802, in Jennifer Tann (ed.), *The Selected Papers of Boulton & Watt*, 1981, pp. 153–56.

12 MRB to Z. Walker jnr, 14 August 1797.

13 Quoted in Richard L. Hills, *James Watt*, Vol. 3, 2006, p. 216.

14 Phillada Ballard, Val Loggie & Shena Mason, *A Lost Landscape: Matthew Boulton's Gardens at Soho*, 2009, p. 25.

15 MB to James Wyatt, 7 July 1796.

16 MB to Sir Joseph Banks, 6 August 1797; Shena Mason, 'The Hôtel d'amitié sur Handsworth Heath: Soho House and the Boultons', in Mason (ed.), *Matthew Boulton: Selling what all the world desires*, 2009, pp. 16–17.

17 J. Watt to MB, 3 July 1793.

18 Rev. John Birch to MB, 25 May 1773.

19 MB to Sir John Sinclair, 12 January 1795.

20 MB to Isaac Hawkins Browne, 8 June 1808.

21 Isaac Riddell to MB, 1 January 1800, quoted in David Brown, 'Matthew Boulton, Enclosure and Landed Society', in Malcolm Dick (ed.), *Matthew Boulton: A Revolutionary Player*, 2009, pp. 45–62.

22 Ibid., p. 50.

23 Roll, op. cit., pp. 225–26, 228–36.

24 A full account of the visit can be found in Olga Baird, 'His Excellency Count Woronzow the Russian Ambassador and the Hardware Man', in Dick, op. cit. The quotations relating to the visit are taken from this article.

25 MB to Mrs C. Matthews, 7 August 1799.

26 Baird, op. cit., p. 99.

27 Mrs C. Matthews to MB, 13 February 1801.

28 Dickinson, op. cit., p. 183.

29 MB to Anne Boulton, 27 December 1800.

30 Quoted in Charles Singer, E.J. Holmyard, A.R. Hall & Trevor I. Williams, *A History of Technology*, Vol. IV, 1958.

31 Jennifer Tann, *The Development of the Factory*, 1970, p. 131.

32 Hills, op. cit., Vol. 3, pp. 152–55.

33 Shena Mason, *The Hardware Man's Daughter: Matthew Boulton and his 'Dear Girl'*, 2005, p. 125.

34 Ibid., pp. 132–38.

35 MB to Anne Boulton, 11 March 1809, quoted ibid., p. 139.

36 JW to MRB, 23 August 1809, quoted in Dickinson, op. cit., p. 194.

Bibliography

Books

Ballard, Phillada, Loggie, Val & Mason, Shena, *A Lost Landscape: Matthew Boulton's Gardens at Soho* (Chichester: Phillimore, 2009).

Barton, D.B., *The Cornish Beam Engine* (Truro: D. Bradford Barton, 1965).

Black, Jeremy, *The British Abroad: The Grand Tour in the Eighteenth Century* (Stroud: The History Press, 2003).

Bradbury, Frederick, *History of Old Sheffield Plate* (Sheffield: J. W. Northend, 1968).

Burton, Anthony & Pip, *The Green Bag Travellers* (London: Andre Deutsch, 1978).

Burton, Anthony, *Remains of a Revolution* (London: Andre Deutsch, 1975).

Burton, Anthony, *Josiah Wedgwood* (London: Andre Deutsch, 1976).

Burton, Anthony, *Richard Trevithick* (London: Aurum Press, 2000).

Clarke, Norma, *Dr Johnson's Women* (London: Pimlico, 2005).

Clay, Richard & Tungate, Sue (eds), *Matthew Boulton and the Art of Making Money* (Studley: Brewin Books, 2009).

Defoe, Daniel, *A Tour Through the Whole Island of Great Britain* (London, 1724–26).

Dick, Malcolm (ed.), *Matthew Boulton: A Revolutionary Player* (Studley: Brewin Books, 2009).

Dickinson, H. W., *A Short History of the Steam Engine* (Cambridge University Press, 1938).

Dickinson, H. W., *James Watt: Craftsman and Engineer* (Cambridge University Press, 1935).

Dickinson, H. W., *Matthew Boulton* (Cambridge University Press, 1937).

Dickinson, H. W. & Jenkins, R., *James Watt and the Steam Engine* (Oxford: Clarendon Press, 1927, repr. Encore Editions, 1981).

Doty, Richard, *The Soho Mint & the Industrialization of Money* (London: Smithsonian Institution/British Numismatic Society, 1998).

Fitton, R.S. & Wadsworth, A.P., *The Strutts and the Arkwrights* (Manchester University Press, 1958).

Fitton, R.S., *The Arkwrights: Spinners of Fortune* (Manchester University Press, 1989).

Fleming, J., *Robert Adam and His Circle in Edinburgh & Rome* (Cambridge MA: Harvard University Press, 1962).

Gibbs, F. W., *Joseph Priestley: Adventurer in Science and Champion of Truth* (London: Nelson, 1965).

Goodison, Nicholas, *Ormolu: The Work of Matthew Boulton* (London: Phaidon, 1974; Christie's, 1999).

Hamilton Jenkin, A.K., *The Cornish Miner* (London: George Allen & Unwin, 1927).

Hills, Richard L., *Power in the Industrial Revolution* (Manchester University Press, 1970).

Hills, Richard L., *James Watt*, 3 vols (Ashbourne: Landmark, 1993–2006).

Hutton, W., *An History of Birmingham* (Birmingham: Thomas Pearson, 3rd edn, 1795).

Jones, Peter M., *Industrial Enlightenment: Science, technology and culture in Birmingham and the West Midlands 1760–1820* (Manchester University Press, 2008).

King-Hele, Desmond, *Erasmus Darwin: A Life of Unequalled Achievement* (London: DLM, 1999).

Mason, Shena, *The Hardware Man's Daughter: Matthew Boulton and his 'Dear Girl'* (Chichester: Phillimore, 2005).

Mason, Shena, *Matthew Boulton: Selling what all the world desires* (Birmingham City Council and Yale University Press, 2009).

Musson, A.E. & Robinson, Eric, *Science and Technology in the Industrial Revolution* (Manchester University Press, 1969).

Prosser, R.B., *Birmingham Inventors and Inventions: Being A Contribution to the Industrial History of Birmingham* (Birmingham, 1881).

Robinson, Eric & Musson, A.E., *James Watt and the Steam Revolution* (London: Adams & Dart, 1969).

Robinson, John Martin, *The Wyatts: An Architectural Dynasty* (Oxford University Press, 1979).

Roll, Sir Eric, *An Early Experiment in Industrial Organisation: Being a History of the Firm of Boulton & Watt, 1775–1805* (London: Longmans, 1930, repr. Cass, 1968).

Schofield, Robert E., *The Lunar Society of Birmingham* (Oxford: Clarendon Press, 1970).

Selgin, George, *Good Money: Birmingham Button Makers, the Royal Mint, and the Beginnings of Modern Coinage, 1775–1821* (Oakland CA: The Independent Institute, 2008).

Singer, Charles, Holmyard, E.J., Hall, A.R. & Williams, Trevor I., *A History of Technology*, Vol. IV (Oxford University Press, 1958).

Tann, Jennifer, *The Development of the Factory* (London: Cornmarket Press, 1970).

Tann, Jennifer, *The Selected Papers of Boulton & Watt*, Vol. I (London: Diploma/Cambridge MA: MIT Press, 1981).

Tann, Jennifer, *Birmingham Assay Office 1773–1993* (Birmingham: Assay Office, 1993).

Timmins, Samuel, *Birmingham and the Midland Hardware District* (London: Robert Hardwicke, 1866, repr. Cass, 1967).

Trevithick, Francis, *Life of Richard Trevithick* (London: E. & F. N. Spon, 1872).

Uglow, Jenny, *The Lunar Men* (London: Faber and Faber, 2002).

Von Tunzelmann, G.N., *Steam Power and British Industrialization* (Oxford University Press, 1978).

Journal Articles

Annals of Agriculture, 16, 1791.

Robinson, Eric, 'Matthew Boulton, Patron of the Arts', *Annals of Science*, 9, 1953.

Robinson, Eric, 'The International Exchange of Men and Machines 1750–1800', *Business History*, 1, 1958.

Robinson, Eric, 'Matthew Boulton and the Art of Parliamentary Lobbying', *Historical Journal*, VII, 2, 1964.

Tann, Jennifer, 'Richard Arkwright and Technology', *History*, LVIII, 1973.

Tann, Jennifer, 'Suppliers of Parts: the Relationship between Boulton & Watt and the Suppliers of Engine Components', *Centenary Trans. Birmingham & Warwickshire Arch. Soc.*, 1974.

Tann, Jennifer, 'Boulton & Watt's Organisation of Steam Engine Production before the opening of Soho Foundry', *Trans. Newcomen Soc.*, 49, 1977–78.

Tann, Jennifer & Breckin, M. J., 'The International Diffusion of the Watt Engine 1775–1825', *Economic History Review*, XXXI, 4, 1978.

Tann, Jennifer, 'Marketing Methods in the International Steam Engine Market: The Case of Boulton and Watt', *Journal of Economic History*, XXXVIII, 2, 1978.

Tann, Jennifer, 'Makers of Improved Newcomen Engines in the late 18th Century', *Trans. Newcomen Soc.*, 49, 1978–79.

Tann, Jennifer, 'Mr Hornblower and His Crew: Watt Engine Pirates at the end of the 18th century', *Trans. Newcomen Soc.*, 51, 1979–80.

Tann, Jennifer, 'Riches from Copper: the Adoption of the Boulton & Watt Engine by Cornish Mine Adventurers', *Trans. Newcomen Soc.*, 67, 1995–96.

Torrens, H.S., 'Some Newly Discovered Letters from Jonathan Hornblower (1753–1815)', *Trans. Newcomen Soc.*, 54, 1982–83.

Tyler, David, 'Humphrey Gainsborough (1718–1776), Cleric, Engineer and Inventor', *Trans. Newcomen Soc.*, 76, No 1, 2006.

Index